THE STORY OF THE NEGRO

VOLUME II

CONTENTS—Volume II

PART III

THE NEGRO AS A FREEMAN

THE STORY OF THE NEGRO
VOLUME II

PART III

THE NEGRO AS A FREEMAN

The Story of the Negro

CHAPTER I

THE EARLY DAYS OF FREEDOM

THE Negro slaves always believed that some day they would be free. From the Bible — the only book the masses of the people knew anything about — they learned the story of the children of Israel, of the house of bondage, and of forty years of wandering in the wilderness, and they easily learned to apply this story to their own case. There was always a feeling among them that some day, from somewhere or other, a prophet would arise who would lead them out of slavery. This faith was the source of the old "freedom songs," which always had for the slaves a double meaning. Interwoven with the religious sentiment and meanings there was always the expression of a desire and a hope, not alone for freedom in the world to come, but of freedom in this world as well.

In their religious meetings, through the medium not only of these songs, but of their prayers as well,

the coloured people expressed their longing for freedom and even prayed for deliverance from slavery,
without apparently arousing the suspicion that they
were thinking of freedom in anything but a spiritual
sense.   The following chorus of the plantation song
will illustrate what I mean:

> Children, we all shall be free,
> Children, we all shall be free,
> Children, we all shall be free,
> When the Lord shall appear.

One of the indications that the slaves on the
plantation believed, near the close of the war, that
freedom was at hand, was the way in which they
began singing, with new fervour and energy, those
freedom songs to which I have referred.

There was one of them which ran this way:

> We'll soon be free,
> We'll soon be free,
> When de Lord will call us home.

The Negroes, in certain parts of South Carolina, sang this song with so much fervour at the
beginning of the Civil War that the authorities
put them in jail, in order to stop it, fearing it might
have the effect of arousing the slaves to insurrection.

Another indication that the masses of the slaves
felt during the war that freedom was at hand was
the interest in which they took, particularly after
the emancipation proclamation had been issued,
in "Massa Linkum," as they called the President of

the United States, and in the movements of the Union armies. In one way and another many of the slaves of the plantations managed to keep pretty good track of the movements of the different armies and, after a while, it began to be whispered that soon all the slaves were going to be free. It was at this time that the slaves out in the cabins on the plantations began to pray for the success of "Massa Linkum's soldiers." I remember well a time when I was awakened one morning, before the break of day, by my mother bending over me, where I lay on a bundle of rags in the corner of my master's kitchen, and hearing her pray that Abraham Lincoln and his soldiers might be successful and that she and I might some day be free.

The plantation upon which my mother lived was in a remote corner of Virginia, where we saw almost nothing of the war, except when some of those who had gone away as soldiers were brought home dead, and it was not until the very close of the war that a party of Union soldiers came through our part of the country and carried off with them a few of the slaves from our community. In other parts of the country, however, freedom came much earlier. Wherever the Union armies succeeded in penetrating the South, work on the plantation ceased, and large numbers of the slaves wandered off on the trail of the army to find their freedom. I have frequently heard older people of my race tell the story of how freedom came to them, and of the sufferings which so many of them endured, during this time.

One of the curious things about the Emancipation Proclamation of January 1, 1863, was that it probably did not immediately confer freedom on a single slave. This was because it was limited in its application to those territories over which the Federal armies had no control. In the Border states and wherever the Union armies were established the institution of slavery remained, nominally at least, as it had been.

On the other hand, wherever the Federal armies entered upon slave territories, no matter what theory the Government held to, it was found impossible in practice to maintain the slave system. The first proclamation of emancipation was, as a matter of fact, General Butler's ingenious phrase which termed the Negro fugitives who came into the Union lines "contraband of war." Theoretically, these fugitives were still merely property of the enemy which had fallen into the hands of the Federal army, but actually to be "contraband" meant to be free, and from that time on Federal officers were everywhere at liberty to receive and protect fugitive slaves who came into their hands.

The result of this was that wherever the Federal armies went slavery ceased. As a consequence thousands of these homeless and helpless people fell into the hands of the Federal commanders. When General Grant entered Northern Mississippi the refugees became so numerous that he detailed Chaplain John Eaton, of the Twenty-seventh Ohio Infantry, afterward colonel of a Negro regiment, to organise them and set them to work picking the cotton which was then ripe in the fields.

In a somewhat similar manner at Fortress Monroe, Virginia, Washington, District of Columbia, Beaufort and Port Royal, South Carolina, Columbus, Kentucky, and Cairo, Illinois, large numbers of the Freedmen had been collected into camps and the problem of dealing with the Negro in freedom was brought, in this way, for the first time definitely before the Northern people for solution. Freedmen were to be governed, to be educated and, in general, to be started in the new life of freedom which was now open to them. The difficulties that presented themselves were appalling, and immediately aroused the deepest sympathy and concern among the people in the Northern states.

As an indication of some of the unusual problems that presented themselves to the Union officers, who were in command at the points I have named, I may refer to an incident which occurred in New Orleans. A free Negro, by the name of John Montamal, had married a woman who was a slave. From the savings of a small business he had purchased his wife for six hundred dollars, so that he stood to her in the relation of owner as well as husband. As a consequence his children were his slaves. At the time

the Union soldiers arrived in the city his only sur-
viving child was a bright little girl of eleven years of
age, who had had the advantages of a school training
and had become a member of the Catholic Church.
Owing to the troublous character of the times the
father had fallen into debt and, in an evil hour, had
mortgaged his daughter to his creditors, believing
that he would be able to redeem her in time to prevent her being sold.   The war prevented his carrying out this plan, and, as a result, the mortgage was
foreclosed and the child sold at auction by the sheriff.
Under these circumstances the man came before
the Provost Court, which had been established by
General Butler, and sought the restoration of his
daughter. Under the laws of Louisiana, which were
nominally, at least, in force at that time, the girl
would have been doomed to slavery, but the Provost
Judge, Colonel Kinsman, promptly decided that
the law was no longer in force and that when
Louisiana went out of the Union she took her "black
laws" with her.

Another anecdote, which illustrates the way in
which Union generals ruthlessly disposed of the old
slave laws, is related by James Parton in his history, "General Butler in New Orleans."   When
the Union soldiers arrived in New Orleans they
found, in the State Prison at Baton Rouge, children
who had been born in the prison of female coloured
convicts.   By the laws of Louisiana these children

were the property of the State, and if General Butler had carried out the law he would have sold them as slaves. When the superintendent applied for orders with regard to these children, General Butler promptly decided that they should be taken care of in the same way as other destitute children, saying that "possibly the master might have some claim upon them, but he did not see how the State could have any."

Thus it was that the work of what was afterward called "reconstruction" began in the South wherever the Union forces obtained possession of the country. In the Department of General Banks, Louisiana, there were 90,000 coloured people; 50,000 were employed as labourers under the direction of the officers of the army. Under Colonel Eaton seven thousand acres of cotton land in Tennessee and Arkansas were leased and cultivated in order to furnish food for the 10,000 people who were not able to take care of themselves. In South Carolina General Rufus Saxton organised Negro regiments, sold confiscated estates, leased abandoned plantations and assisted in the building up of the Negro schools that had been started under Edward L. Pierce.

March 3, 1865, what was known as the Freedmen's Bureau was organised under General Oliver O. Howard, to carry on the work that had been begun under the Federal generals at the different refugee camps. For the next four years this Freedmen's

Bureau, so far as concerned the Freedman and his relation to his former master, was in itself a pretty complete sort of government. In 1868 there were 900 bureau officials scattered throughout the South, ruling directly and indirectly several millions of men and women. During that time 30,000 black men were sent back from the refugee and relief stations to the farms and plantations. In a single state 50,000 contracts for labour were signed under the direction of the agents of the Bureau. The total revenue of $400,000 was derived from the coloured tenants who had leased lands under the control of the Bureau.

It was under this Bureau that the Negro schools were started in every part of the South. Fisk, Atlanta and Howard universities were established during this time and nearly $6,000,000 was expended for educational work, $750,000 of which came from the Freedmen themselves. Before all its departments were finally closed something like $20,000,000 was expended by the Bureau in the different branches of its service.

One of the results of the organisation of the Freedmen's Bureau was to give employment to a large number of ambitious coloured men, and many representatives of the Negro race, who afterward became prominent in politics, gained their first training in this direction as agents of the Freedmen's Bureau. Among others who went into politics through this door were Hiram R. Revels, the first coloured man to enter the United States Senate, and Robert C. DeLarge, who was a member of the Forty-second Congress from South Carolina.

Hiram R. Revels was born at Fayetteville, North Carolina, September 1, 1822. His parents seem to have been free Negroes. At any rate they had been permitted to give him some education while he was a boy. After he became of age he went North, entered the Quaker Seminary in Union County, Indiana, and finally, about the year 1847, graduated from Knox College, at Galesburg, Illinois. He became a preacher and lecturer throughout Indiana, Illinois, Ohio, and Missouri and, at the breaking out of the war, he was serving as pastor of the Methodist Church in Baltimore. He assisted in raising the first coloured regiment that was organised in the State of Maryland, and afterward organised a second coloured regiment in Missouri. In 1864 he was at Vicksburg, where he assisted the Provost Marshal in managing the Freedmen's affairs. He spent the next two years in Kansas and Missouri, preaching and lecturing, and finally settled at Natchez, Mississippi, where General Adelbert Ames, the Military Governor, appointed him an alderman of the city. In January, 1870, he was chosen United States Senator and on February 25th, took his seat in Congress.

The announcement that a coloured man had been

elected to the Senate of the United States created a great deal of surprise and comment, and the appearance of the new Senator from Mississippi, who was to take the place that had been occupied by Jefferson Davis, President of the Southern Confederacy, was waited with great interest. Strenuous efforts were made to resist, on the ground that it was unconstitutional and unprecedented, the determination of the Senate to allow him to take his seat. Charles Sumner made a speech in favour of the admission of the coloured Senator in which he said: "The vote on this question will be an historical event, marking the triumph of the great cause." Senator Henry Wilson, the second Senator from Massachusetts, accompanied Mr. Revels to the Vice-president's chair where he took the oath. The chamber and galleries were crowded with spectators eager to witness the event, which was to give formal notice to the world that the revolution, which changed the Negro from a slave into a free man, had been completed. In the same year two other Negroes, Joseph H. Rainey from South Carolina and Jefferson Long from Georgia, were admitted to Congress. During the next few years coloured men were representing, either in the Senate or in the House of Representatives, every one of the seceding states with the exception of Texas and Tennessee.

The Freedmen's Bureau went out of existence in 1869 with the proposal by Congress of the Fifteenth

Amendment.* When the bill bringing the Bureau into existence was under discussion, in 1865, Senator Davis, of Kentucky had described it as a measure "to promote strife and conflict between the white and black races . . . by a grant of unconstitutional power." This puts in a sentence the objections that were made to the organisation of the Bureau in the first instance and the criticisms that have been passed upon it since. It was unfortunate that the Freedmen's Bureau did not succeed in gaining the sympathy and support of the Southern people. This was the more unfortunate because, during the four years of its existence, the Freedmen had learned to look to this Bureau and its representatives for leading, support and protection. The whole South has suffered from the fact that the former slaves were first introduced into political life as the opponents, instead of the political supporters, of their former masters. No part of the South has suffered more on this account, however, than the Negroes themselves. I do not mean to say that this rupture could have been avoided. It was one of the unfortunate consequences of the manner in which slavery was brought to an end in the Southern states.

In the early days of their freedom, in spite of the rather harsh legislation of certain of the Southern

---

* The Freedmen's Bureau went out of existence January 1, 1869, with the exception of its educational work, which was continued to 1872. The Fifteenth Amendment was proposed by Congress February 27, 1869. It was ratified by twenty-nine states, March 30, 1870. . . . See "The Freedmen's Bureau," W. E. Burghardt Du Bois, *Atlantic Monthly*, March, 1901.

legislatures, the temper of the Southern Freedmen was conciliatory. The first move to obtain some part in the government was made by the Free Negroes of New Orleans. On November 5, 1863, the free coloured people of New Orleans held a meeting and drew up an address to Brigadier-general Shepley in which they refer to the fact that there are among them "many of the descendants of those men whom the illustrious Jackson styled 'his fellow-citizens,' when he called upon them to take up arms to repel the enemies of the country," adding that they were at that time paying taxes on property of which the assessed value was more than nine million dollars. In consideration of these fact and others they ventured to ask that they be permitted to assist in establishing, in the new convention, a civil government for the state.

The next year in that corner of the State of South Carolina occupied by the Federal troops, of which Beaufort is the centre, a mass State Convention was held to which the people of the state were invited, "without distinction of colour," to elect delegates to the Baltimore Presidential Convention. These delegates were not, however, allowed to take part in the proceedings of the Convention. From this time on, numerous meetings of the coloured people were held in different parts of the South and of the North. In 1865, a state convention of coloured people was held in South Carolina "to confer together and to deliberate on our intellectual, moral, industrial, and political condition, particularly as affected by the great changes in the state and country." This convention issued an address to the white people of the state in which they declared, among other things, that "notwithstanding we have been born and reared in your midst and were faithful while your greatest trials were upon you, and have done nothing since which could justly merit your dis-approbation," that they had been denied the rights of citizenship which are freely accorded to strangers. The address concludes with the moderate request that the provisions of the "black code," which have denied them the opportunities of education, equal rights before the court, and imposed burdensome reg-ulations upon their personal liberty may be repealed.

There were some such slight evidences in other parts of the country of a disposition on the part of an element of the coloured people and of the Southern white people, to come to terms with each other in order to establish a form of government which would be fairly satisfactory to both races. For instance, the coloured citizens of Tennessee were invited, in 1867, to take part in the political meetings of both parties, and a convention of Coloured Conservatives which met at Nashville, April 5, 1867, adopted among others the following resolutions:

Resolved, That we do not desire to be an element of discord in the community in which we live; that to seek to unite the coloured race against the white, or the poor against the rich, would only bring trouble; that we believe the common good of both depends on the spirit of harmony and justice of each toward the other.

Resolved, That, believing the spirit and tendencies of radicalism are unfavourable to these aims, we take our stand with the true Union Conservatives of Tennessee and invite our race throughout the state to do the same.

Resolved, That our right to vote involves the right to hold office, that its denial is unjust, and that our interests and rights as free men require also that we should have the right to sit upon juries.

The year before, October 1, 1866, Governor Worth, of North Carolina, had spoken in a conciliatory manner to a convention of coloured people assembled at Raleigh. He declared that he was ready to protect them in all their rights and urged them to be industrious, to educate their children, and to keep out of politics, seeing, as he said, "the strife and struggle in which party politics have involved the whites." He added that the general feeling of the men who had been their masters was kindly toward them, and added that "the whites feel that they owe you a debt of gratitude for your quiet and orderly conduct during the war, and you should endeavour to so act as to keep up this kindly feeling between the two races."

Bishop James W. Hood of the A. M. E. Zion Church, who had recently come to the South, was chairman of this convention. Bishop Hood was born in Chester County, Pennsylvania, May 30, 1831. He entered the ministry in 1860, and is said to have been the first regularly appointed missionary of the

Negro race sent to the Freedmen in the South where, it is stated, he founded in North and South Carolina and Virginia more than six hundred church organisations.

Among the Negroes of the Northern states who had gotten their political education under the influence of the Northern abolitionists, the trend of sentiment was naturally much more radical than in the Southern states.

June 15, 1863, a convention of coloured people was held at Poughkeepsie, New York, at which J. W. C. Pennington, a Presbyterian minister, presided. At this convention resolutions were passed, pledging the support of coloured soldiers to the Union cause and expressing the confidence that the Negro soldiers would receive the "protection and treatment due to civilised men."*

On October 3, 1864, a national convention of coloured people was held at Syracuse, New York, to take into consideration the future of the coloured race in America. This convention was the successor of other national conventions of the coloured people which had been held in different parts of America since the first National convention held in Philadelphia, June, 1831. The radical temper of this convention is, perhaps, best represented in a letter written by Frederick Douglass in accepting an invitation to be present. In this letter he demanded "perfect

* Appleton's Annual Encyclopedia, 1864, p. 842.

equality for the black man in every state before the law, in the jury-box, at the ballot-box, and on the battlefield"; and that, in the distribution of officers and honours under the Government, "no discrimination shall be made in favour of or against any class of citizens, whether black or white, of native or foreign birth."

On February 7, 1866, a delegation of coloured men, including George T. Downing, Lewis H. Douglass, William E. Matthews, John Jones, John F. Cook, Joseph E. Otis, A. W. Ross, William Whipper, John M. Brown, and Alexander Dunlop, headed by Frederick Douglass, called upon President Johnson to urge upon him the propriety and necessity of granting to coloured people the rights and privileges of citizenship that had hitherto been and was still denied them.

In reply to the President's statement that the policy they proposed would lead to a race war, and that he did not propose to make himself responsible for more bloodshed, the committee drew up an address to the country in which they brought forward the argument that if the hostility of the two races was actually as great as President Johnson had stated the Negro must be given the ballot "as a means of defence." This address gave public expression to the theory upon which Congress acted when in the following year Negroes were permitted to vote for delegates to the constitutional conventions in all the seceding states.

At this time the Fifteenth Amendment had not been proposed to Congress and there were only six Northern states which permitted the Negro to vote. In Ohio, Indiana, and Illinois, many of the provisions of the "black code," were still in force. Only a few weeks before this time on February 25, 1866, Negroes voted for the first time in the District of Columbia.

Meanwhile the progress of events in the South had been hastened by what the newspapers called a "race war," at Memphis in May, and another and still more bloody riot in New Orleans in which thirty-seven Negroes had been killed and one hundred and nineteen wounded. All this helped to bring into power in Congress the radical party in the North, and this party now proceeded to impose its Government upon the South with the aid of Negro votes.

Negroes sent two hundred and seven delegates out of eight hundred and thirty-four to the constitutional conventions which met, in 1867 and 1868, in Virginia, North Carolina, South Carolina, Georgia, Florida, Alabama, Mississippi, and Texas.* Texas was represented by the smallest number of Negroes. The proportion was nine Negroes to eighty-one white delegates. In South Carolina the Negroes were in control, the proportion being seventy-six blacks to forty-eight whites. Among the other members of

* Rhodes's "History of the United States," 1850-1877, Vol. VI., p. 88.

the South Carolina State Convention of 1867, was
Robert Smalls, who first became known during the
Civil War as the black pilot of the famous Confederate ship, the *Planter*, which he boldly steered
out of the Charleston harbour and turned over to
the Federal fleet on the morning of May 13, 1862.
Robert Smalls was born a slave at Beaufort, South
Carolina, April 5, 1839. In 1851 he came to Charleston, where he worked in the ship-yards as a "rigger,"
and thus became familiar with the life of a sailor.

In 1861, he was employed on the Confederate
transport, the *Planter*. I have more than once
heard Mr. Smalls tell the story of how he succeeded
in taking this ship out of the harbour under the
guns of the fort and at the same time managed to
carry his wife and family to freedom.

Up to this time the *Planter* was being used as the
special dispatch boat of General Ripley, the Confederate Post Commander at Charleston. On the
night of May 12th, all the officers went ashore and
slept in the city, leaving on board a crew of eight men,
all coloured.

This was the opportunity Smalls had been looking for. He spoke to the members of the crew and
found them willing to help him. Wood was taken
aboard, steam was put on, and, with a valuable
cargo of guns and ammunition intended for Fort
Ripley, the *Planter* moved from her dock about two
o'clock in the morning, steamed to the North Atlantic

wharf, where Small's wife and two children, together with four women and one other child and three men, were waiting to go on board.   By this time it was nearly 3:30 o'clock in the morning.   The ship was started on its voyage, carrying nine men, five women and three children.   Two of the men, who had first agreed to go with the ship, at the last moment concluded to remain behind.

The transport blew the usual salute in passing Fort Johnson, and proceeded down the bay.   When approaching Fort Sumter, Smalls stood in the pilot house leaning out the window with his arms folded across his breast, and his head covered with a big straw hat which the commander of the ship usually wore.   Here again the usual signal was given, and the ship headed toward Morris Island, and passed beyond the range of the guns of Fort Sumter before any one suspected anything was wrong.   The *Planter* steered directly toward the Federal fleet, and was nearly fired upon by one of the Federal ships before the flag of truce was noticed.

As soon as the vessels came within hailing distance of each other, Mr. Smalls explained who they were and what was their errand.   Captain Nichols, of the ship *Onward*, boarded the vessel, and took possession. Smalls was transferred to another ship; and was employed for some time as a pilot in and about the neighbouring waters, with which he was familiar. Later, in the war, for meritorious conduct, he was promoted to the rank of captain and was given charge of the *Planter*, which he had so successfully carried out of Charleston harbour. In September, 1866, he carried this boat to Baltimore where it was put out of commission and sold.

After the war Mr. Smalls was elected in 1868 to the House of Representatives of the State Legislature. In 1870 he was elected to the Senate of South Carolina, and afterward served three terms in Congress. He was appointed Collector of the Port of Beaufort, by President Harrison, a position which he was still holding in 1908.

One of the surprising results of the Reconstruction Period was that there should spring from among the members of a race that had been held so long in slavery, so large a number of shrewd, resolute, resourceful, and even brilliant men, who became, during this brief period of storm and stress, the political leaders of the newly enfranchised race. Among them were sons of white planters by coloured mothers, like John M. Langston, P. B. S. Pinchback, and Josiah T. Settle, who had given their children the advantages of an education in the Northern states. Mr. Pinchback's father was Major William Pinchback, of Holmes County, Mississippi. His mother, Eliza Stewart, claimed to have Indian blood in her veins. When he was nine years old young Pinchback and his brother Napoleon were sent to Cincinnati by their father to attend Gilmore's High School. After his father died, Mr. Pinchback's mother came to Cincinnati, and it was there he grew to manhood.

Josiah T. Settle's father was one of those men, of whom there were considerable number in the South, who brought their children by slave mothers North in order to free them. In fact, in Mr. Settle's case, his father not only freed him but married his mother. Mr. Settle got his early education in Ohio, and in 1868 entered Oberlin College. The following year he went to Howard University, where he graduated in 1872. Mr. Settle was active in politics in Mississippi during a portion of the Reconstruction Period, being engaged in the practice of law at Sardis, Panola County, Mississippi. In 1885, he went to Memphis; was appointed assistant prosecuting attorney of the criminal court of Shelby County, and is still practising law in that city, where he is one of the directors of the Negro bank at that place, the Solvent Savings Bank.

Blanche K. Bruce, senator from Mississippi from 1875 to 1881, was born a slave in 1841 in Prince Edward County, Virginia. He received his early education along with his master's son. After freedom came he taught school for a time in Missouri, and studied for a short time at Oberlin College. In 1869, he became a planter in Bolivar County, Mississippi, where he held a number of offices, including that of sheriff and superintendent of public schools. In 1881, President Garfield appointed him Registrar of the United States Treasury. His son, Roscoe Conklin Bruce, graduated with honours from Harvard University; was for a time head of the Academic Department of Tuskegee Institute; and afterward had charge of the coloured schools in Washington, District of Columbia.

Perhaps the most brilliant and, I might add, the most unfortunate of these men of the Reconstruction Period was Robert Brown Elliott, who was born in Boston, Massachusetts, August 11, 1842. His parents were from the West Indies and, while he was still a young boy, they returned to their home in Jamaica. There young Elliott had the advantage of a good schooling. He was sent to England, and in 1853 entered High Holborn Academy, London. Three years later he went to Eton, from which he graduated in 1859. He adopted law as his profession and after some years of travel in South America and the West Indies, settled in Charleston, South Carolina, where he became editor of the Charleston *Leader*, afterward known as the *Missionary Record*, owned by Bishop Richard H. Cain. He soon entered politics and was elected to the Lower House of the State Legislature in 1868.

In 1869, Mr. Elliott was appointed Assistant Adjutant-general of the State, which position he held until he was elected to the Forty-second Congress. He was a member of the Forty-third Congress, but resigned that position to accept the office of sheriff. In 1881, he was appointed special agent of the United States Treasury, with headquarters at Charleston. He was transferred from there to New Orleans, Louisiana. But the fall of the Reconstruction governments in the South carried disaster to him, and he died August 9, 1884, in comparative obscurity and poverty.

Frederick Douglass says of Robert Brown Elliott: "I have known but one other black man to be compared with Elliott, and that was Samuel R. Ward, who, like Elliott, died in the midst of his years." Samuel R. Ward was, in 1848, editor of the *Impartial Citizen*, published in Syracuse, New York.

Altogether, the Negro race has been represented in Congress by two Senators and twenty Representatives. In addition to those already mentioned, Richard H. Cain served as a Representative of South Carolina in the Forty-third and Forty-fifth Congress; H. P. Cheatham represented North Carolina in the Fifty-second and Fifty-third Congresses. Jere Haralson represented Alabama in the Forty-fourth Congress. Jefferson Long was the Representative of Georgia in the Forty-first Congress. John Hyman was a member of the Forty-fourth Congress for North Carolina, and James E. O'Hara represented the same state in the Forty-eighth and Forty-ninth Congresses. Thomas H. Miller was a member of the Fifty-first Congress, and George W. Murray of the Fifty-third and Fifty-fourth Congresses. Both these men were elected from South Carolina. James T. Rapier was elected to the Forty-third United States Congress from Alabama. Benjamin S. Turner represented the same state in the Forty-second Congress. Josiah T. Walls was elected to represent Florida in the Forty-second, Forty-third, and Forty-fourth Congresses. The last man to represent the Negro race in Congress was George H. White, of North Carolina.

In a speech on the subject of the Spanish-American War, January 26, 1899, Mr. White made a sort of valedictory address, which is in many respects so interesting, and created so much comment at the time it was delivered, that I am disposed to quote a portion of it here. Referring to Negro Congressmen, Mr. White said:

Our ratio of representation is poor. We are taunted with being uppish; we are told to be still, to keep quiet. How long must we keep quiet? We have kept quiet while numerically and justly we are entitled to fifty-one members of this House; and I am the only one left. We have kept quiet when numerically we are entitled to a member of the Supreme Court. We have never had a member and probably never will; but we have kept quiet. We have kept quiet while numerically and justly, according to our population as compared with all other races of the world, so far as the United States are concerned, we should have the recognition of a place in the President's Cabinet; but we have not had it. Still we have kept quiet, and are making no noise about it.

We are entitled to thirteen United States Senators, according to justice and according to our numerical strength, but we have not one and, though we have had two, possibly never will get another;

and yet we keep quiet. We have kept quiet while hundreds and thousands of our race have been strung up by the neck unjustly by mobs of murderers. If a man commits a crime he will never find an apologist in me because his face is black. He ought to be punished, but he ought to be punished according to the law as administered in a court of justice. But we keep quiet; do not say it, do not talk about it. How long must we keep quiet, constantly sitting down and seeing our rights one by one taken away from us ? As slaves it was to be expected, as slaves we were docile and easily managed; but as citizens we want and we have a right to expect all that the law guarantees to us.

Speaking a little later of the progress which the Negro race has made, Mr. White said some things which seem to me to express very accurately the sober second thought of the Negro people upon their condition in this country, and give a just and proper expression to the legitimate aspiration of the American Negro. He said:

We are passing, as we trust, from ignorance to intelligence. The process may be slow; we may be impatient; you may be discouraged; public sentiment may be against us because we have not done better, but we are making progress. Do you recollect in history any race of people placed in like circumstances who have done any better than we have ? Give us a chance and we will do more. We plead to all of those who are here legislating for the nation that while your sympathy goes out to Cuba — and we are legislating for Cuba — while your hearts burst forth with great love for humanity abroad, remember those who are at our own door. Remember those who have worked for you; remember those who have loved you, have held up your hands, who have felled your forests, have digged your ditches, who have filled up your valleys and have lowered the mountains, and have helped to make the great Southland what it is to-day. We are entitled to your recognition. We do not ask for domination. We ask and expect a chance in legislation, and we will be content with nothing else.

This speech of Mr. White marks the end of an episode in the history of the American Negro. In considering the relation of the Negro people to this period it should be remembered that, outside of a few leaders, Negroes had very little influence upon the course of events. It was, to a very large extent, a white man's quarrel, and the Negro was the tennis ball which was batted backward and forward by the opposing parties.

Even as a boy I can remember that all through the days of Reconstruction I had a feeling that there was something in the situation, into which the course of events had pushed the Negro people that was unstable and could not last. It did not seem possible that a people who yesterday were slaves could be transformed within a few days into citizens capable of making laws for the government of the State or the government of the Nation.

There were a good many others who felt as I did.

One of the best illustrations that I happen to remember of the sanity of not a few coloured people on the subject of Reconstruction is Lewis Adams, the man who was more largely responsible, perhaps, than any one else for the location at Tuskegee of the Negro school which now bears the name of the Tuskegee Normal and Industrial Institute.

Lewis Adams lived in Macon County, Alabama, during the days of Reconstruction, and there was no coloured man in the state, I dare say, who had more influence over the masses of the coloured people than did he.   During this period Mr. Adams could have been elected a member of the Legislature and, I have no doubt, could have been sent to Congress had he made the slightest effort in that direction. He refused, however, to be a candidate for any office, because, as he told me, he saw the futility and the shallowness of it all.   He saw there was no logical foundation upon which the political activity of the Negro could rest and, for that reason, he preferred to devote himself to furthering the education of his people and to building up his own interests.   The results show that he was right.   When he died, on April 28, 1905, he was among the most honoured, respected, and successful coloured men in Macon County.   On the other hand, men who had chosen to travel the political road had not only failed to succeed but some of them died unknown, forgotten, after passing their later years in obscurity and poverty.

CHAPTER II

SOME years ago I was asked by the editor of a well-known English magazine to write an article on what he termed the "Racial Feuds" in the southern part of the United States. I was compelled to reply that I could not write such an article as he desired because, so far as I had been able to learn, no such thing as a feud existed between the races in the Southern states. I said to him, as near as I can remember, that I had frequently heard of feuds among certain of the white people living somewhere in the mountains of Tennessee, but so far as I knew there never had been such a thing as a feud between the black and the white people in the South, and that, in fact, the trouble between the races in the South was of quite a different character.

I mention these facts here to emphasise an observation I have frequently made in regard to reports that are printed and spread abroad in regard to the relations between the white man and the black man in the Southern states. As a rule, the world has heard and still hears the worst that happens; it rarely hears of the best. It hears of the riots and the lynchings, but it knows very little of the friendly and helpful relations which exist between individuals of both races in every community in the Southern states.

In the chapter preceding this I have written something about the manner in which, directly after the war, the two races became divided, politically, so that up to the present time there is a white party and a black party in the Southern states. I told something of the manner in which this black party arose and gained power in the South, and referred briefly to some of the riots and disturbances which this division between the races caused. The story of the evils which came upon both races as a result of what is sometimes referred to as "Negro domination" has been frequently told. The animosities that were kindled between the races at that time have not yet died out, and there has been very little disposition on the part of the politicians, black or white, to allow them to die out. But the fact is that the good relations between the Freedmen and their former masters, which existed directly after the war, were never wholly destroyed by the political contentions of the Reconstruction Period, and in consequence of the emphasis that has been placed upon the disasters of that period by the historians and others who have written about it, the existence of the friendly relations to which I have referred has been too frequently overlooked.

As an illustration of what these friendly relations between the Freedmen and their former masters sometimes were, I am reminded of an old coloured man by the name of Matthews, whom I ran across some years ago, when I was visiting a little town in western Ohio. When I met this man he was about sixty years of age, and in early life he had been a slave in Virginia, where he had learned the trade of carpentry. It frequently happened in Virginia, as it did in other parts of the South, that after a slave had learned a trade he would buy his own time, so that he might go about the country working for whom he chose, making his own contracts and keeping for himself the money that he earned. In such cases the slave would usually plan to save his money until he could buy his freedom. This was the case with Matthews.

About 1858, Matthews proposed to his master that he would pay $1,500 for himself, a certain amount to be paid in cash and the remainder to be paid in instalments. Such a bargain as this was not uncommon in Virginia at that time. Matthews's master, having learned to have implicit confidence in his slave, permitted him, after this contract was made, to seek work wherever he could secure the best pay. This went on for some time until Matthews secured the contract for the erection of a building in the State of Ohio. While he was at work in that state the war broke out, but Matthews

remained, and continued to work at his trade.   In
1863, he was declared a free man by Abraham
Lincoln's Proclamation of Emancipation.   At that
time he still owed his former master, according to
his contract made before the war, $300.   In telling
me the story, Matthews said that he was perfectly
well aware that, by the Proclamation of Emancipation, he was released from all legal obligations
to pay this money to his master.   He knew that, in
the eyes of nine-tenths of the world, he would be
released from all moral obligations to pay a single
cent of the unpaid balance.   But he said he wanted
to begin his life of freedom with a clean conscience.
In order to do this, he walked from his home in Ohio,
a distance of three hundred miles, much of the way
over mountains, and placed in his former master's
hand every cent of the money that he had promised
years before to pay him for his freedom.

The story which I have just related is an instance
of a kind of thing that very frequently happened
directly after the War.   I could relate hundreds of
instances which have come to my knowledge in
which former slaves have shown their fidelity to their
former masters and have assisted them in their
poverty, and sympathised with them in their troubles,
long after slavery had been abolished.   In stating
these facts I am not seeking to apologise in any way
for the institution of slavery, neither do I mean to
suggest that the Negro slaves were ever satisfied with

their conditions in slavery. I think there is in the mind and heart of every human being an ever-present longing for freedom, no matter how comfortable, in other respects, his condition in servitude may be. I have often heard it said that some coloured people were better off in slavery than in freedom, but, in all the contact I have had with members of my race in every part of the country, I have never found an individual, no matter what his condition, who did not prefer freedom to servitude.

I remember an acquaintance of mine telling me of an old coloured man he had met somewhere in North Carolina, who had spent the greater part of his life in slavery. My friend, who had known the institution of slavery only through the medium of books, was anxious to find out just what the thing seemed like to a man who had lived in slavery most of his life. The old coloured man said that he had had a good master, who was always kind and considerate; that the food he had to eat was always of the best quality and there was enough of it; he had nothing to complain of in regard to the clothing that was provided or the house that he lived in. He said both he and his family always had the best medical attention when they fell ill. To all appearances, as near as any one could judge, the old man must have been a great deal better off in slavery than he was in freedom. Noticing these things, my friend became more inquisitive and wanted to know whether, after all, there was not a feeling deep down in his heart, that he would rather be back in slavery, with all the comforts that he had enjoyed there, than be free. The old man shrugged his shoulders, scratched his head, thought for a second, and then said: "Boss, dere's a kind of looseness about dis y'ere freedom which I kinder enjoys." It seems to me that the old man has expressed the matter about as tersely and as accurately as it is possible to do.

I have referred to the manner in which the Freedmen have stood by their former masters in the troubles that came upon them during the war and afterward. I want to emphasise, just as strongly, that the Southern white men, who owned slaves, have stood by them and helped and protected them in freedom — in like manner and in the same degree.

In the spring of 1909, I made a trip, in company with a number of well-known and successful coloured men, through the State of South Carolina, spending a week in visiting all the principal cities where I was likely to meet the coloured people of the state in the largest numbers. The purpose of this visit was the same as that of similar journeys of observation that I have made at different times in other parts of the country. I wanted to see for myself the conditions of the members of my race, and, if possible, to say a word of counsel and encouragement, which might help them in their struggle for better things. I was surprised to learn that, in spite of all that I had heard and in spite of all that I had read about the bitter experiences South Carolina went through during the Reconstruction Period, the relations between individual coloured men and individual white men throughout that state were friendly and helpful to a degree that few people outside of the State of South Carolina had comprehended.

On the car in which we travelled, for instance, were a number of prominent and successful coloured men of South Carolina and the neighbouring state of North Carolina. During the week that we were together I learned, directly and indirectly, a great deal about the history of these men and the manner in which they had achieved success in the different lines in which they were working. I recall that, in almost every case, each one of these men attributed a large part of their success to the friendship or to the assistance which they had received from some white man. One of the leading men in this party, who was as responsible as any one else for the success of our campaign, was Richard Carroll, the founder of an industrial home for Negro orphans, and one of the organisers of an association that, in 1908, held the first successful Negro state fair in South Carolina. Mr. Carroll told me that one of the men who had been his constant personal friend and assisted him in all that he had attempted to do for the benefit of the Negro race was United States Senator

Benjamin Tillman, who has the reputation of being the most bitter opponent of the Negro, with perhaps one exception, in the Southern states.

Another man who accompanied us upon this trip was John Merrick, of Durham, North Carolina, the founder of a Negro insurance company, The North Carolina Mutual and Provident Association, which has written insurance, since its organisation in 1898, for over 160,000 members, paid $500,000 in benefits and owns real estate in South Carolina and in North Carolina to the value of something like $50,000. This company owns a block of buildings in Durham, where the home office of the company is located, which, I am informed, is assessed at $30,000, and in order to do business in South Carolina, the officers have had to deposit $10,000 cash with the insurance commissioner to protect the company's contracts in that state.

John Merrick was born at Clinton, North Carolina, in 1859. His mother was a house servant for Judge Almon McCord. Merrick was brought up in Raleigh, North Carolina, where he learned the trade of bricklayer. Because this trade left him without work during the winter, he gave it up and became a barber. After that he went from Raleigh to Durham and made his first start in business for himself there with money he borrowed from a white man, Mr. J. S. Carr. While he was in the barber business at Durham, he made the acquaintance of Mr.

J. B. and Mr. Ball Duke, of the Duke Tobacco Company. These men became interested in him and assisted him not only in his personal affairs, but in the work that he tried to do for the members of his own race. They gave him money at different times to help build a church. They gave him money with which to endow twenty-one beds in the Lincoln hospital for coloured people, which is established at Durham, and they afterward gave $5,000 as an endowment for this hospital. It was not, perhaps, entirely a personal interest in Mr. Merrick that led them to give this money through him to these different institutions. The Duke Tobacco Company employs two thousand or more coloured people in its factories at Durham. They wanted to help the coloured people whom they employed, and because they trusted Mr. Merrick and had confidence in him they gave this money to the coloured people largely upon his suggestion and advice.

Among the other people who accompanied us upon this South Carolina trip was Bishop George W. Clinton, of Charlotte, North Carolina, who was one of a group of young coloured men that entered the University of South Carolina, when it was open to coloured students directly after the war. Bishop Clinton, who, as a young man, lived through a large part of the Reconstruction Period in South Carolina, gave me a great deal of interesting information in regard to the happenings of that time. Among other things he told me a story which illustrates the point that I am trying to emphasise, namely, that in spite of the antagonisms of that period, the individual friendly relations between the races, particularly between the Freedman and his former master, remained in many instances firm and unshaken.

One of his first teachers, he said, was Irving Clinton, a white planter and lawyer, and a brother of his father's master. Bishop I. C. Clinton, who, though he has the same name and title, is no relative of Bishop George W. Clinton, was a slave of this man, he said, and before the war had been for many years the foreman of his plantation. Bishop Clinton, he said, had learned to read while he was a slave; he had been taught by his master. After emancipation the relations between the Freedman and his former master remained intimate and friendly. In fact, Bishop I. C. Clinton became, before his death, the spiritual advisor of his former master; was present at the bedside when his old master died; and erected, at his own expense, in the Presbyterian cemetery, at Lancaster, South Carolina, a monument to his former master and lifelong friend. I may add that Bishop I. C. Clinton was a man of very little learning, so far as the books were concerned. He had had one year's training, I believe, at Hampton Institute, but he was a man of great influence and apparently of great common sense. He died in October, in 1904, at the age of seventy-eight.

I have referred to some individual cases of friendship between white men and black men to show what the character of some of these relations is. The best indication that these friendly relations are more frequent than ordinarily supposed, is the fact of the success that the Negro has made in the South in getting property, and in doing away with the burden of illiteracy with which he entered freedom. It would not be possible for Negroes to own as much property as they do in the South at the present time, unless the majority of the white people were disposed to encourage them to get it. It would not have been possible to reduce the illiteracy in the race from 90 to 47 per cent. if the white people in the South had not been willing to support, to some extent, Negro schools.

It is not possible to determine with exactness just how much property Negroes own, in the United States, at the present time. In most parts of the South, no effort is made to separate tax lists of Negroes from those of white people. The State of Georgia is, however, an exception in this respect, and it is possible to study from records of the Comptroller General's office the progress of the race in that state. The figures obtained in Georgia, however, may be used for estimating the progress in the

South, because it has been found that on the whole
the progress of the Negroes in Georgia runs parallel
to the progress of Negroes in the other Southern
states.   I do not mean by this that Negroes in some
states are not gaining property more rapidly than
they are in others; I do mean that, on the whole,
they seem to be gaining in Georgia at about the
same rate they are throughout the South, taking all
the Southern states as a whole.

In 1866, a year after the close of the War, the
Negroes to Georgia owned about ten thousand acres
of land, to the value of $22,500.   In the next ten
years, they increased the amount of land in their
possession more than forty-five times, having, in
1876, 457,635 acres of land, the tax value of which
was $1,234,104.

The rapid increase in land-getting during this
period is easily accounted for. A good many
Negroes had served in one way or another in the
Civil War, and the Freedmen's Bureau had paid
out something like $7,000,000 in bounties to Negro
soldiers.   During the first ten years after the War
a large part of this money was invested in land in
the Southern states.   During the next ten years,
from 1876 to 1886, Negroes increased their holdings
in farm land by nearly 100 per cent., having at the
close of that period 802,939 acres of land, the assessed
value of which was $2,508,198.   During the next
ten years the holdings of Negro farmers increased

to 1,043,847 acres, with an assessed value of $4,234,848.

During the next period of ten years, from 1896 to 1906, the increase in the holdings was slower. In 1906 the amount of property owned by coloured people in Georgia was 1,420,888 acres, but the value of that property had increased from four to seven millions. The last available statistics give, in 1907, the land-holdings of Georgia Negroes as 1,449,624 acres, valued at $7,972,787. These figures do not include the amount of property owned by Negroes in the form of city lots; neither do they include the various forms of personal property on which they pay taxes.

The increase in the value of this class of property has gone on at about the same rate as that of the property in farm lands. For instance, the value of city property owned by Negroes in 1866 is given at $70,000, but in 1907, the value of city and town property owned by Negroes in that state amounted to $6,710,189, while the total assessed value of all Negro property in Georgia had increased during that period from $450,000 to $25,904,822. This does not include the value of church and school property which, according to a careful investigation of Professor Monroe N. Work, made while he was connected with the Georgia State Industrial College, amounts to something like $7,000,000.

Some efforts have been made to study the progress

of the Negro land-owner in Virginia. Negroes have made great progress all over that state in the matter of land-getting but they have done better, perhaps, in Gloucester County than in any other part of the state. According to the census of 1900, the coloured population of Gloucester County was a little less than the white. According to the public records, when an investigation was made a few years ago, the total value of the land owned by coloured people amounted to $87,953.55. The total assessed value of land at that time was $666,132.33. At the same time the coloured people paid taxes upon $79,387 worth of buildings and improvements, while the total assessed valuation of buildings and improve-ments in the county was $466,127.05. To state it differently: the Negroes of Gloucester County, beginning forty years before in poverty, had in 1905, at the time of this investigation, reached the point where they owned and paid taxes upon one-sixth of the real estate in that county. This property is held very largely in the shape of small farms, varying in size from ten to one hundred and fifty acres. A very large proportion of these farms contain about ten acres.

I have always believed that in proportion as the industrial, not omitting the intellectual, condition of my race was improved, in the same degree would their moral and religious life improve.

Some years ago, before the home life and economic condition of the people had improved, bastardy **was** common in Gloucester County. In 1903, there were only eight cases of bastardy reported in the whole county, and two of those were among the white population. During the year 1904, there was only one case of bastardy within a radius of ten miles of the courthouse.

Another gratifying evidence of progress appears in the fact that there is very little evidence of immoral relations existing between the races. In the whole county, during the year 1903, about twenty-five years after the work of education had gotten under way, there were only thirty arrests for misdemeanors; of these sixteen were white, fourteen coloured. In 1904, there were fifteen such arrests — fourteen white and one coloured. In 1904, there were but seven arrests for felonies; of these two were white and five were coloured.

I ought, perhaps, to add that the majority of the teachers in this county were trained at Hampton Institute, and have been teaching there for a number of years. For the most part the teachers of Gloucester County are not mentally superior, but what they lack in methods of teaching and intellectual alertness is more than made up for by their moral earnestness and by the example which they set in their own lives for the people whom they teach. Most of these teachers are natives of the county, and what is more important, most of them own property in the county.

Recently a careful study has been made of the progress which Negro farmers have made in Macon County, Alabama, where the Tuskegee Institute is located. In 1880, a year before the school opened, the census reported 593 farm-owners in the country surrounding Tuskegee Institute. Of this number not more than 10 per cent. were owned by Negroes. Twenty years later the census showed 517 farm-owners in the county, of whom 30 per cent. were Negroes. From 1900 to 1908 the amount of property owned by Negroes in Macon County increased more rapidly than at any other period. The number of Negro farm-owners increased from 167 in 1900 to 421 in 1908. Negroes paid taxes on 55,976 acres of land assessed at $236,989. More than one-seventh of the land and more than one-sixth of the land value is held by Negro farmers. In addition to this there are 288 Negro owners of town property, which is about one-sixth of the value of the town property in the county. To sum up, then, of the $2,061,108 worth of real property in Macon County $325,474 worth is owned by Negroes.

One explanation of the rapid progress which Negro farmers have made in recent years in Macon County may be found in the efforts that have been made to build up the country schools. During the years from 1904 to 1908, largely under the stimulus and encouragement of Tuskegee Institute, the Negro farmers in Macon County raised something over $7,000 to build schoolhouses and lengthen the school terms. This was supplementary to the funds that were given to support the schools by the state. During that same period a special effort was made to bring the influence of the Agricultural School at Tuskegee to bear directly upon the work of the farms in the surrounding territory. The result of all this has been to draw into the county a class of farmers who wanted the advantages of good schools for their' children, and to largely increase the productiveness of their farms. I think I can safely say, that whatever the opinion of people in other parts of the South may be, the people of Macon County, both black and white, have been convinced by the results obtained that Negro education can be made to pay.

I have referred to the progress which Negroes are making in Georgia and in certain other parts of the South, where the statistics are available. From my own observation I should say that the advance in the places I have mentioned is not as exceptional as it might appear. From all that I can learn Negroes are making quite as much progress in North Carolina and Mississippi, Texas and Oklahoma as they are in Georgia and Alabama. As near as I can estimate, Negro farmers are increasing their acreage in land at the rate of 5 per cent. annually.

On the other hand, the taxable value of Negro property seems to be increasing at the rate of about 11 per cent. per annum.

Using all the statistics at hand, it is safe to say that Negro farmers in 1909 owned, in the Southern states, not less than thirty thousand square miles of land.   This is an amount of territory nearly equal to five New England states, Vermont, New Hampshire, Massachusetts, Connecticut, and Rhode Island.   From the best estimate I have been able to find I should say that Negroes in the United States own at the present time not less than $550,000,000 worth of taxable property.   If it is true, as I have stated in another place, that the free coloured people of this country owned before the War something like $25,000,000 worth of property, it is safe to say that $525,000,000 worth of property has been acquired by the coloured people of the United States since freedom.

It is difficult for one, who has not lived in the South and has not closely studied the life of the Negro on the Southern farms and plantations, to clearly understand the actual progress that the figures I have referred to stand for.   As a matter of fact, they represent the work that the masses of the Negro people have done for their own emancipation.   It is a mistake to assume that the Negro, who had been a slave for two hundred and fifty years, gained his freedom by the signing, on a certain date, of a certain paper by the President of the United States.   It is a mistake to assume that one man can, in any true sense, give freedom to another.

Freedom, in the larger and higher sense, every man must gain for himself. In this larger and higher sense the Negro is, slowly but surely, gaining his freedom in every state, in every city, and in every village and on every plantation in the South. Here and there this progress seems to halt. Sometimes there seems to be a retrograde movement but, on the whole, the work of emancipation goes steadily forward.

One of the most interesting examples in my experience of this kind of emancipation is that of a coloured farmer of my acquaintance in Alabama. When he was "turned loose," as he put it, at the end of the Civil War, he was about sixty years of age, and at that age, he began life, as a great majority of my race began at that time, with nothing. He did not own a house; he had but little clothing, and no food but a bag of meal and a strip of bacon. He had gotten out of slavery, however, a close and intimate acquaintance with the soil, and the habit of work.

After freedom came he left the plantation on which he had been a slave and went to work on an adjoining place as a "renter." He told me that when he was first free he felt that he had to move about a little, just to find out what freedom was like. But he soon found that in most respects there was very little difference between his condition in freedom and his condition in slavery. The man of whom he rented furnished him rations, directed his planting, and kept after him to see that he made his crop. At the end of the year the charges for rent and interest had eaten up all that he had earned, so that from one year to another he was not any better off than he had been the year before. When he did come out with a little money to his credit the storekeeper soon got it all, and, if he fell sick or anything happened to his family, he sometimes found himself in debt at the end of the year, and then he was worse off than if he had nothing.

One of the chief privileges of freedom he found to be the opportunity for getting into debt, but after he had succeeded in getting into debt he learned that he had lost even the privilege which had remained to him of moving from one plantation to another. The reason for this is that, as a rule, the Negro farmer who rents has no security to give for the money he borrows except his own labour. In order to secure this labour for the payment of debts the custom, and frequently the law in the Southern states, prevents a tenant from leaving the plantation until he has "paid out of debt," as the saying is, or until some other planter has bought him out of debt. This condition, which has grown up naturally and, I might almost say, necessarily, out of the relations between the white land-owner and his Negro tenants, represents a kind of serfdom, and it is these same conditions that so frequently bring about the cases of peonage, of which one occasionally hears in the Southern states. This serfdom, however, is merely one of the stages through which a society, in which slavery has existed, has usually worked its way to freedom.

Gradually something of all this that I have described began to dawn upon the mind of the old coloured farmer. He saw that he was making no headway and that his condition might easily become worse. It was about this time that he began coming to our annual Negro Conference at Tuskegee Institute. There he heard the stories of other Negro farmers, some of whom had worked themselves out of this condition of partial slavery that I have described. As he listened to these stories, he began to realise that what had been possible for others was possible for him also. He began to think for the first time in his life of getting a home of his own. A place, as he told me, where if he drove a nail or planted a tree it would stay there and could be handed down to his children. He began thinking about the land on which he was working, and a passionate desire to own and improve it took possession of him. He wanted to be in a position where he could afford to improve his surroundings and preserve for his children the improvements that he made.

In order to get more out of the soil he arose early in the morning before daybreak, and he and his

wife and his children were out in the field all day
and late at night. In the midst of this work the
rented mule, which he had been using to make his
cotton crop, died. This was a terrible blow to him,
but it proved his economic salvation, for it determined him to have an ox or mule that he could
call his own next year.

The old farmer talked the matter over with his
wife and between them they agreed upon this plan:
they would do all the work they could during the
day with their hoes, and after dark, by the light of
the moon, the old man would put the harness that
the mule had worn on his own back and, while his
wife held the plow, he pulled it through the furrow
as well as he could. This method of cultivating the
soil was so unusual that he did not care to attract
the attention of his neighbours by working in this
way during the day.

At the end of the season he found that he had
cleared enough to buy an ox. I have heard the old
man tell more than once how proud he felt when
he owned an ox that he could call his own, something, at any rate, that was absolutely free of debt
and no man had a claim upon it. With the aid
of this ox, he and his wife and his children made
the next year a larger crop and, when the cotton
had been picked, he had in his possession more
money than he ever had before in his life. With
this money he bought a mule. Working the mule

and the ox together, he made a still larger crop, and the next year purchased another mule.

Without detailing step by step the method by which the old man went forward, I might say that before many years had gone by he had become the owner in fee simple of over two hundred acres of land. He was living in a good house and had surrounded himself with most of the necessities and some of the comforts of life. Not only was this true, but I learned afterward that he had been able to put considerable money in the local bank, of which he eventually became a stockholder. There were few men of either race who had the confidence and respect of the community in a larger degree than did this man, who emancipated himself in the manner in which I have described.

The story which I have just related is typical of hundreds of other coloured farmers, whom I have known personally, and whose stories have been related from year to year at the annual Tuskegee Negro Conference. Some of these farmers, who have told their stories at the Conference, are men who have made an impression upon the communities in which they live by the success which they have achieved. One of these men, whose name, I remember, is Alfred Smith, known as "the cotton king," of Oklahoma. He was born a slave on a Georgia plantation, but went out to Kansas directly after the War, and eventually moved into Oklahoma.

He is known all over that state for the success he has made in cotton raising. He has a number of times taken the first prize for cotton raised in Oklahoma. He has taken the prize for his cotton in Liverpool, and, in 1900, gained the first prize at the World's Exhibition in Paris, France.

One of the best-known farmers in Georgia is Deal Jackson, of Albany, who owns and works two thousand acres of land upon which he employs forty-six families. For a number of years past he has gained a reputation throughout Georgia by bringing the first bale of cotton to market. One of the most successful farmers in the State of Alabama is a coloured man by the name of John J. Benson, who owns something like three thousand acres of land in Elmore County. He is living on the plantation upon which he was born a slave. He is famous throughout the county not only for his success in raising cotton but quite as much for his success in breeding horses and raising cattle. His son, William E. Benson, is the head of a corporation which owns over nine thousand acres of land adjoining John Benson's plantation.

Negro farmers have not only been successful in getting hold of the land but they have been successful, in one or two instances, at any rate, in greatly improving their methods of farming. There is a farmer by the name of Sam McCord, in Wilcox County, Alabama, who has become famous through-

out Alabama from the fact that, while he farms
only two acres of land, he raises on that two acres
every year four bales of cotton, besides considerable
corn and fodder. This is the more remarkable
when it is remembered that the average yield per
acre in Alabama is a little more than one-third of
a bale.

Few people, who are not themselves members of
the Negro race, realise to what extent the masses
of the coloured people feel that they must be led
and guided; that they have no power within themselves to accomplish anything, unless they are controlled and directed by some one else. In the early
days of freedom the masses of the people felt that
it was hardly possible for coloured people to be
their own masters. They felt that it was somehow
unnatural to find themselves controlled and directed
by one of their own race. I never realised to what
extent this was true until I attempted to organise
the Normal and Industrial Institute at Tuskegee.

After I came to Alabama, in 1881, and before I
attempted to take any definite measures toward
founding the Tuskegee Institute, I spent several
weeks travelling about among the people in the
county, explaining to them my plans and seeking
to interest them in what I proposed to do. They
listened to me patiently and respectfully, but I
could see that, deep down in their hearts, they had
the feeling that white people might accomplish some

such thing as I proposed, or that coloured people, under the direction and guidance of white people, might do so, but that it was hardly possible for Negroes to succeed in any such enterprise. For that reason they halted and hesitated, and doubted my ability and their own, to carry out the plans I proposed to them.

After we had succeeded in erecting our first building at Tuskegee, however, I could see that we had made an impression upon the people. I can remember how they would come in from the surrounding districts, men, women, and children, to look over the school and see what we had done. It was touching to me to observe the manner in which they would enter the different rooms, treading lightly and cautiously, as if they were afraid they would hurt the floors or, perhaps, that the floors would somehow or other harm them. Then they would stop and look about in a kind of bewildered amazement, as if they were not quite sure whether what they saw was real, and as if in order to test it, they would take hold of the door knobs, put their hands on the glass of the window panes, feel of the blackboards, and then stop and gaze wonderingly again at the plastered walls, the desks and the furniture. It was difficult for them to believe that the buildings and the school grounds really belonged, as I tried to explain, to them. It seemed impossible to them that all this could have been brought into existence for the benefit of Negroes. I was compelled to tell them, over and over again, that I wanted them to feel that the school grounds and the school buildings were theirs, and that I wanted them to have a part in the direction and in the upbuilding of everything connected with the school.

It took some years to really convince the masses of the people in our neighbourhood that what I said to them was literally true. But at last the idea that Tuskegee is theirs has entered deep into the minds and hearts of the members of my race, not only in our immediate neighbourhood, but I believe, also, to a large extent throughout the South. At the present time I think that every coloured man and woman in the South not only feels proud of what Tuskegee has accomplished, but that he feels, also, a little more alive, a little more able to go ahead and do something in the world than he did before our institution came into existence.

It is this feeling on the part of the members of my race that has given to me, and to others who are working with me, the desire to go forward and make our institution bigger and better and more useful, in order that it may help complete the work of this larger emancipation, which began before the Civil War destroyed slavery as a political institution, and has been going on steadily everywhere in the Southern states since that time.

CHAPTER III

ONE of my most vivid boyish recollections is of the period just previous to the end of slavery, when my stepfather, who at that time was, I take it, a man of about fifty years of age, would return to his family at Christmas time and tell us stories of his adventures during his long absence from home. I recall that I would sit for hours in rapture hearing him tell of the experiences he had had in a distant part of Virginia, where he and a large number of other coloured people were employed in building a railway. Although he was employed merely as a common labourer he had learned something as to the plan and purposes for which this railway was being built and he had some idea of the great changes that it was intended to bring about, and he told it all with a great deal of interesting circumstance.

In my boyish ignorance at that time, I used to wonder what interest he could have in a railway of that kind; whether or not he owned any part in it; and how it was he was so much interested in the

building of a railroad that he could remain away
from home for five or six months and sometimes
longer at one time. All through the country, in our
part of Virginia, Christmas was a season of great
rejoicing, on account of the home-coming of a large
number of coloured people who had been at work in
different industries in different parts of the state.
Some of them had been hired out to work on the
farms, some were employed on the railroads, and
others were mechanics, and when they came home
at Christmas time they brought with them stories,
anecdotes, and news of what was going on in different parts of the state.

I am reminded of these facts at this time because
they gave me the first idea I had of the extent to
which the labour of the coloured man, both in the
shops and in the fields, has been employed in the
building up of the civilisation of the Southern states.
The Negro was first employed in the severe pioneer
work of clearing the forests, and planting and har-
vesting the crops. After that he was employed in
building railways; in digging the coal and iron from
the mines; in laying out the streets, and erecting the
buildings in the cities. He is to-day very largely
depended upon for labour in the iron, mining and
manufacturing districts, like Birmingham, Alabama, as well as on the great cotton plantations in
Mississippi, Arkansas, and Texas.

Not only has the Negro performed this labour,

but he has performed it cheerfully, faithfully, and, on the whole, as far as his education and training would permit, he has performed it well. The white people of the South, who have known the Negro best, know and value the service that the Negro race has performed in the South. Although they have not always come forward publicly to defend the Negro against the charges that are frequently made against him, they know, deep down in their hearts, that they owe the Negro a debt of gratitude for what he has done, and they have expressed this feeling to individual Negro men and Negro women, not only in words, but in every-day acts of kindness and good will, particularly toward those who at one time belonged to their families or have in some way or other gained their friendship.

It is largely owing to the manner in which the Negro and the white man were brought together in slavery that there is to-day no place in the world where the Negro has made himself a more valuable and efficient labourer than he has in the Southern states. At the same time there is no place in the world where, in spite of complaints that one sometimes hears, there is a more general desire to retain the Negro as a labourer, and no place where there is more opportunity for Negroes to engage in all kinds of labour, common and skilled, or to enter into business pursuits.

Although the slaves that were first imported from

Africa were, as a rule, rude and unskilled in the industrial arts of the white man, yet the native African was not wholly without skill in the crafts, and it was not very long before some of the dark-skinned strangers had mastered the trades. Among the slaves of Robert Beverly, who was clerk of the House of Burgesses, in Virginia, in 1670, was a carpenter valued at about thirty pounds. About this same time Ralph Wormeley, a man of considerable distinction in his time, who died in 1701, owned a cooper and a carpenter, each valued at thirty-five pounds. Negroes were employed as iron miners and ship-carpenters, wheelwrights, coopers, tanners, shoemakers, millers and bakers before the Revolutionary War. As early as 1708 Negro mechanics had become common enough in Pennsylvania to arouse the opposition of the free white workmen, who at that time petitioned the Legislature against the practice of hiring out slaves to work in certain of the trades.*   In the early part of the nineteenth century the number of Negro mechanics in the District of Columbia was considerable, and one of the men who assisted in laying out and surveying the District of Columbia in 1791 was Benjamin Banneker, the Negro astronomer, who is said to have constructed the first clock that was made in America.

Benjamin Banneker was born November 9, 1731, in Baltimore County, Maryland, near the village

---

* "The Negro Artisan," Atlanta Publications, No. 7, p. 15.

of Ellicott's Mill.   He is often referred to as a man of pure Negro ancestry, but the facts seem to be that his grandmother, on his mother's side, was a white woman, by the name of Molly Welsh, who was sent out from England in an early day as a Redemptioner, and after she had served her master for seven years, purchased a small farm and two slaves.   One of these slaves, whose name was Banneker, she gave his freedom and married.

Benjamin Banneker seems to have been a great favourite with his grandmother, who taught him to read.   At this time there was a "pay school" in the neighbourhood, to which a few coloured children were admitted, and Banneker got a part of his education there.   He early seems to have shown an inclination for mechanics, and about the year 1754, with the imperfect tools he was able to command, he constructed a clock, which not only told the time but struck the hours.   Three years later the Ellicott flour mills were erected on the banks of Patapsco River, near his home.   The construction of these mills was a source of great interest and instruction to Banneker and, in this way, he made the acquaintance of Mr. George Ellicott, who opened to him his library and furnished him with astronomical instruments in order that he might pursue further the studies he had already begun in the subject of astronomy.

From this time on Banneker, who still cultivated a little farm inherited from his father, devoted himself entirely to his scientific studies. He made the acquaintance, through correspondence, with scientific men in all parts of the world. It was after his return home after helping to lay out the District of Columbia, in 1791, that he got out his first almanac for the year 1792. Before this almanac was printed he sent a copy of the manuscript to Thomas Jefferson, with a letter of explanation. In reply, Thomas Jefferson said, among other things: "I have taken the liberty of sending your almanac to Monsieur de Condorcet, Secretary of the Academy of Sciences of Paris, and member of the Philosophical Society, because I consider it as a document to which your whole colour had a right, for their justification against the doubts which have been entertained of them."

Although after 1830 a number of restrictions were put upon the Negro mechanics, limiting the extent to which they might be educated, particularly in knowledge of books, still, as a rule, these laws were not strictly enforced and the number of coloured mechanics continued to increase. In Virginia Negroes worked in the tobacco factories, ran the steamboats, and were employed in numerous kinds of skilled labour. In Charleston and some other places Negroes were employed in cotton factories. Frederick Law Olmsted, who made a journey through the Southern states in 1856, says that he was told in Louisiana that master mechanics often bought up slave mechanics and acted as contractors.

In Kentucky, slaves worked in the hemp-bagging factories, in tobacco factories, and in the iron works on the Cumberland River. Ex-Governor Lowry, of Mississippi, says that before the War the Negro mechanics became masters of their respective trades, as a result of long service under the direction of white mechanics. "During the existence of slavery," he adds, "the contract for qualifying a Negro as a mechanic was made between his owner and the master workman."*   In Alabama, there was, some time before the War, as I have heard, an enterprising white man who converted his plantation to an industrial school for slaves. In other words, he would buy untrained slave boys and give them instruction in the different trades that were used upon the plantations, then sell them again at a much larger price than he paid for them. It was not unusual, in fact, for a well-trained mechanic to sell for as high as two thousand dollars while an able-bodied field-hand would sell for eight hundred to one thousand dollars. I mention these facts because they show that, even in slavery, the value of education was clearly recognised.

One of the best mechanics I ever knew was Lewis Adams, whose name I have mentioned in the previous chapter. He was a first-class tinner, shoemaker, and harnessmaker, and could do anything

---

* Quoted in "The Negro Artisan," Atlanta University Publications, from *North American Review*, p. 14.

from repairing a watch to mending an umbrella. After the Tuskegee Institute was started, he became the first teacher of the trades. During the early days of the school he taught three distinct trades, and was not only our tinner, shoemaker, and harnessmaker, but for some time, also, our engineer. As illustrating the extent to which the slave obtained education in the trades, Mr. Adams once said that there were in Macon County before the War twenty-five Negro carpenters, eleven blacksmiths, three painters, two wheelwrights, three tinsmiths, two tanners, and fourteen shoemakers. Of these mechanics, he said:

As a rule, they lived more comfortably than the other class of Negroes. A number of them hired their time and made money; they wore good clothes and ate better food than the other class of people. A very small number of them were allowed to live by themselves in out-of-the-way houses. All the master wanted of them was to stay on his place and pay over their wages. As a rule, a white man contracted for the job and overlooked the work. These white men often would not know anything about the trades, but had Negro foremen under them who really carried on the work.

One of the men who learned his trade in slavery was J. D. Smith, who, a few years ago, was a stationary engineer in Chicago. In a study of the "Negro Artisan," published by Atlanta University, in 1902, he is quoted as saying:

On every large plantation you could find the Negro carpenter, blacksmith, brick and stone mason. These trades included much

more in those days than they do now. What is now done by
machinery was wrought then by hand. Most of our wood-work
machinery has come into use since the days of slavery. . . .
The carpenter's chest of tools in slavery time was a very elaborate
and expensive outfit. His "kit" not only included all the tools
that the average carpenter carries now, but also the tools for performing all the work done by various kinds of wood-working
machines. . . . The carpenter in those days was also the
cabinetmaker, the wood-turner, and coffin-maker, and generally
the patternmaker, and the maker of most things which were made
of wood. The blacksmith was expected to make anything and
everything wrought of iron. He was, to all intents and purposes,
the machinist, blacksmith, horseshoer, carriage and wagon ironer
and trimmer, gunsmith, wheelwright, and frequently whittled and
ironed the hames, the plough-stocks, and the single-trees for the
farmers. He was an expert, also, at tempering edged tools and
many of the slaves had secret processes of their own for tempering
tools which they guarded zealously.

Negro machinists had also become numerous before the downfall
of slavery. Slave-holders were generally the owners of all the
factories, the machine shops, the flour mills, sawmills, gin-houses,
and crushing machines; they owned all the railroads and shops
connected with them. In all these, the white labourer and
mechanic had almost entirely been supplanted by slave mechanics
by the time of the breaking out of the Civil War. Many of the
railroads in the South had their entire train crews, except con-
ductors, but including engineers and firemen, made up of slaves.*

At the close of the slavery period the Negro artisan,
to a very large extent, had a monopoly of the trades
in the Southern states. After slavery disappeared
the Negro boy and girl no longer had the same opportunity to learn the trades they had had in slavery
time. At the same time, as the country developed,

---

* "The Negro Artisan," Atlanta Publications, No. 7, p. 16.

and as new machinery and new methods of doing things were introduced, there was a greater demand for skilled labour than, there had ever been before. Wherever machinery was introduced to perform work which had previously been performed by hand labour, it generally happened that the white man was employed to do that kind of work.

For instance, the building up of the cotton mills in the South and the rapidly increasing demand for labour that it caused, drained large portions of the country districts of their white population to furnish labour for these factories. All this produced great changes in conditions in the Southern states. It has seemed to many persons that the Negro, in losing his monopoly in the trades, was losing also his position in them. After a careful study of the facts, I have come to the conclusion that this is not true. What the facts do seem to show is that there is in process a re-distribution of the coloured population among the different trades and professions. There were fewer negroes engaged in farm labour in 1900 for instance, but there is a larger proportion of the Negro population engaged in the other four general classes of labour than there was in 1890.

When the census was taken in 1900, 62.2 per cent. of all the Negroes in the United States over ten years of age were engaged in gainful occupations, while, at the same time, only 48.6 per cent. of the

white population over ten years of age were so
engaged.   This does not mean that the Negroes, as
a race, are more industrious than the white people;
it means that a larger number of those who should
be in school, preparing themselves to perform more
efficient labour, are at work performing unskilled
and inefficient labour.   The actual number of
Negroes engaged in each of the main classes of the
occupations, in 1890 and in 1900, was as follows:

	1890	1900
Agricultural pursuits	1,984,310	2,143,176
Professional service	33,994	47,324
Domestic and personal service . . .	956,754	1,324,160
Trade and transportation	145,717	209,154
Manufacturing and mechanical pursuits	208,374	275,149

While these figures show that a larger number
of Negroes is employed in all the main classes
of occupations, it does not mean that the percentage
of the Negro population engaged in these different
kinds of labour was larger in 1900, in all classes,
than it was in 1890.   As a matter of fact, the percentage of Negroes engaged in agricultural pursuits was nearly 6 per cent. less in 1900 than it was
in 1890, as the following statement indicates:

	1890	1900
Agricultural pursuits	59.6	53.7
Professional service	1.0	1.2
Domestic and personal service	28.7	33.0
Trade and transportation	4.4	5.2
Manufacturing and mechanical pursuits	6.3	6.9

While it is true that these figures show a decreased percentage of Negroes engaged in agriculture, still a closer study of the figures indicates that the loss has been in the class of agricultural labourers. There are something over 18,000 less Negroes engaged as agricultural labourers in 1900 than in 1890. On the other hand there has been a gain in the number of Negro farmers, both as to number and as to their percentage of the total farmers. There were 590,666 Negro farmers in 1890, and 757,822 in 1900. Negro farmers were 11.1 per cent. of the total number of farmers in 1890, and 13.3 per cent. in 1900.

Of the 3,998,963 Negroes engaged in gainful occupations, considerably more than one-half were engaged in agricultural pursuits in 1900. The next largest class, that of domestic and personal service, employed 1,324,160 persons. Although there were 64,562 more Negro servants and waiters in 1900 than in 1890, the per cent. which they formed of the total number of Negroes engaged in this kind of service decreased from 42 per cent. in 1890 to 35.1 per cent. in 1900. In other words, although there was a considerable gain in the total number and percentage of Negroes engaged in this kind of service, the chief gains were in those of trades like that of barbers and hair-dressers, boarding-house and hotel keepers, janitors, and sextons, launderers and laundresses, nurses and mid-wives, and in the class of unspecified domestic and personal service.

These figures indicate the direction which this re-distribution of Negro labourers among the different trades has taken.

Manufacturing and mechanical pursuits gave employment to 275,149 Negroes. This class included carpenters and joiners, stone and brick masons, painters, glaziers, and varnishers, paper hangers and plasterers, plumbers, gas and steam fitters, roofers and slaters, brick and tile makers, glass workers, marble and stone cutters, potters, fishermen and oystermen, miners and quarry men, butchers, bakers, butter and cheese makers, confectioners, millers, blacksmiths, iron and steel workers, machinists, steam-boiler makers, stove, furnace, and grate makers, tools and cutlery makers, wheelwrights, wire workers, boot and shoemakers and repairers, harness and saddle makers and repairers, leather curriers and tanners, trunk and leather-case makers, bottlers and soda-water makers, brewers and maltsters, distillers, and rectifiers.

Other kinds of manufacturing and mechanical pursuits, in all of which Negroes were found engaged, are cabinet makers, coopers, saw-mill and planing-mill employees, glass workers, clock and watch makers and repairers, gold and silver workers, tin plate and tinware makers, bookbinders and paper-box makers, engravers, printers, lithographers and pressmen, operatives in paper and pulp mills, bleaching and dye works, carpet factories, carpet, cotton, hosiery, and knitting, silk, and woollen mills, dress-makers, hat and cap makers, milliners, seamstresses, tailors, broom and brush makers, charcoal, coke and lime burners. Negroes were also engaged as engin-eers and firemen, glovemakers, model and pattern makers, photographers, rubber factory operatives, tobacco and cigar factory operatives and uphol-sterers. In all these manifold occupations, except fifteen, the number of Negroes employed increased in the period from 1890 to 1900.

Negroes lost numbers in the trades of carpentry, plastering, brick and tile making, marble and stone cutting, blacksmithing, wheelwrighting, bootmaking and shoemaking, harness and saddle making, leather currying and tanning, trunk, valise and leather-case making, engraving, hosiery and knitting and woollen milling. But the same census shows that in more than half of these trades, owing, per-haps, to the larger use of machinery, there has been a decrease in the total number of persons employed, whether white or coloured. This indicates another reason than that of racial competition for the redis-tribution in the trades.

I have referred to the trades in which there appears to be a falling off of Negro employees; let me say a word concerning some of the trades in which the Negro has made exceptional gains. The num-ber of Negro miners in 1890 was 15,809. By 1900 this number had been increased to 36,568, a gain during ten years of 20,759, or 132 per cent. In 1890, the number of Negroes engaged as brick and stone masons was 9,647. In 1900, this number had been increased to 14,387, an increase of 4,740 or 49 per cent. In the meantime, the number of white men reported as engaged in this occupation had decreased 1.8 per cent.

The number of dressmakers in 1890 was 7,479. The number in 1900 was 12,572, an increase during the decade of 65.3 per cent; meanwhile the number of white dressmakers in 1890 was increased to 17.4 per cent., which is between one-third and one-fourth of the increase of the coloured dressmakers. In 1890, the number of Negro iron and steel workers was 5,790. In 1900 the number was 12,327, an increase of 6,537, or 112.7 per cent.; meanwhile the number of white iron and steel workers had increased 100 per cent. The number of Negro stationary engineers and firemen in 1890 was 6,326. In 1900, they had increased to 10,277, or 62.4 per cent. During the same time the increase for the white engineers and firemen was only 60 per cent.

The rapid increase of the Negro labourers in the iron and steel industries was undoubtedly due to the rapid development of that industry in the Southern states. Perhaps this industry, together with the coal and iron mining, has drawn more heavily than other industries upon the labouring population of the country districts. Some figures and observations, indicating the progress that the Negro has made in these industries, were furnished to me by Mr. Belton Gilreath, of the Gilreath Coal and Iron Company, and the Union Coal and Coke Company, of Birmingham, Alabama, who, after a very careful inquiry, has found that Negroes in the Birmingham region mine about 90 per cent. of the iron ore and about 50 per cent. of the coal.

"Twenty years ago," he says, "when the mines were first being opened in this district, the ore-mining was done by white miners with coloured labourers, mostly foreigners, who in turn taught some of the white men here. After a while, the Negro labourers began to be the miners, and now Negroes have almost completely monopolised the iron ore-mining. Negroes perform both the work of labourers and miners until about 90 per cent. of the ore-miners are coloured."

Mr. Gilreath added that in the coal mining industry Negroes have likewise made progress, but are not mining as large a proportion of the coal as they are of the ore. "As near as I can estimate," he said, " from the best information I am able to secure, one-half the coal produced is gotten out by coloured miners."

According to the census for 1900, 209,154 Negroes were employed in occupations which are classified under "trade and transportation." This class includes: agents, bankers, and brokers, bookkeepers and accountants, clerks, and copyists, commercial travellers, draymen, hackmen, teamsters, foremen and overseers, hostlers, hucksters and peddlers, livery-stable keepers, merchants and dealers, messengers, errand and office boys, officials of banks and corporations, packers, and shippers, porters and helpers, salesmen and saleswomen, steam railway employees, stenographers and typewriters, street railway employees, telephone and telegraph linemen, telegraph and telephone operators. In nearly all these occupations Negroes have made considerable gains. Among other facts I note that the number of Negro draymen and hackmen, teamsters, and so forth, increased from 43,963 in 1890 to 67,727 in 1900, an increase of 54 per cent. The increase among the whites for the same period was 45.9 per cent.

In 1900 there were over 200,000 Negroes engaged in occupations requiring skill in some form or other. These were: miners and quarry men, 36,568; saw-mill and planing-mill employees, 33,266; dress-makers and seamstresses, 24,110; carpenters and joiners, 21,114; barbers and hair-dressers, 19,948; tobacco and cigar operatives, 15,349; brick and stone masons, 14,387; iron and steel workers, 12,327; engineers and firemen, 10,227; blacksmiths, 10,104; brick and tile makers, 9,970. In addition to these there were 2,585 Negro operatives in factories and mills, 52 architects, designers and draughtsmen, 185 electricians, 120 civil engineers and surveyors, 1,262 machinists, 198 tool and cutlery makers, 342 cabinet makers, 109 clock and watch makers, 66 gold and silver workers, 86 bookbinders, 22 engravers, 1,845 men and women tailors, 15 glove makers, 24 model and pattern makers, 247 photographers, and 1,045 upholsterers.

A thing that should be considered is that Negroes are, more and more every year, becoming themselves the employers of Negro labour. When Negroes go into business they employ other Negroes as clerks, bookkeepers, agents, and salesmen. All these things tend to draw coloured people from the trades and occupations in which they were formerly employed. The Negro barber is a good illustration of what I mean. The census of 1900 shows that there were not only a larger number but a larger percentage of barbers at that time than there were ten years before. During this same period, however, there has been a very large increase in the number of white barbers not only in the North but in the South. In many cases, particularly in the South, white barbers have taken the places of the Negro barbers, who formerly had a monopoly of that trade. In spite of this fact, as I have said, the number of Negro barbers has steadily increased. The explanation is that a much larger number of barbers are now employed by Negroes than there were a few years

ago.   The whole number of barbers increased from
1890 to 1900 to 54 per cent., while the number of
Negro barbers increased during that period only
14 per cent.

A little earlier in this chapter I made the statement that, with the growth of factories and the
introduction of machinery into the Southern states,
to perform work that had previously been performed
by hand, the white man rather than the Negro was
used to perform that kind of labour.   In recent
years, however, there has been a growing disposition
to employ Negro labour in the factories.   For
example, in 1900 a silk mill was established in
Fayetteville, North Carolina, by the firm of Ashley
and Bailey, who are the owners of a number of silk
mills in different parts of the North.

This firm decided, after carefully considering the
matter, to try the experiment of using Negro labour
in the spinning and weaving of silk.   In order to do
this they purchased a considerable tract of land
just outside of Fayetteville, and started to build up
there a Negro colony.   They rented to each family
they employed a tract of land and a house.   They
erected a schoolhouse, in which there was a nine
months' school, and built a church for the use of
the colony.   They obtained the services of an ener-
getic Negro minister to bring together a number of
Negro families and settle them on the land and in
the houses they had erected.   After that they

invited the children to take employment in the mills. These mills, which employ about five hundred persons, are now conducted under the direction of a white superintendent, who has under him a coloured foreman, who is in charge of the mill which spins the thread.

Under the direction of these two men some five or six hundred children, from twelve to sixteen years of age, have been trained until they have become very satisfactory mill operatives. The superintendent, Mr. G. W. Kort, says it will take a number of years to bring these children up to the point where they will equal the trained and disciplined operatives in the Northern mills. He says, also, that the company has found certain special difficulties in controlling these children, most of whom have come directly from the farm to take up their work in the mills. Most of these difficulties can be traced back to the irregularities in the home life of the parents. Nevertheless, the Fayetteville silk mill has been a success, and is no longer, I understand, to be considered an experiment.

Negro labour has also been tried successfully in a number of hosiery mills. One of these is located in Savannah, Georgia, and another in Durham, North Carolina. In 1897, a group of coloured men in Concord, North Carolina, organised the Coleman Manufacturing Company, and erected a cotton mill,.

which employed for a time some two hundred coloured boys and girls.   Just after the mill had been fairly started, however, Mr. Coleman, the man who organised the company, died, and the mill was sold to a company of white men who decided to employ white labour.

From the ranks of Negro mechanics, there have come from time to time a number of Negro inventors. The first of these inventors, to whom the Patent Office records refer, is Henry Blair, of Maryland, who was granted a patent for a corn harvester in 1834, and another patent for a similar invention in 1836.   This man was probably "a free person of colour," as slaves were not allowed to take out patents for inventions in those days.   The rule in regard to the inventions of slaves was laid down, in 1858, by the Commissioner of Patents and con- firmed by the Attorney-general of the United States. The circumstances were these: A Negro slave, liv- ing with his master in the state of Mississippi, per- fected a valuable invention which his master sought to have patented.   His application was refused on the grounds that he was not the inventor.   He then sought to have the invention patented as assignee of his slave, but under the law a slave could not hold property and therefore could not assign this invention to his master.   The case was appealed to the Attorney-general, and, as I have said, he confirmed the decision of the

Commissioner of Patents. The result of this law was that neither the slave nor his master could secure the protection of the Government for any invention that a slave succeeded in making.

In 1862 a Negro slave belonging to Jefferson Davis, President of the Southern Confederacy, invented a propeller for vessels, which was finally put into use, it is said, by the Confederate navy. A Negro slave in Kentucky is said to have invented the hemp-brake, a machine in which the hemp fibre is separated from the hemp stalk. Negro mechanics also have been the builders of some of the most important buildings erected in the South before the War. When I was in Vicksburg, Mississippi, a few years ago, my attention was called to the courthouse, that was erected before the War, and is still the most imposing building in the city. I was told that this building was planned and built under the direction of a Negro slave.

A few years ago, in 1899, an attempt was made to find out from the Patent Office at Washington, and through inquiries directed to prominent patent attorneys in different parts of the United States, the number of patents that had been taken out by coloured inventors. Something over three hundred and seventy patents, taken out by two hundred and seven inventors, were found to have been taken out by coloured men. Elijah McCoy, of Detroit,

Michigan, had taken out at that time twenty-eight patents on appliances to be used for lubricating engines and locomotives. This was the largest number of patents taken out by any coloured man. The next largest number of patents was taken out by Granville T. Woods, an electrician. Mr. Woods has patented many valuable improvements in telegraph and telephone instruments. One of his telephone inventions was sold to the American Bell Telephone Company. Another important series of inventions, covering machinery to be used in soling shoes, was made by J. E. Matzeliger. These included a lasting machine, a nailing machine, a tack-separating mechanism, and a mechanism for distributing tacks.*

One interesting fact in regard to the Negro mechanic in slavery time is that the demand for more efficient and more skilled labour made the slave mechanic a freer and more independent person than the other slaves. In a recent study of the condition of slave labour in the Charleston District, Professor Ulrich B. Phillips, of the University of Wisconsin, has pointed out that, all through the South and particularly in the cities where the demand for skilled labour was greatest, there was a constant disposition on the part of slave-owners to do away, in one way or another, with the restrictions

---

* "The Negro as an Inventor," N. E. Baker, and "Twentieth Century Negro Literature," pp. 399-413.

that were imposed upon the intellectual progress and personal freedom of their slave mechanics. Upon this point, Professor Phillips says:

The system had to be made flexible by giving to every trustworthy slave, who was capable of self-direction, a personal incentive to increase his skill and assiduity. Under such conditions the laws which impeded industrial progress were increasingly disregarded and became dead letters. Slaves by hundreds hired their own time; whites and blacks, skilled and unskilled, worked side by side, with little notice of the colour line; trustworthy slaves were practically in a state of industrial freedom; and that *tertium quid*, the free person of colour, always officially unwelcome, was now regarded in private life as a desirable resident of a neighbourhood, provided he were a good workman. The liberalising tendencies were fast relieving the hard-and-fast character of the régime, so far at least as concerned all workmen who were capable of better things than gang and task labour.

The great mass of the common Negroes, it is true, were regarded as suited only for the gangs and unfit for any self-direction in civilised industry; but even in this case a few thinking men saw vaguely from time to time that a less expensive method of control ought to be substituted for chattel slavery, involving as it did the heavy capitalisation of lifetime labor as a commodity.*

Under the influence of the conditions here described a considerable portion of the slaves were gradually making their way out of slavery. Many of them purchased their freedom and moved North; others, though nominally slaves, were practically free. They were allowed to purchase their own time, and in many cases engaged in business for themselves. Such was the case, for instance, of

---

* *Political Science Quarterly*, September, 1907, vol. xxii., pp. 427–429.

the father of Mr. R. R. Taylor, Director of Mechanical Industries, at Tuskegee Institute.   Mr. Taylor's
father was the son of a white man who was at the
same time his master.   Although he was nominally
a slave, he was early given liberty to do about as he
pleased.   While he was still a young man in Wilmington, North Carolina, he made the acquaintance of a white man who owned a sailing vessel,
and they entered into a sort of partnership together.
The young coloured man collected and bought up
naval stores and other merchandise which he
turned over to his partner, who carried them off in
his ship and sold them.   In this way they made a
considerable amount of money together so that after
all the losses of the war, Mr. Taylor's father was able
to send him through one of the best technical training schools in the United States, the Boston
Institute of Technology.   I could mention a hundred other cases which illustrate the way men and
women, though nominally slaves, succeeded in
reaching a condition that was very close to that of
freedom.

It was not an unusual thing in slavery days for a
coloured man and a white man to go into business
together.   Negro and white artisans worked side by
side during slavery, and the freedom to labour
and to engage in business, without prejudice, has
always existed.   In all the ordinary forms of
business and of labour there is no prejudice

against the Negro. I should rather say that, other things being equal, a Southern white man who has a job of work to do would prefer to have a Negro perform it.

If slavery had continued as it began, merely an industrial system, a method of obtaining and directing labour, it is very likely that the slaves would have succeeded finally in working out their own freedom; but slavery had become, with the course of time, not only an industrial but also a political system and, by the beginning of the nineteenth century, many people in the South had begun to feel that it was absolutely necessary to preserve this system. In order to do this they found it necessary to pass laws which would limit and set bounds to the progress which the slaves were making. It was in the interest of this system that laws were passed to prevent masters emancipating their slaves. It was in the interest of the same system that laws were passed limiting the direction in which slave labour might be employed and the extent to which slaves might be instructed in the trades and in books. For instance, North Carolina allowed slaves to learn mathematical calculation, but not reading and writing. A law was passed in Georgia that no one should permit a Negro "to transact business for him in writing." In 1830, Mississippi passed a law which forbade employment of slaves in printing-offices, and, in 1845, the Legislature of Georgia declared that slaves and free Negroes could not take contracts for building and repairing houses.*

These restrictions bore most heavily upon the class of industrious and ambitious slaves. It was largely from this class that the fugitives, who, at the beginning of the nineteenth century, began to make their way northward, were recruited. It was from the sufferings of these fugitives and the hardships which they endured in order to preserve their liberty, that the Northern people became acquainted with the evils of slavery in the South. Many of the fugitive slaves, like Frederick Douglass, Bishop Loguen, and William Wells Brown, joined in the anti-slavery agitation in the North, and by their eloquence helped prepare the North for the struggle with slavery that was soon to take place. Thus the effect of the laws made in the South, to suppress the efforts of the Negro slaves to be free, produced conditions in the North which finally resulted in the destruction of the slavery system.

Perhaps it is fair to say that the real cause of the downfall of slavery was not so much the hardships that it imposed upon the masses of both races, black and white, but the fact that it attempted to build up a dam that would hold back and restrain the forces that were making for progress inside the system itself. No page of history, I venture to say, better illustrates the fact that it is not possible to pass a

---

* "The Negro Artisan," Atlanta University Publications, No. 7, p. 15.

law to permanently stop the progress of civilisation. The hardest and most ungrateful task, that any individual or any race can undertake, is that of holding down and under another individual or another race that is trying to rise.

CHAPTER IV

NEGRO CRIME AND RACIAL SELF-HELP

NEGRO crime in the United States reached its highest point in the years of financial strain, beginning in 1892 and ending in 1896. The United States Census Statistics of Crime show that from 1870 to 1890 there was an enormous increase of Negro criminality, particularly in the Northern states. The total number of Negro criminals enumerated in the Census of 1870 was 8,056; in 1880 this number had increased to 16,748; in 1890 it was 24,277; and in 1904 it was 26,087. This meant that for every one hundred thousand Negroes in the United States there were, in 1870, 162 criminals; in 1880, 248 criminals; in 1890, 325 criminals. Fourteen years later, however, in 1904, the number of Negro criminals to every one hundred thousand of the Negro population had fallen to 282.

Some time between 1890 and 1904 the wave of Negro criminality which, up to that time, had seemed to be steadily increasing, reached its highest point and began to recede. Between these two periods no census figures for the whole country are available, but a special study of the criminal statistics of cities, North and South, shows that about 1894 and 1895 there was a marked decrease in Negro crime.

Statistics for Washington, District of Columbia, from 1881 to 1902, showed that the maximum rate of 184 police arrests per thousand of Negro population was reached in 1893. In Charleston, South Carolina, the rate of arrests reached its maximum of 92 per thousand in 1902. Cincinnati, Ohio, reached its maximum rate of 276 per thousand of the Negro population in 1894. In Savannah, Georgia, the highest rate of 165 was not reached until 1898. In Chicago the rate of arrests of Negroes reached its maximum of 586 per thousand in 1892, the year of the World's Fair. At this time, there was a considerable transient population in Chicago, and, as the rate of Negro criminality per thousand is estimated on the basis of the permanent population, these figures are like to be misleading.

The rate of arrests in St. Louis, Missouri, reached its maximum, when the number of arrests per thousand of the Negro population was 269. Statistics from the cities of New York and Philadelphia, the only cities for which data covering the period prior to 1866 are available, show that the rate of Negro arrests per thousand of the Negro population was about as great prior to 1866 as it was in 1902. The maximum rate for New York was reached in 1899 when the number of arrests per thousand of the Negro population was 111. The rate of arrests per thousand of the Negro population in Philadelphia has, at no time previous to 1902, been greater than it was in 1864, when there were 150 arrests per thousand of the Negro population.

The thing that makes these figures the more signif-icant is the fact that it is, as a rule, in the large cities that much the larger proportion of crimes is com-mitted. At any rate, it is in the cities that the larger proportion of crimes committed gets into court and is recorded. Furthermore, it is in the cities that the larger proportion of the increase of recorded crime has taken place during the period that I have men-tioned. This is, no doubt, the reason why statistics show that there are more Negro criminals in the North than in the South. Seven-tenths of the Negroes in the Northern states live in the cities having at least more than 2,500 inhabitants, and more than one-third of the Negroes in the Northern states live in cities having more than one hundred thousand inhabitants.

A comparison of the criminal statistics of the Northern and Southern states will illustrate what I mean:

Negro Prisoners in Northern States:

1870	1880	1890	1904
2,025	3,774	5,635	7,527

Negro Prisoners per 100,000 of Negro Pop. in Northern States:

1870	1880	1890	1904
372	515	773	765

Negro Prisoners in Southern States:

1870	1880	1890	1904
6,031	12,973	19,244	18,550

Prisoners per 100,000 of Negro Pop. in Southern States:

1870	1880	1890	1904
136	221	284	220

The increase in the amount of Negro crime in the United States during the period of 1870 to 1890 was so rapid and so marked that it made a great impression on the public, North and South.   A thing that helped to emphasise these facts and make them seem more serious than they actually were, particularly in the Southern states, was the outbreak, at this time, of mob-violence so savage and so terrible in its manifestations, as to attract, for a time, the attention of the whole civilised world.   From 1882 to 1892 the number of persons lynched in the United States increased from 114 to 235 per annum.   From that time on to 1903 the number decreased to 104 per annum. The total number of Negroes lynched during this period of twenty-two years was 2,060; the total number of whites lynched during the same period was 1,169.   In the case of the Negroes there was an average of 93 and 7-11 per year; in the case of the whites the average was 53 and 3-22 per year.

Of the 2,060 put to death in this way during this period, 1,985, or more than 96 per cent., were lynched in the Southern states.   The offences for which these people suffered death from the wild vengeance of the mob were not, as has been supposed, in the majority of cases assaults upon women. A little more than one-third of the lynchings were due to assaults, attempted assaults, upon women or insults to them. The larger number were occasioned by the crime of murder.

The minor offences for which Negroes were lynched were such things as robbery, slander, wife-beating, cutting levees, kidnapping, voodooism, poisoning horses, writing insulting letters, incendiary language, swindling, jilting a girl, colonising Negroes, political troubles, gambling, quarrelling, poisoning wells, throwing stones, unpopularity, making threats, circulating scandal, being troublesome, bad reputation, drunkenness, rioting, fraud, enticing a servant away, writing letters to white women, asking a white woman in marriage, conspiracy, introducing small-pox, giving information, conjuring, concealing a criminal, slapping a child, passing counterfeit money, elopement with a white girl, disobeying ferry regulations, running quarantine, violation of contract, paying attention to a white girl, resisting assault, inflammatory language, forcing white boys to commit crime, lawlessness.*

These cases of mob-violence and the crime which occasioned them, were, as I have said, widely advertised by the press through the North and through the South. And they helped to give the impression that the Negroes in the South were much more

* "Lynch Law," Cutler, p. 167.

lawless than they were in other parts of the country, much more lawless than other races in the same stage of civilisation as the Negro. As a matter of fact, as may be seen from the statistics I have given, the Negro criminals in the North were always much more numerous, in proportion to the Negro population, than they were in the South. Furthermore, as I hope to show later in this chapter, the amount of crime committed by other peoples who have come here from Europe, and particularly from the South of Europe, where the social conditions are in some sense comparable to the social conditions of the Negro in the South, is considerably larger in proportion to the number of population they represent, than is true in the case of the Negro.

The single fact to which attention was directed, as a consequence of this outbreak of mob-violence, was that the number of Negro criminals, in proportion to the Negro population, was three times as great as that of the white criminals in proportion to the white population, and that Negro crime was increasing with much greater rapidity than was the crime committed by whites.

One of the wholesome results of these outbreaks of mob-violence and of the discussion that they aroused, has been to direct the attention of earnest men and women of the Negro race to a study of the actual facts and their causes, in the hope of improving conditions by getting at the sources of Negro crime. The attention of Negro teachers and students was first called to these facts by the Hampton Negro Conferences, and studies were begun under the direction of these Conferences as early as 1898. Some years later, in 1903 and 1904, a study of Negro crime was made under the direction of W. E. Burghardt Du Bois, Professor of Sociology at Atlanta University. This study of Negro crime, which was published in 1904, is all the more interesting because it was made under the direction of a Negro and represents, in so very large a degree, the results of the studies and observations of Negro students and teachers upon the sources of crime among the people of their own race.

Referring to the work that Negro schools are doing in the way of studying the social conditions of the Negro people, I am reminded of something said to me a few years ago by a gentleman who had been devoting some months to travel through the Southern states, in order, to gather material for a book upon the subject of the Negro and his relations to the white man in the South. He told me, among other things, that he had been greatly surprised to observe to what extent educated coloured men, in all parts of the country, had taken up in a serious and systematic way the study of the social conditions of their own people. He said that he had been informed in the North that educated Negroes had little or no interest in studying the conditions of their own people, but were interested rather in getting as far away as they were able from the masses of the Negro race. On the other hand, he had been told in the South that Negroes were so wholly ignorant and unreliable that if he wanted to really get at the truth about the Negro he must get his information from a white man.

When he came to meet the educated Negroes in the Southern states, however, he had learned that they were not only well-informed in regard to the conditions of their own people but that they frequently seemed to have gained a deeper insight into the actual conditions of the Negro people, and to have a more accurate knowledge of the situation, as it looked to a man from the outside, than many white men he had met. He added that, considering the persons he referred to were in many instances the sons and daughters of slave parents, and that few of them had had opportunities for study that men and women of the white race have had, this seemed to him an evidence of very genuine progress on the part of the Negro race.

The study of Negro crime to which I have referred is interesting, however, not merely as an indication of the serious interest that educated Negroes have begun to take in the condition of the Negro race, but it is interesting also for the new facts which were first brought to light in this study, and have since been confirmed by a census of crime published by the United States Census Bureau in 1907.

One of the facts brought out by this census concerns the method of enumeration used by the Census
Office. For instance, up to 1904 it had been the
practice, in taking the census of crime, to count all
persons who were in jails or prisons on a certain day.
The result was supposed to give the relative number
of criminals in different parts of the country and so
indicate the comparative amount of crime committed
in these different places.

A closer study of the statistics shows, however,
that it has been customary to sentence prisoners for
longer terms in some parts of the country than in
others, even though the crime committed was of the
same character or class. This is true, for instance,
of the Southern states as compared with the Northern
states. The result has been that an undue amount
of crime has been credited, by this method of enumeration, to the Southern states.

I can, perhaps, make this point clear by an illustration. Consider the case of a man who is engaged
in raising chickens, and who, for some reason or
other, desires to confine a certain number of his
chickens, while the others are allowed to run loose.
He has, let us suppose, two breeds, and he puts
five chickens of each breed into the hen-yard every
day, with, however, this difference, that the chickens
of one breed are confined in the hen-yard one week,
while the chickens of the other breed are confined
two weeks. Now it is evident that if you put five

chickens of each breed in the hen-yard every day, you will have, at the end of the first week, an equal number of each breed, namely, thirty-five. From that time on, however, the number of chickens in the hen-yard which are confined two weeks will be larger than that of the breed confined one week. So that at the end of the second week there will be still only thirty-five chickens of the first breed, while there will be seventy of the second. In other words, there will be twice as many of the second in confinement as of the first breed.

The result is the same whether we are counting chickens in a hen-yard or prisoners in a penitentiary. This illustrates, in a simple way, how it is that in the Southern states, where the sentences imposed upon criminals are heavier than they are in the Northern states, the number of criminals enumerated at any one time will be disproportionately large.

In order to correct this error it was determined, in the Census of 1904, not merely to enumerate the persons found in confinement at any particular date, but to obtain figures as to the number of commitments, that is to say, to find out the number of persons who had been sent to jail during the period of a year. By this means, the Census of 1904 took account not merely of those who happened to be in the jails or the prisons at a given period, but also of those who had come in during the year, and, either because they had been able to pay their fines or because they served their sentences, had been released.

The results showed at once some striking changes in the statistics of crime, and materially corrected some wrong impressions as to the relative amount of crime committed in the different sections. For example, the number of prisoners enumerated according to the earlier method gave the North Atlantic states in 1904, 27,389 prisoners. The number of commitments for that same year was 76,235. In other words, according to the second method of enumeration, there was 48,846 more crimes committed in the Northern states than there appeared to be by the first method of counting. This was an increase of nearly 200 per cent.

On the other hand, in the South Atlantic states there were 11,150 prisoners enumerated, but only 10,643 had been committed to prison during the year. By this method of reckoning it appeared that there were 507 criminals less than were shown by the earlier method of enumeration. The same differences appear when the South Central states are compared with the North Central states and the Western states. By the census enumeration, it appeared that there were 14,614 prisoners in the penitentiaries and jails in the South Central states while only 10,206 had been committed to prison during the year. This was a decrease of 4,408. In the North Central states, reckoning by the methods of enumeration, there were 21,000 prisoners, but by the method of commitment there were 38,603. In other words, there appeared to be 17,603 more criminals by this latter method of enumeration than by the former. In the Western states there were 7,619 prisoners enumerated, but there were 14,004 commitments during the year.

One explanation of these differences is, as I have said, that in the Southern states the sentences are longer than they are in the Northern states. I do not know exactly why the Southern courts impose heavier sentences upon prisoners than the Northern courts. Perhaps it is because the crimes committed in the South are more serious than those committed in the North and deserve heavier punishment. But that, of course, is no reason why we should count those crimes twice in making up our estimates of the criminal population, as I fear has, in effect, sometimes been done in comparing the amount of crime committed in the South with the amount of crime committed in the North.

The method of computing crime which has made so large a difference in the apparent amount of crime committed in the South, as compared with the North, has been responsible for crediting a disproportionate amount of crime to the Negro. For instance, in the South Atlantic states, 8,281 criminals were enumerated as in jails and prisons in 1904. In the same year, however, only 6,847 prisoners had been committed to prison. In the South Central states, 10,269 prisoners were enumerated in the prisons and jails during the year 1904. At the same time it was found that only 6,066 prisoners had been committed during that year. In other words, if we were to estimate the amount of Negro crime in the South by the number of persons found in the prisons and jails, there would be 5,643 more criminals found for the year 1904 than if we had counted the actual number of Negroes arrested, convicted and committed to prison. The reason here again is that Negroes in the South are given longer sentences than white men. For example, 50 per cent. of the Negroes convicted of crime in the South Atlantic states were sentenced to terms of one year or more, while only 38 per cent. of the white men so convicted were sentenced to terms of a year or more.

No doubt, also, there is a difference in the crimes committed by the white and black population. It is said that, in the South, stealing and all crimes against property are punished relatively with more severe sentences than crimes of violence, or crimes against the person, as they are termed. An illustration of this is given in an article upon the " Negro in Crime," in the *Independent* for May 18, 1899, where the following items clipped from the Atlanta *Constitution*, of January 27, are quoted. The items are:

Egbert Jackson (coloured), aged thirteen, was given a sentence of $50, or ten months in the chain gang, for larceny from the house·

The most affecting scene of all was the sentencing of Joe Redding, a white man, for the killing of his brother, John Redding. . . .

Judge ———— is a most tender-hearted man, and heard the prayers and saw the tears, and tempered justice with moderation, and gave the modern Cain two years in the penitentiary.

The two cases I have just cited are, perhaps, exceptional, but they illustrate the kind of crime upon which the Southern courts are disposed to put the emphasis. At the time the crimes referred to in these clippings were committed, there were, so far as I know, no juvenile courts in any of the Southern states, and with the exception of the Virginia Manual Labour School, started in 1897, no reformatories to which Negro children could be sent. Where the principle of the juvenile court has been established, an offence committed by a child, such as the one referred to in the foregoing quotation, is not considered a crime in the same sense in which an offence committed by an adult person is so considered. The imposition of heavier sentences for minor offences and especially the disposition of Southern courts to impose relatively heavier penalties on children, has had the effect of largely increasing the number of Negroes in the jail and prison population.

It should be remembered, in this respect, also, that among the members of the Negro race, owing, no doubt, to the condition of the home surroundings, to poverty, and, perhaps, also, to the fact that mothers are so frequently employed away from home, a much larger proportion of Negro criminals are children than is true with the white race. This makes the system which prevailed a few years ago, and still continues in a less degree, of sending children, particularly Negro children, to the penitentiaries and the chain-gang, bear so heavily upon the members of my race. When children are sent to prison, they are not only subjected, during the period when they are most impressionable, to the influences of evil companions, but they sometimes get to thinking of the prison as a place to which they naturally belong, and where they expect to spend the larger part of their lives. It is a very serious matter when a race or a class of people reaches the point where it begins to feel that it is looked upon by those to whom it has been taught to look for guidance and control, as a criminal people.

A few years ago, when I was in Kentucky, I remember hearing a story which struck me as peculiarly pathetic. One morning the officers of the State Prison found, in counting over their prisoners, that they had one too many. Upon investigation, they discovered a young coloured boy, who had been discharged from prison a few days before, had actually broken into the prison during the night, apparently in order to find a place to sleep. As I remember the story, the boy said, when questioned, that after leaving the prison he had wandered about till he was very hungry, and as he had no place to stay he finally decided to come back and crawl into the stockade, where there were at least people who knew him, and where he could find a place to sleep. From all that I could learn, this boy had lived so long in prison that he had come to feel more at home there than he did outside.

Another reason why prison sentences are longer in the South than they are in the North is because, under the convict-lease system, crime has been or has seemed to be immensely profitable, not only to the states but to individuals. For instance, in 1900, the state of Georgia received $61,826.32 from the earnings of prisoners. From 1901 to 1903, the net income was $81,000 a year. In 1904, new contracts were made for a period of five years beginning April 1, 1904, which netted the state on an average of $225,000 per annum.

It is only slowly that the public has begun to realise that the new form of slavery, represented by the convict-lease system, has made the condition of the convict-slave infinitely worse than was possible under a system of slavery in which the slave belonged to his master for life. Gradually, however, the evils of a system which made crime profitable have been coming to light. In 1908, Georgia, seeing the horrible conditions that existed in the convict camps, abandoned its old methods of disposing of convict labor and has since that time employed convicts in building the public roads. The conditions that formerly existed in Georgia still exist, however, in several of the other Southern states.

In most cases where an effort has been made to determine the relative criminality of the Negro it has been customary to compare the Negro with the white man. Because the white man stood higher in the scale of civilisation, was better educated, had a better home and was more respected, this comparison has been to the disadvantage of the Negro.

The criminal statistics of 1890 showed, for example, that there were 104 white and 325 Negro criminals in the United States for every one hundred thousand of the respective races. In other words, the crimes of Negroes were more than three times those of the whites. In the Northern states, the ratio was even greater, the crimes of Negroes being more than five times those of the whites.

In 1904, however, when the races were compared upon the basis of the actual number of persons committed to prison during the year, it was found that the commitments per hundred thousand were 187 for the whites and 268 for the Negroes. That is to say, the two races stood to each other, in respect to the amount of crime committed by each, in about the ratio of one to one and one-half. In the Northern states, Negro crime, instead of being five times, was a little more than four times that of the whites.

By the census of 1890 it appeared that the Negro

offenders in Southern states compared with the white
offender in those states, were in the ratio of 2 to 9.
That is to say, in those states, comparing the races
by the methods I. have described, there were four
and one-half times as much crime committed by
Negroes as by whites. In 1904, however, considering the actual number of both races committed to
prison, it appears that the Negro crime, compared
with the white, was in the ratio of less than three
and one-half to one — a decrease of 21 per cent.

In looking further into the statistics of crime
with special reference to the nationality of the criminals, I have found that among the foreign-born
people in the United States, the different nationalities
range themselves, at very diverse distances, on two
sides of the general average of crime committed by
the foreign population as a whole. On the one side,
there are nationalities which fall far below the
average. On the other hand, there are others which
rise far above that average.

In comparing the Negro with the immigrants now
coming into the United States in such large numbers
from the South of Europe, we are comparing him
with races which in Europe have been, and still in
America are, living in the conditions that are in many
respects comparable to those in which the masses of
the Negro people now live. The people to whom
I refer are, in many instances, less advanced in education in books than the majority of the coloured

people in the Southern states, though they are, no doubt, far ahead of them in some of the more fundamental things.

For instance, among the Italian people, as a whole, more than 38 per cent. of the population can neither read nor write. Of the people who come into the United States, particularly from Sicily and Southern Italy, no doubt a much larger per cent. are illiterate. In Russia, more than 70 per cent. of the population are without education. In other parts of Southern Europe, like Roumania, 89 per cent. of the people are wholly illiterate.

A good many of these people are now coming into certain parts of the South. The following comparison, therefore, of the relative criminality of these different races as compared to the Negro is peculiarly interesting:

Nationality	Number in U. S. according to census 1900	Prison commitments in 1904	Commitments per 1,000 of each nationality
Mexicans . . .	103,410	484	4.7
Italians . . .	484,207	2,143	4.4
Austrians . . .	276,249	1,006	3.6
French . . .	104,341	358	3.4
Canadians . .	1,181,255	3,557	3.0
Russians . . .	424,096	1,222	2.8
Poles	383,510	1,038	2.7
Negroes . . .	8,840,789	23,698	2.7

There is another class of crimes with which the Negro has been more associated in the public mind than any other. I refer to the assaults upon women, to which attention has so often been directed because they have so frequently been made the occasion of, or excuse for, outbreaks of mob-violence, not only in the Southern states but in the Northern states as well. The total commitments for rape, in 1904, were 620; of this number 450 were by white persons, 170 by coloured, and 111 by persons of foreign birth.

The number of cases of rape committed by coloured people, including all the races in the United States classed under that title, was 1.8 per hundred thousand of the total coloured population. The total number of commitments for the white population was 0.6 per hundred thousand of the white population. The number of commitments for this crime per hundred thousand of the foreign population was 1. In other words, the number of commitments for rape was proportionately three times as great for the coloured population as it was for the whites. It was nearly twice as great, proportionately, as that for the foreign population.*

A comparison of the coloured committed for this crime with that portion of the foreign-born population which is nearest to the coloured in respect to education and social condition shows, however, that the Negro is by no means the worst offender in respect to this crime. The following table shows the number of commitments per hundred thousand for

---

* The census for 1904 does not separate the Negro from the other coloured populations in respect to the crime of rape.

this crime of the foreign-born people to whom I
have referred: :

Italians	. . . . 5.3	Hungarians	. . 2.0
Mexicans	. . . 4.8	French 1.9
Austrians	. . . 3.2	Russians	. . . 1.9

For other portions of the foreign-born population
the percentage is less. For example, among the
Canadian-born population statistics indicate for
every one hundred thousand of the population that
1.2 are guilty of assaults on women. For other
foreign-born portions of the population the figures
are Polanders 1.0, Germans 0.4, Irish 0.3.

While it is true that the Negro furnishes a proportionately large number of the crimes of assault
upon women, I do not think it is true, if we are to go
by the statistics, that there is any more disposition on
the part of men of the Negro race to commit this
crime than on the part of men of other races.
While no statistics can possibly determine this fact,
I have taken the trouble to find out what per cent. of
the major offenders, that is to say, of the men who
committed the worst crimes, were sent to prison for
the crime of rape during the year 1904. From these
figures it appears that only 1.9 per cent. of the coloured
offenders committed for major offences were committed for the crime of rape. On the other hand,
2.3 per cent. of the white and 2.6 per cent. of the
foreign major offenders were committed in 1904
for that crime. The following table will show the

per cent. of major offenders of the races to whom
I have already made reference, who were committed
for this offence:

Hungarians .	. .	4.7	Canadians . . .	3.0
Italians .	. . .	4.4	Mexicans . . .	2.7
Austrians	. .	4.2	Poles	2.1
French .	. . .	3.1	Germans . . .	1.8
Russians .	. . .	3.0	Irish	1.3
	Coloured	. . 1.9		

As a further confirmation of the facts which these
statistics show, I might mention that in the South
Atlantic states, where 35.7 per cent. of the total population are Negroes, the rate of commitments per
100,000 of the population for assault on women is
0.5. On the other hand, in the Western Division,
where only 0.7 per cent. of the total population are
Negroes, the commitments for rape amount to 1.4
for each 100,000 of the population. In the North
Atlantic states, where Negroes represent 1.8 per cent.
of the population, the number of commitments for
this crime per hundred thousand is 0.9. In the South
Central states, where 29.8 per cent. of the population
are Negroes, the number of commitments for rape
per hundred thousand is 0.7.

It may be said that the reason the commitments
for assaults upon women are lower in those regions
where the Negro population is proportionately larger,
is due to the fact that the men who commit these
crimes are summarily executed by lynch law. The

fact is, however, that were the total number of Negroes lynched for rape in the United States in 1904 added to those arrested and committed to prison, it would not change these percentages more than a quarter of one per cent.

Before concluding what I have to say on the subject of Negro crime I want to add a word in regard to the work that Negroes, sometimes in association with their white neighbours and sometimes independently, have done and are doing to get at and destroy the sources of crime among members of their race.

Immediately after the Atlanta Riot, September 22, 1906, during which ten white people and sixty coloured people were wounded, and two white and ten coloured people were killed, there came forward two men, among others, with definite measures of "re-construction." These men were ex-Governor W. J. Northen and Charles T. Hopkins.

Ex-Governor Northen set on foot what was at first known as the "Christian League," an organisation composed of leading coloured men and leading white men, formed for the purpose of putting down mob-violence. Charles T. Hopkins, a prominent young lawyer of Atlanta, organised, in association with Reverend H. H. Proctor, pastor of the First Coloured Congregational Church, and some others, what was known as the Civic League, the purpose of which was to bring leading coloured men and leading white men of the city together in order to coöperate in doing away with the conditions which had brought about the Atlanta Riot.

One of the first things that this dual organisation did was to defend in the courts a Negro named Joe Glenn, who had been charged with an assault upon a woman. In fact, he had been identified by the woman upon whom the assault was committed, and the members of this organisation, both white and coloured, believed that Joe Glenn was guilty. Their purpose was merely to secure for him a fair and speedy trial. Upon examination into the evidence, however, they came to the conclusion that the man was not guilty, and succeeded not only in proving his innocence before the trial was ended, but in finding the man who was guilty, and thus, undoubtedly, saved the life of an innocent man.

The Civic League confined its operations to the city of Atlanta, but ex-Governor Northen sought to extend the influence of his organisation throughout the state of Georgia and into adjoining states. Up to 1909, he had organised eighty-three of what came to be known as the Christian Civic leagues. These organisations were located mainly in counties containing the larger Negro populations, and were composed of the very best people in the state, white and black.

One of the indirect results of this "re-construction" movement was the erection, under the direction of Reverend H. H. Proctor, and at a cost of $50,000, of a handsome institutional Negro church. This church was dedicated in February, 1909. It was intended to do a work among the coloured people that would attack the causes of racial friction and make mobs like that of 1906 impossible.

Before this time, however, Negro people themselves, with very little assistance from their white neighbours, had undertaken a kind of work intended to remedy the evils in their present condition. All over the South, and in many parts of the North, wherever the Negroes live in large numbers, coloured orphan asylums have been established to care for the neglected children from among whom Negro criminals are so frequently recruited. As near as I have been able to learn, there are not less than fifty or sixty of such asylums already in existence in different parts of the United States. A number of these, like the Carrie Steele Orphanage, of Atlanta, have been started upon the small savings and pious faith of some good coloured woman.

Carrie Steele, the founder of the orphanage at Atlanta, which bears her name, was born a slave in Georgia. For many years she was employed at the Atlanta Union Depot. Here she had an opportunity to see something of the dangers to which homeless and neglected coloured children were subjected. In order to raise money to carry out the plan she then formed of establishing an orphans' home, she wrote a little book, which was the story of her life. This book found a ready sale among the charitably disposed people, and with the proceeds a home was organised in 1890. This institution began with five orphans. In 1906, it was caring for ninety-seven children, and had an income of $2,000 a year, a portion of which is paid by the coloured people and the remainder by the city.

In 1897, a Negro reformatory association was organised in Virginia by John H. Smythe, former minister to Liberia. It had a Negro board of directors, and an advisory board of seven white people, and its purpose, as stated, was to "rescue juvenile offenders." The association purchased a large tract of land, amounting to four hundred and twenty-three acres, which had been part of the "Broadneck" estate in Hanover County, Virginia. For a number of years this reformatory was supported by private philanthropy, but eventually it became a state institution.

In conclusion, I want to say a word here about a work that the Negroes of Birmingham, Alabama, have undertaken, at the suggestion and under the direction of Judge N. B. Feagin, of the Municipal Court.

Judge Feagin is not only a lawyer, but a student of sociology. Some years ago, when he first became judge of the Municipal Court, there was no way of disposing of children convicted in the City Courts except to send them to the chain-gang. In 1898, however, there was established at East Lake, about twenty miles from Birmingham, a reformatory for white boys.

The large number of juvenile offenders who found their way into courts were, however, Negro children. Nothing had been done, up to this time, to keep them out of prisons and chain-gangs. Every year large numbers graduated from the prisons into the ranks of professional criminals. In 1903, an attempt was made to remedy this by passing a juvenile court law, but it failed. March 12, 1907, however, a law was passed making it a misdeameanor to send any child under fourteen years of age to jail or prison. If there had been practical means for executing this law, it would have effected a revolution in the treatment of criminal children in Alabama. But, as in the case of the Negro children, no such means existed; the law was repealed the following August.

Meanwhile, Judge Feagin determined to establish, upon his own responsibility, a modern system of dealing with criminal children in Birmingham. He found that there are thirty Negro churches in Birmingham. He determined to call the preachers of these churches together and explain his purpose to them. He then asked them if they could not induce the women of their congregation to raise two dollars per month to support a coloured probation officer. He said if they would do that, instead of sending the coloured children, who were brought into his court, to the chain-gang, he would send them back to their homes or to the homes of relatives and friends, on probation.

A coloured probation officer was appointed and the city divided into thirty districts, in which three women from each of the thirty Negro congregations in the city were appointed to coöperate with the probation officer in looking after the children on probation. In order to arouse interest in this plan, an association was formed of the coloured women of the thirty different churches, and Judge Feagin went around to the different Negro churches to speak to the people in order to assist the association, in this way, in raising money to support the voluntary probation officer he had appointed.

So far as the plan outlined was carried out, it concerned only those children who were brought into the court for the first time. It was necessary to devise some means for taking care of those who were guilty of a second offence. Judge Feagin decided that the way to dispose of them was to send them to the country districts. He then announced this plan in the papers and declared that wherever he could find a coloured farmer of good character, who would take these children and put them to work, he would turn them over to him, under certain conditions, which were named.

About twelve miles from Tuscaloosa, the former capital of Alabama, there is a Negro farmer by the name of Sam Dailey, who owns five hundred and thirty-five acres of land. This man, reading of Judge Feagin's proposal, came to see him and made a proposition to set aside one hundred and twenty-five acres of his farm, on which he would employ the children whom Judge Feagin sent him. Sam Dailey has been receiving these boys since 1903. With the aid of funds which he has been able to collect and from the profits of the farm he has established a school, which is conducted by a coloured preacher employed for that purpose. During this time, and up to 1909, he had had on his farm over one hundred Negro boys. Some few of them have run away. Several have been sent back to their relatives in the city. Others have become permanently settled in the farming districts and are making good citizens.

As a result of the interest aroused in this work, two other reformatories for juvenile offenders of the Negro race have been started. One of these is on the outskirts of Birmingham, and the other is at Mount Meigs, a few miles from Montgomery. At the time this is written, the probation officer, Reverend J. D. James, is supported not merely by the contributions he receives from the coloured churches, but also from two of the coloured secret orders in Birmingham. It is the hope of Judge Feagin and those who are associated with him that the work which is being done will eventually receive the sanction and support of the state, and that the juvenile court law, which was passed and repealed, will then be reënacted.

CHAPTER V

IN THE spring of 1907, Colonel Henry Watterson, of Louisville, Kentucky, the noted Democratic editor and statesman, made an address at a great meeting in Carnegie Hall, New York City, in the interest of Negro education in the South. Speaking of the work that has been accomplished in this direction since the War, he said: "The world has never yet witnessed such progress from darkness into light as the American Negro has made in the period of forty years."

When the Negro was made free and became an American citizen, it is safe to say that not more than 5 or, at most, 10 per cent. of the race could read and write. In 1900, at the end of less than forty years of freedom, 55½ per cent. could both read and write. If Negro education has made as much progress in the last ten years, as it did from 1890 to 1900, it is safe to say, at the present time, that not more than 32 per cent. of the Negro population is without some education in books. As Mr. Watterson said, no race in history can show a similar record.

What was it that so aroused a whole race, a nation within a nation, numbering at the present time ten millions of people, to make such strides in education? How has this work been done?

Perhaps the best answer I can make to this question is to relate my own experience. When I was a boy in Virginia, I used sometimes to accompany the white children of the plantation to the schoolhouse, in our neighbourhood. I went with them to carry their books, to carry their wraps, or their lunches, but I was never permitted to go farther than the schoolroom door. In my childish ignorance, I did not understand this. During the hours when the white children were not in school, we played and chatted together about the house or in the fields. We rode together our wooden horses; we fished together in the nearby streams; we played marbles, town-ball, "tag," and wrestled together on the parlour floor. And yet, for some reason I did not understand, I was debarred from entering the little schoolhouse with the children of my master.

The thing made such an impression upon my mind, that I finally asked my mother about it. She explained the matter to me as best she could, and from her I heard for the first time that learning from books in a schoolroom was something that, as a rule, was forbidden to a Negro child in the South. The idea that books contained something which was forbidden aroused my curiosity and excited in me a desire to find out for myself what it was in these books that made them forbidden fruit to me and my race.

From the moment that it was made clear to me that I was not to go to school, that it was dangerous for me to learn to read, from that moment I resolved that I should never be satisfied until I learned what this dangerous practice was like. What was true in my case has been true in the case of thousands of others. If no restriction had been put upon Negro education, I doubt whether such tremendous progress in education would have been made.

When I became free all the legal restrictions against my getting education were removed. Nevertheless I heard it stated in public speeches that the Negro was so constituted that he could not learn from books, and that time, effort and money would be thrown away in trying to teach him to master the studies of the ordinary school curriculum. When I heard this, I resolved again that, at the price of any sacrifice, I would do my part in order to prove to the world that the Negro possessed the ability to get an education, and to use it. If I had heard no such prediction regarding the ability of the Negro to get education, I question whether I would have been any more interested in mastering my school studies and text-books than the ordinary white boy.

Directly after the War the whole race was conscious that a large part of the American people doubted the ability of the Negro to compete with other races in the field of learning. But when the Negro heard people freely discussing his abilities and making predictions about his future he determined to see to it that these predictions should not be fulfilled.

My experience is that it is very unsafe to make predictions either in regard to races or in regard to individuals. Sometimes the mere statement of a prophecy tends to bring about its own fulfillment. In this case, if the predictions made are evil, the prophets become, to a certain extent, responsible for their consequences. At other times predictions stimulate the people, in regard to whom they are made, to do something entirely different than the thing predicted. But in that case, of course, the predictions do not become true. In either case prophecy is likely to be unprofitable.

In order to gain a just idea of the distance the Negro has travelled during the years since freedom came we should compare his progress with that of the people of some of the countries of Europe that have been free for centuries. For example, in Italy, 38.30 per cent. of the population can neither read nor write. In Spain the percentage of illiteracy is 68.1 per cent.; in Russia, 77 per cent.; in Portugal, 79 per cent.; in Brazil, 80 per cent.; in Venezuela,

75 per cent.; and in Cuba 56.6 per cent. By comparison, the progress of the American Negro represents a remarkable achievement.

In the early days, when slavery was still merely an economic and not yet a political institution, there seems to have been no special restrictions put either upon the education of slaves or of free Negroes. If Negroes did not obtain an education it was because there were few opportunities in the Southern colonies for any one to receive an education. In fact, before the Revolution, there was no such thing as a public school system in any colony south of Connecticut. The colonies were opposed in principle to public schools. It was considered an interference on the part of the state to undertake the education of the younger children, who were supposed to be taught at home.

People in England who sent out the first colonies were interested, however, in the religious education of the Indians and as the number of slaves increased they became interested in the education of the Negroes, who, at that time, were also a "heathen" people. In fact, the first public school in Virginia, which was started about 1620, was erected for the benefit of these native Americans. The Indian War of 1622 destroyed this school, however, and thus little or nothing was done to educate either the Indian or the Negro in the English colonies until the year 1701, when a society was organised in England to carry the gospel and its teachings to the Indians and Negroes in America. In June, 1702, Reverend Samuel Thomas, the first missionary of this society, in reporting upon his work in South Carolina, said that he "had taken much pains, also, in instructing the Negroes, and learned twenty of them to read."

In 1704, Elias Neau, a French Protestant, established a catechising school for the Indian and Negro slaves in New York. His work continued successfully until 1712, when a conspiracy of the Negro slaves was discovered in New York, which was said to have had its origin in Mr. Neau's school. Upon the trial, however, it appeared that the guilty Negroes were "such as never came to Mr. Neau's school. And what is very observable," the chronicle adds, "the persons whose Negroes were found most guilty were such as were declared opposers to making them Christians." In 1738, the Moravian or United Brethren first attempted to establish missions exclusively for Negroes. In the Moravian settlement at Bethlehem, Pennsylvania, a painting is preserved of eighteen of the first converts made by these missionaries in America prior to 1747. Among the number are Johannes, a Negro of South Carolina, and Jupiter, a Negro from New York.

The religious instruction of Negroes was begun by the Presbyterians in Virginia in 1747. In a letter written in that year, Reverend Samuel Davis refers to "the poor, neglected Negroes who are so far from having money to purchase books that they themselves are the property of others." A little further on in this same letter, speaking of the eagerness of the Negro slave to hear the gospel and to learn to read, he says:

There are multitudes of them in different places who are willing and eagerly desirous to be instructed and to embrace every opportunity of acquainting themselves with the doctrines of the gospel; and though they have generally very little help to learn to read, yet to my agreeable surprise many of them, by dint of application in their leisure hours, have made such progress that they can intelligently read a plain author, and especially their Bibles, and pity it is that any of them should be without them.*

Two years earlier than the date of this letter, in 1745, the Society for Propagating the Gospel in Foreign Parts established a school in Charleston, South Carolina. It had at one time as many as sixty scholars and sent out annually about twenty Negroes, "well instructed in the English language and the Christian faith." This school was established in St. Philip's Church and some of its scholars were living as late as 1822, when the Denmark Vesey Conspiracy resulted in the closing of the schools for free Negroes as well as for slaves.

It seems probable that prior to the Revolution some attempt was made to teach the Negroes, wherever they were brought into touch with the Church. In this way, the Negro Sunday-schools

* "The Gospel Among the Slaves," W. P. Harrison, p. 51.

gave the Negroes the first opportunity for education and his first school book was the Bible. In 1747, when slavery was introduced into the colony of Georgia, respresentatives from twenty-three districts met in Savannah and drew up resolutions in regard to the conduct of masters toward their slaves. Among other things they declared in substance "that the owners of slaves should educate the the young and use every possible means of making religious impressions upon the minds of the aged."

In 1750, the Reverend Thomas Bacon, who was himself a slave-holder, established in Talbot County, Maryland, a mission for the poor white and Negro children. The majority of the colonied children who attended this school were slaves.*

In the Methodist Conference of 1790 the question was raised: "What can be done in order to instruct poor children, white and black, to read?" to which the following reply was made:

Let us labour as the heart and soul of one man to estab-lish Sunday-schools in or near the place of worship. Let persons be appointed by the bishops, elders, deacons, or preachers to teach gratis all that will attend and have a capacity to learn, from six in the morning till ten, and from two in the afternoon till six, where it does not interfere with public worship. The Council shall compile a proper school book to teach them learning and piety.

The opposition to the teaching of the slaves seems to have begun in South Carolina. In 1740 that

* "A Pioneer in Negro Education," Bernard C. Steiner, in the *Independent*, August 24, 1899.

state passed a law imposing a fine of one hundred pounds upon any one who should teach any "slave or slaves in writing in any manner whatsoever." In 1770 Georgia passed a similar law punishing with a fine of twenty pounds any person teaching a slave to read and write.

Immediately after the Revolution there was a feeling all over the United States that slavery was soon to pass away. About 1792, however, a Yankee schoolmaster, Eli Whitney, invented the cotton-gin. This invention suddenly made Negro slave labour valuable, particularly in the new states of the Southwest. From this time on, the feeling that slave labour was necessary to the economic life of the Southern states grew to a conviction that slavery was to be a permanent institution in the Southern states.

The change in public opinion is reflected in the laws. In 1819, Virginia passed an act prohibiting all meetings of slaves, free persons, and mulattoes, in the night, or any school or schools for teaching them reading and writing in either day or night. Ten years later, Georgia passed a law forbidding any person of colour from receiving instruction from any source. In 1830, Louisiana forbade free Negroes entering the state and passed a law against the printing and distribution of seditious matter among people of colour and against their being taught. A year later Mississippi passed a law against any coloured person, free or slave, from preaching the gospel. The next year Alabama passed a law against teaching any free person of colour or slave and, in 1835, North Carolina abolished the schools for free persons of colour, which up to that time had been taught for the most part by white teachers. The law passed in North Carolina at this time provided that no descendants of Negro parents, to the fourth generation, should enjoy the benefit of the public school system. Similar laws were passed in Mississippi and Missouri.

In spite of this fact Negroes continued, in one way or another, to keep alive the little tradition of learning they had already possessed. In New Orleans, and in Charleston, South Carolina, there were clandestine schools in which the children of free Negroes had an opportunity to get some sort of an education. In New Orleans it had long been the custom for planters, who had children by slave mothers, to send them abroad to France or to some of the Northern states for their education. One of the most interesting, as well as one of the most pathetic, chapters in American history is that which has to do with this class of white men who felt in honour bound to support, educate and protect their illegitimate offspring. To do this meant in many cases ostracism, loss of property, and reputation.

In 1833, the city of Mobile was authorised by

an act of legislation to grant licence to suitable persons to give instruction to the children of the Creole Negroes in that city. This act applied only to the county of Baldwin and to the city of Mobile. The basis for it was the treaty between France and the United States by which all the rights and privileges of citizens were guaranteed to them. It should be remembered, also, that schools for free coloured people were never abolished in Maryland, Kentucky, Tennessee, Florida and Texas.

The census of 1860 shows that there were 1,355 free coloured children attending school in Maryland. The schools were such as the coloured people could support, from the African Institute on Saratoga Street, Baltimore, with its hundred or more scholars, "to the half-dozen urchins learning their words under the counter of a little tobacco shop in Annapolis." One of these, known as the Wells school, was established in 1835 by Nelson Wells, a coloured man, who applied the income of $7,000 to its support.

The coloured people who got sufficient education during the days of slavery to read their Bible may be divided into four classes: those who were taught by their owners in spite of law; those who had white fathers; those who, in some way or other, obtained their freedom; those who literally stole their education. There were always a few cases in all the states where the master or mistress, or some other member of the family, took sufficient interest in some individual slave to teach him to read. Sometimes this was done out of mere curiosity, just to see if the Negro could learn. I have met dozens of former slaves who told me their owners taught them to read, and described the great precautions sometimes taken to keep the fact that such teaching was going on from other members of the same family and from the neighbours.

The desire to read the Bible was a plea that usually touched the heart of the more kindly disposed master. To this day there is an intense longing among a number of the older people to learn to read the Bible before they die. No matter how the slaves obtained their knowledge of reading and writing, in every case it was like bringing the germs of an infectious disease into the household; it spread. Among the free Negroes of Charleston, the learning that the older people had obtained previous to 1822 was handed down from generation to generation until the War brought freedom to the slave and the free Negro alike.

During his journey through Northern Mississippi, Frederick Law Olmsted one day stopped to talk with a small planter who seemed to have an exceptionally good class of slaves. Mr. Olmsted referred to the fine appearance of his Negro labourers, whereupon the following conversation as reported by Mr. Olmsted ensued:

"Well, I reckon it's my way o' treatin' 'em, much as anything. I never hev no difficulty with 'em. Hen't licked a nigger in five year, 'cept maybe sprouting some of the young ones sometimes. Fact, my niggers never want no lookin' arter; they just tek ker o' themselves. Fact, they do tek a greater interest in the crops than I do myself. There's another thing — I 'spose 'twill surprise you — there ent one of my niggers but what can read; read good, too — better'n I can, at any rate."

"How did they learn?"

"Taught themselves. I b'lieve there was one on 'em that I bought, that could read, and he taught all the rest. But niggers is mighty apt at larnin', a heap more'n white folks is."

I said that this was contrary to the generally received opinion.

"Well, now, let me tell you," he continued; "I had a boy to work, when I was buildin', and my boys jus' teachin' him night times and such, he warn't here more'n three months, and he larned to read as well as any man I ever heerd, and I know he didn't know his letters when he come here. It didn't seem to me any white man could have done that; does it to you, now?"

"How old was he?"

"Warn't more'n seventeen, I reckon."

"How do they get books — do you get them for them?"

"Oh, no; get 'em for themselves."

"How?"

"Buy 'em."

"How do they get the money?"

"Earn it."

"How?"

"By their own work. I tell you my niggers have got more money 'n I hev."

"What kind of books do they get?"

"Religious kind of books ginerally — these stories; and some of them will buy novels, I believe. They won't let on to that, but I expect they do it." *

When slaves living on the distant plantations in the back country of Mississippi succeeded in learning to read it is not difficult to understand that in the cities, where exceptional opportunities were given to the slaves employed in the household services of their masters, a considerable number should in one way or another learn to read and write. Frederick Douglass, in the story of his life, has given a description of the manner in which he learned to read, which is probably typical of other slaves in the same class as himself. He says:

The frequent hearing of my mistress reading the Bible aloud, for she often read aloud when her husband was absent, awakened my curiosity in respect to this mystery of reading, and roused in me the desire to learn. Up to this time I had known nothing whatever of this wonderful art, and my ignorance and inexperience of what it could do for me, as well as my confidence in my mistress, emboldened me to ask her to teach me to read. With an unconsciousness and inexperience equal to my own, she readily consented, and in an incredibly short time, by her kind assistance, I had mastered the alphabet and could spell words of three or four letters. My mistress seemed almost as proud of my progress as if I had been her own child, and supposing that her husband would be as well pleased, she made no secret of what she was doing for me. Indeed, she exultingly told him of the alphabet of her pupil, and of her intention to persevere in teaching me, as she felt her duty to do, at least to read the Bible. Master Hugh was astounded beyond measure, and probably for the first time proceeded to unfold to his wife the true philosophy of the slave system, and the peculiar

* Olmsted, "The Cotton Kingdom," vol. ii, pp. 70, 71.

rules necessary in the nature of the case to be observed in the management of human chattels. Of course he forbade her to give me any further instruction.

In learning to read, therefore, I am not sure that I do not owe quite as much to the opposition of my master as to the kindly assistance of my amiable mistress. I acknowledge the benefit rendered me by the one, and by the other, believing that but for my mistress I might have grown up in ignorance.

Filled with the determination to learn to read at any cost, I hit upon many expedients to accomplish that much-desired end. The plan which I mainly adopted, and the one which was the most successful, was that of using my young white playmates, with whom I met on the streets, as teachers. I used to carry almost constantly a copy of Webster's spelling-book in my pocket, and when sent on errands, or when playtime was allowed me, I would step aside with my young friends and take a lesson in spelling.

Fortunately, or unfortunately, I had earned a little money in blacking boots for some gentlemen, with which I purchased of Mr. Knight, on Thames Street, what was then a very popular school book, namely, "The Columbian Orator," for which I paid fifty cents. I was led to buy this book by hearing some little boys say they were going to learn some pieces out of it for the exhibition. This volume was indeed a rich treasure, and every opportunity afforded me, for a time, was spent in diligently perusing it.*

In another portion of his narrative, Mr. Douglass describes how he used to pick pieces of waste paper from the gutters of Baltimore, and try to read them. Sometimes he made use of other devices for getting the knowledge he wanted. For example, he would bet the white boys, with whom he frequently played, a marble or a piece of candy that they could not read an advertisement he found

---

* "Life and Times of Frederick Douglass," written by himself, pp. 69-75.

on the fences or on the side of a house. This
wager would tempt the white boys, of course, to
spell out and read these advertisements, and as
they did this young Douglass was able to learn
from them what the words of the advertisement
meant. This same method of learning to read was
adopted by more than one ambitious slave boy.

It sounds strange to-day, but it was nevertheless
true that up to a few years before the Civil War
there was almost as much opposition to Negro
education in the North as there was in the South.
In 1882, John F. Slater, of Norwich, Connecticut,
gave a million dollars to be used in the education
of the Negro race. Up to that time this was the
largest sum that had ever been given at one time
for a like purpose. Yet, fifty years before, in
the neighbouring town of Canterbury, Prudence
Crandall, a young Quaker schoolmistress, who
ventured to open a school for coloured children,
was mobbed by some of the inhabitants of that
town, and so great was the opposition to the school
that a special law was passed, making it a crime
to open a school for Negroes in that state.

In 1831, when the first national coloured convention assembled at Philadelphia, it was determined
to establish a college for coloured people, and the
Reverend Samuel E. Cornish, a coloured Presbyterian clergyman, was appointed agent to secure
funds. In the course of the next year, he succeeded

in raising $3,000 for establishing "a school on the manual labour plan." Arthur Tappan, the philanthropist, succeeded in buying several acres of land in the southern part of New Haven, Connecticut, and had completed arrangements for erecting a building. As soon as it was discovered, however, that it was proposed to erect a Negro school in New Haven, there was a great outcry and protest from the citizens. At a public meeting, at which the mayor presided, it was resolved by a vote of seven hundred to four, that "the founding of colleges for educating coloured people is an unwarrantable and dangerous undertaking to the internal concerns of other states and ought to be discouraged," and that "the mayor, aldermen, common-council, and freemen will resist the establishment of the proposed college in this state by every lawful means."

About this time, the Noyes Academy, of Canaan, New Hampshire, opened its doors to coloured students. Several young men entered the academy, and for a time the coloured people believed that they had found a school where they might obtain advanced education in the United States. On the 3rd of July, 1835, however, a town meeting was called and a committee was chosen to "remove the academy." A little more than a month later, this committee, aided by some three hundred persons and a hundred yoke of oxen, proceeded to literally carry out the instruction of the town meeting. In many other of the Northern states, particularly in Ohio, Indiana and Illinois, even where there was no law prohibiting the education of Negroes, no provision was made for educating them in the public schools.

In spite of the opposition which manifested itself from time to time against Negro education, there was a steady increase in the number of Negro schools in most of the large Northern cities. I have already referred to the school established by Anthony Benezet, in 1750. This first noted teacher of Negroes, who died May 3, 1784, left in his will property to put this school on a permanent foundation. The school was continued in the charge of a committee of Friends, and received donations from time to time, one donation of three hundred pounds coming from a coloured man by the name of Thomas Shirley. In 1849, it appeared from a statistical study of the condition of coloured people at Philadelphia, made at that time, that there were among others the following schools for coloured persons: A grammar school with 463 pupils; five other schools with 911; an infant school in charge of the abolition society with 70 pupils; a "moral reform" school with 81 pupils. In addition to the public schools there were also about 20 private schools with 296 pupils, making an aggregate of more than 1,800 pupils receiving an education of one kind or another.

In 1832, ten thousand dollars was left by the will of Richard Humphreys, an ex-slave-holder, to establish "An Institute for Coloured Youth." The school was accordingly started in 1837. A farm was purchased in Bristol Township, Philadelphia County, in 1839, but later sold, and a school building erected on Lombard Street, Philadelphia. In 1852, the school was opened and conducted for a time by Charles L. Reason, of New York. Ebenezer D. Bassett, afterward for nearly eight years Minister and United States Consul-general at Porte au Prince, Haiti, was for many years the principal of this school. A few years ago, sufficient funds were raised to enable the school to carry out the original purpose of its founder and it was removed to Cheyney, Pennsylvania, and transformed into an industrial school for the special purpose of training teachers.

The circumstance that a number of free persons of colour were frequently kidnapped in New York City resulted in the formation in an early day of "The New York Society for Promoting the Manumission of Slaves and for Protecting Such of Them as Have Been or May Be Liberated." The same gentlemen who organised this society became the Board of Trustees of what was known as the New York African Free School, which was, or afterward became, the first public school in New York City. This school was located on Cliff Street, between

Beekman and Ferry streets, and was opened in 1786 with forty pupils. In 1824, when General Lafayette was in this country, he visited this school, and a little coloured boy, who afterward became Dr. James McCune Smith, was delegated to make an address to him in behalf of the students.

This school and others established by the society continued to flourish until 1832, when they, with their 1,400 students, were formally turned over to the public school society and became part of the public school system of the city. The first normal school for coloured teachers was established in 1853, with John Peterson, a coloured man who had long been a teacher in the coloured schools of New York, principal.

The first coloured school for Negro children in Ohio was established in 1820. Owen T. B. Nickens, a public-spirited and intelligent Negro, was largely responsible for bringing these schools into existence. In 1844, the Reverend Hiram S. Gilmore founded the "Cincinnati High School" for coloured youth, and in 1849, the Legislature passed an act establishing public schools for coloured children. The law provided that the school funds should be divided among the white and coloured children, but for a long time this law was not enforced, until, under the leadership of John I. Gaines, the coloured people took the matter to the court. In 1856, a law was passed giving the coloured people the right by ballot to elect their own trustees, and in 1858, Nicholas Longworth built the first school house for coloured people, giving them a lease for fourteen years, during which time they were to pay the $14,000, which the building cost.

The first separate school for coloured children in Massachusetts was established at the home of Primus Hall, in Boston, in 1798. This school continued to be held in the house of Primus Hall until 1806, when the coloured Baptists erected a church on Belknap Street, and fitted up the lower rooms as a school for coloured children. This school continued until 1835, when a coloured school-house was erected from a fund left for that purpose by Abiel Smith. This became the famous "Smith schoolhouse." This Smith schoolhouse continued in existence until 1855, when a law was passed abolishing separate schools for coloured children.

Although slavery was not abolished in the District of Columbia until April 16, 1862, the free coloured people, who were very numerous in the District, early succeeded in establishing and maintaining schools for their children. The first schoolhouse built for coloured pupils was erected by three coloured men named George Bell, Nicholas Franklin and Moses Liverpool. All these men had been slaves in Virginia, and not one of them knew a single letter of the alphabet. From this time on, the number of schools increased rapidly with the increase of the free coloured population. One of the most noted of the early coloured teachers was John F. Cook. He had been born a slave, but had been purchased by his aunt, Alethia Tanner, who at the same time purchased his mother, Laurena Cook, and four other children. John F. Cook learned the shoemaker's trade in his boyhood and worked very hard after the purchase of his freedom to make some return to his aunt for the money she had spent in setting him free. He picked up the rudiments of an education in the Treasury Department, and thereupon began teaching school. During the Snow Riot of September, 1835, his schoolhouse was destroyed, and, to escape the mob, he fled to Pennsylvania. In the next year he returned, re-opened his school on a more generous plan than before, and kept it up until his death, March 21, 1855, when the work was taken up by his sons, John F. and George F. T. Cook.

Among the other noted teachers in Washington before the War were Louisa Park Costin, the daughter of William Costin, who was for twenty-four years the messenger for the bank of Washington, and who was well known and respected by all the old residents of Washington, District of Columbia. Another was Maria Becraft, who was the head of the first seminary for coloured girls in the District of Columbia. This seminary was established, in 1827, in Georgetown, under the auspices of Father

Vanlomen, who was the pastor of the Holy Trinity Catholic Church. In 1831, Maria Becraft gave up her school to the care of one of the girls she had trained. In October of that year she joined the convent of the coloured Catholic Sisters at Baltimore, where she was known as Sister Aloyons.

'Little struggling schools, that sprang up here and there in the cities North and South before the Civil War, served to give the rudiments of an education to a few coloured people, but it was not until after 1865, when four millions of Negro slaves were made free, that the education of the race really began. I shall never forget the strange, pathetic scenes and incidents of that time. Nothing like it, I dare say, had ever before been seen. It seemed that all at once, as soon as they realised that they were free, the whole race started to go to school, but not in the usual orderly fashion. It was as if four million people had been shut up where they could not get food until they had reached the starving point, and then were suddenly released to find food for themselves.

The primer, the first reader, and most frequently of all, the Webster's blue-back speller, suddenly, as if by a miracle, made their appearance everywhere. Even before the thousands of Negro soldiers had been disbanded, they inveigled their officers into becoming their schoolmasters, and scores of Negro soldiers in every regiment were learning to read and to write and to cipher. On every plantation, and in nearly every home, whether in the town or city, the hidden book that had been tucked away under the floor or in an old trunk or had been concealed in a stump, or between mattresses, suddenly came out of its hiding-place and was put into use.

I can recall vividly the picture not only of children, but of men and women, some of whom had reached the age of sixty or seventy, tramping along the country roads with a spelling-book or a Bible in their hands. It did not seem to occur to any one that age was any obstacle to learning in books. With weak and unaccustomed eyes, old men and old women would struggle along month after month in their effort to master the primer in order to get, if possible, a little knowledge of the Bible. Some of them succeeded; many of them failed. To these latter the thought of passing from earth without being able to read the Bible was a source of deep sorrow.

The places for holding school were anywhere and everywhere; the Freedmen could not wait for schoolhouses to be built or for teachers to be provided. They got up before day and studied in their cabins by the light of pine knots. They sat up until late at night, drooping over their books, trying to master the secrets they contained. More than once, I have seen a fire in the woods at night with a dozen or more people of both sexes and of all ages sitting about with book in hands studying their lessons. Sometimes they would fasten their primers between the ploughshares, so that they could read as they ploughed. I have seen Negro coal miners trying to spell out the words of a little reading-book by the dim light of a miner's lamp, hundreds of feet below the earth. In the early days of freedom, public schools were not infrequently organised and taught under a large tree. Some of the early school-houses consisted of four pieces of timber driven into the ground and brush spread overhead as a covering to keep out the sun and rain. It was a simple and inexpensive schoolhouse, but I am sure that the students were more earnest than many who have since had much greater advantages.

The night school became popular immediately after freedom. After a hard day's work in the field, in the shop, or in the kitchen, men and women would spend two or three hours at night in school. A great many of the Freedmen got their first lessons in reading and writing in the Sunday-school. In fact, there were frequently more spelling-books in the Sunday-school than Bibles. I, myself, got my first knowledge of the alphabet by perusing a spelling-book in the Sunday-school.

A teacher in the first few years of freedom was likely to be any one who knew something some one else did not know. Sometimes it happened that some would be able to read better than they could write; others would be able to write better than they could read. In that case the former became teachers of reading and the latter became teachers of writing. As may well be understood, there was very little organisation in these first schools; they were just groups of people moved by a common impulse in coming together for study. But almost before the proclamation of freedom had been issued, white teachers of all classes and both sexes began to pour into the South from the Northern states. Along with them came numbers of Negro men and women who had escaped from slavery and, having gained some education in the North, now returned to the South to become the teachers of their race. It should be added, also, that many of these teachers were Southern white people, who, when they found no other occupation directly after the war, were glad to turn to teaching the Freedmen in order to eke out a livelihood.

It was during this same period that the people of the Northern states, through their religious and missionary organisations, began sending not merely teachers, but money, books, and clothing to provide for the schools and for the pupils in the Negro schools that were springing up everywhere. It was during this period that many of the most noted schools in the Southern states were founded. Berea

College had been established since 1856, by the Reverend John G. Fee, a Kentucky minister who had been converted to anti-slavery views by taking a course at Lane Seminary, Cincinnati, Ohio. In 1865, Lincoln Institute, at Jefferson City, Missouri, was founded with the assistance of contributions of the Sixty-second and Sixty-fifth United States coloured regiments, who generously contributed something over $6,000 of the wages they received from the Government to help establish the school. The same year Shaw University was started at Raleigh, North Carolina. In 1866, Hampton Institute was founded by General S. C. Armstrong, and in the same year Fisk University was established at Nashville, Tennessee. The next year Atlanta University was established at Atlanta, Georgia; Biddle University, at Charlotte, North Carolina; and Howard University, named after General O. O. Howard, at Washington, District of Columbia; two years later, in 1869, Straight University, at New Orleans, Louisiana; Tougaloo University, at Tougaloo, Mississippi; Talladega College, at Talladega, Alabama; and Clafin University, at Orangeburg, South Carolina.

In speaking of the contribution which the people of the United States made at this time to the education of the Negro in America, it should not be forgotten that Negro education has contributed something in return to the people of the United States. It was through the Negro that industrial education in this country had its start. Neither in the North nor in the South, before the starting of Hampton Institute in Virginia, was any systematic instruction in the industries given in any kind of educational institution. The success of the Hampton and Tuskegee institutes in giving industrial education to the Negroes led the way to the introduction of industrial education into the Northern schools and white schools in the South, as well as in many other parts of the world.

The desire for education among the Freedmen was a veritable fever for the first ten or twelve years after emancipation. Since that time I do not think the desire for education has diminished among the coloured people, but the methods for obtaining it have become more profitable and less picturesque. This is shown particularly in the effort which the coloured people are making everywhere to add to the meagre funds which are given them by the states in order to prolong their school terms, to secure better teachers, and build comfortable schoolhouses. Negro parents will still make all kinds of sacrifices, frequently depriving themsevles not merely of the comforts, but many times of the necessities of life, in order that they may have the satisfaction of seeing their children able to read and write.

All sorts of devices are now employed in the

coloured communities to eke out the salary of the coloured school-teacher. In some communities teachers will impose an extra tax of ten cents per month for every student who comes to school. In other cases each family will take turns in boarding the teacher for a day or for a week. Sometimes they will donate a pig, a chicken, a dozen eggs, a fish, or a rabbit to help the school-teacher out. A method that is now growing in popularity, for the purpose of meeting the expenses of a first-class school, is what is known as the "school farm." This means that three or four acres of land will be secured near the schoolhouse and on a given day, usually Saturday, parents and children come together to plant, plough, or harvest the cotton which is to be sold to increase the length of the school term.

Some idea of the difficulty under which the coloured schools labour in the South may be gathered from the fact that, while in the Northern and Western states something like five dollars per pupil is spent every year for the education of the children of school age, in several of the Southern states only fifty cents per pupil is expended for coloured children. While a number of office-seekers in the South, complaining about the burden of education under which the South laboured, have been advocating that no money be spent for the education of the Negro, and that everything possible be done to check his advancement in this direction, a few courageous State Superintendents of Public Instruction in the South have begun to point out that, not only is the Negro not a burden upon the South so far as his education is concerned, but in some instances Negro taxpayers are supporting white schools. In a careful study made of the statistics of education some years ago in Florida, the superintendent in that state came to the conclusion that "the schools for Negroes not only were not a burden upon the white people, but four thousand five hundred and twenty-seven dollars contributed for Negro schools from other sources was in some way diverted into the white schools." Speaking of the conditions in middle Florida, where the Negro population is most dense and the educational conditions are at their worst, he said:

The usual plea is that this is due to the intolerable burden of Negro education, and a general discouragement and inactivity were ascribed to this cause. The figures show that the education of the Negro in the middle of Florida does not cost white people of that section one cent. . . . It is the purpose of this paragraph to show that the backwardness of the education of the white people is in no degree due to the presence of the Negro, but that the presence of the Negroes has actually been contributing to the sustenance of white schools.

At a meeting of the Conference for Southern Education, in Atlanta, Georgia, in the spring of 1909, Charles L. Coon, Superintendent of Schools at Wilson, North Carolina, read a paper on "Public

Taxation and Negro Schools," in which he attempted to show, for the whole South, what he had previously shown for North Carolina, that the Negroes were not only not getting their share of the public education fund, which they were entitled to under the law, but their education was not, as has so often been asserted, a piece of philanthropy on the part of whites to the coloured race. He found, by the study of actual statistics, that while Negroes represented 40.1 per cent. of the total population of the eleven Southern states they received only 14.8 per cent. of the money spent for education. In Mississippi, where Negroes represent 58.7 per cent. of the population they received 21.9 per cent. of the school funds. In Louisiana, where they represent 47.2 per cent. of the population, they received 8.6 per cent. of the school funds.

After a careful study of all the available statistics, Mr. Coon reaches the conclusion, to put it in his own words, "that the Negro school of the South is not a serious burden on the white taxpayer. On the contrary, if all the Negro children of the Southern states were white, it would cost to educate them just about five times as much as it does now to give the same number of Negroes such education as they are getting."

Mr. Coon points out, and quotes articles from several Southern papers to support him, that the Negro is not only almost the only dependable labourer in the Southern states, but even those people who are most ready to abuse him "as a burden and a curse" are loud in their complaint "whenever any one attempts to lure him away."

In 1891, the Negroes of North Carolina listed $8,018,446 worth of property. In 1898, they listed $21,716,922, an increase of 171 per cent. in seventeen years. The property listed by the whites during that time increased only 89 per cent. In other words, the taxable value of property of Negroes increased in seventeen years nearly twice in proportion to that of the white people. In Georgia, in 1891, Negroes listed $14,196,735 worth of property. In 1907, they listed property to the value of $25,904,822, an increase of 82 per cent. The taxable property of white people increased during this same period only 39 per cent. This again indicates that the ratio of increase of Negro property in Georgia during the last sixteen years has been twice that of the property of the white people.

"Such facts as these," says Mr. Coon, in concluding his report, "give us glimpses of the economic importance of Negroes, and abundantly justify us in hoping that the senseless race prejudice which has for its object the intellectual enslavement of Negro children will soon pass away. I do not believe that any superior race can hope for the blessings of heaven upon its own children while it begrudges more light and efficiency for those of an inferior race."

In all that has been said, bearing upon what the Negro has done to help himself in education through the public schools in the South, the fact should not be overlooked that he owes much to the Southern white people. Especially is this true in the large cities and towns of the South, where generous provision has been made for the education of the Negro child in the public schools. While in the country districts, as a rule, the schools are poor, almost beyond description, still in not a few country districts broad-minded and courageous Southern white men have seen to it, and are seeing to it, that the Negro gets a reasonable chance for education in the public schools. It should also be stated that while the Negro at present is paying in a large part for his own education in the public schools, in the years immediately following emancipation he paid very little and during this time the burden of his education fell heavily upon the Southern white people.

It should be remembered also that it is only within the past fifty or sixty years that many of the Northern states have begun to have a system of education which sought to educate all the people irrespective of race or colour. The world is slow to learn that when we attempt to stop the growth of our fellow-man, we are doing the thing that will most surely stop our own growth. How much faster the world would go forward if every one should learn, once for all, that nothing is ever permanently gained by any attempt to retard or stop the progress of any human being!

CHAPTER VI

THERE are about twenty national Negro secret societies in America. The older and better known of these are the Masons, the Odd Fellows, Knights of Pythias, United Brothers of Friendship, Improved Benevolent and Protective Order of Elks, Knights of Tabor, Benevolent Order of Buffaloes, Ancient Order of Foresters, The Grand United Order of Galilean Fishermen, Good Samaritans, Nazarites, Sons and Daughters of Jacob, The Seven Wise Men, Knights of Honour, Mosaic Templars of America, and the True Reformers.

In addition to these there are a number of smaller organisations, most of them local in character, but quite as interesting in their workings and history as the larger organisations.

The Masonic order, which is the oldest, and so far as its history is concerned, the most interesting of these orders, had its origin in the following manner: During Revolutionary days there lived in Boston a Negro of exceptional ability, named Prince Hall. On March 6, 1775, he and fourteen other Negroes were initiated into the secrets of Free Masonry by an army lodge attached to one of the regiments of British soldiers stationed there.   According to a custom of the day, these fifteen coloured men were authorised to assemble as a lodge, to walk on St. John's Day, and to bury their dead with due form. They, however, could do no "work" and make no Masons until they were warranted.

On March 2, 1784, the members of this lodge applied to the Grand Lodge of England for a warrant.   It was issued to them on September 29, 1784, as "African Lodge, No. 459," with Prince Hall as master, but because of various delays it was not received until April 29, 1787.   The lodge was formally organised May 6, 1787.

The original warrant establishing Masonry among the Negroes in America is, considering the time and the circumstances under which it was issued, a document of such historical interest that I venture to reproduce it here in full.   The text is as follows:

To all and every our right worshipful and loving Brethren, we, Thomas Howard, Earl of Effingham, Lord Howard, etc., etc., acting Grand Master under the authority of His Royal Highness, Henry Frederick, Duke of Cumberland, etc., etc., Grand Master of the Most Ancient and Honourable Society of Free and Accepted Masons, send greeting:

Know Ye, that we, at the humble petition of our right trusty and well-beloved Brethren, Prince Hall, Boston Smith, Thomas Sanderson and several other Brethren residing at Boston, New England, in North America, do hereby constitute the said Brethren into a regular Lodge of Free and Accepted Masons under the title or denomination of the African Lodge, to be opened in Boston aforesaid, and do further, at their said petition, hereby appoint the said Prince Hall to be Master, Boston Smith, Senior Warden, and Thomas Sanderson, Junior Warden, for the opening of the said Lodge and for such further time only as shall be thought proper by the brethren thereof, it being our will that this appointment of the above officers shall in no wise affect any future election of officers of the Lodge, but that such election shall be regulated agreeable to such by-laws of said Lodge as shall be consistent with the general laws of the society, contained in the Book of Constitutions; and we hereby will and require you, the said Prince Hall, to take especial care that all and every one of the said Brethren are, or have been, regularly made Masons, and that they do observe, perform and keep all the rules and orders contained in the Book of Constitutions; and further, that you do, from time to time, cause to be entered in a book kept for the purpose, an account of your proceedings in the Lodge, together with all such rules, orders and regulations as shall be made for the good government of the same; that in no wise you omit once in every year to send us, or our successors, Grand Master, or to Roland Holt, Esq., our Deupty Grand Master, for the time being, an account in writing of your said proceedings, and copies of all such rules, orders and regulations as shall be made as aforesaid, together with a list of the members of the Lodge, and such a sum of money as may suit the circumstances of the Lodge and reasonably be expected towards the Grand Charity. Moreover, we will require you, the said Prince Hall, as soon as conveniently may be, to send an account in writing of what may be done by virtue of these presents.

Given at London, under our hand and seal of Masonry, this 29th day of September, A. L. 5784, A. D. 1784.

By the Grand Master's Command,

R. HOLT, D. G. M.

Witness: WM. WHITE, G. S.

By the terms of this decree Prince Hall became the first Grand Master of the first Grand Lodge of Negro Masons in the United States, and in 1797 issued a licence to thirteen men of colour who had been made Masons in England and Ireland to assemble and work as a lodge in Philadelphia. At Providence, Rhode Island, under Hall's authority, a lodge was organised for Negro Masons who resided in that vicinity. In 1808, these three lodges joined and formed the African Grand Lodge of Boston, which was afterward called the Prince Hall Lodge of Massachusetts.

The second coloured Grand Lodge was called the "First Independent African Grand Lodge of North America, in and for the commonwealth of Pennsylvania." Some time after this, the Hiram Grand Lodge of Pennsylvania was organised, and in 1847, these three Grand Lodges united in forming a National Grand Lodge. From this time this order has grown steadily among the Negroes of the United States until, in 1904, there were 1,960 Masonic lodges with 45,835 members.

It is an interesting fact in the history of these lodges that Negro Masons formed a part of the funeral procession of the first President of the United States, George Washington.

The Negro Masons, like other secret orders formed in the United States before the Civil War, encountered all the difficulties under which free Negroes laboured at that time. It is said, however, that they often received indirect recognition by white Masons. For example, the first Kentucky lodge of coloured Masons, known as Mount Moriah, No. 1, was organised by residents of Louisville in 1850. It was organised under the jurisdiction of Ohio, and for three years, on account of the "black laws," which forbade the assembling of free people of colour, met in New Albany, Indiana. After that time the lodge removed to Louisville. Shortly after, the rooms of the order were forcibly entered by the police and twenty-one of the members were arrested. On arriving at the prison, however, the jailors, it is said, refused to receive them. The judge of the court, who was consulted, ordered them discharged upon their personal recognisance to appear for trial the next morning. The next morning when they appeared in a body for trial, they found the entrance to the courthouse guarded by police, by whom they were denied admission. They were told to quietly go their way, say nothing, and they would not again be disturbed. The explanation given by the coloured Masons to this extraordinary proceeding is that the jailors and the judge were Master Masons.

The next secret order to be formed in the United States was the Odd Fellows. In 1842, certain members of the Philomathean Institute of New York and of the Library Company and Debating Society of Philadelphia, applied for admission to the International Order of Odd Fellows, but were refused on the ground of their colour. Peter Ogden, however, who had joined the Odd Fellows in England, secured from the English order a charter for the first American Negro lodge of Odd Fellows, which was called the Philomathean, No. 646, of New York. This lodge was organised March 1, 1843. The Negro Odd Fellows in America are still under the jurisdiction of England and regularly represented in the general meetings of the order. In 1904, there were 4,643 lodges in the United States, with 285,931 members.

Two other national secret organisations were organised in the United States before the War. One of these was the Galilean Fishermen. Another was the Nazarites. The United Brothers of Friendship was organised at Louisville, Kentucky, August 1, 1861. It was first a benevolent organisation and later became a secret order. The Knights of Pythias of the World was first organised in Washington, District of Columbia, February 19, 1864.

No other city in the South has been the birth-place of so large a number of coloured secret and beneficial orders as Baltimore, Maryland. There are societies still existing in Maryland that date back as far as 1820. They were formed in order that the members might help one another in sickness, and provide for a decent burial through a system of small but regular payments. Twenty-five of these societies were formed before the war. From 1865 to 1870, seventeen more were added to this number, and since 1870 it is said that at least twenty more have been added to these.

In 1884 a meeting was held of many persons connected with these societies in order to arouse a more general interest in their work. At this meeting forty of these societies claimed an aggregate membership of 2,100. It was stated at this time that nearly fourteen hundred members had been buried by these orders, and more than $45,000 paid out for funeral expenses. Something like $125,000 had been paid as sick dues, and thirty of the societies paid $27,000 to widows. Among the other items of expense were $10,700 for house rent and $11,300 paid for incidental expenses. There had been paid back to members of the societies, from unexpended balances, $40,000, and there remained in the banks and in the hands of the treasurers, $22,800. Five of these societies had considerable sums invested. In one case the amount was nearly $6,000. The total amount of money handled had been nearly $200,000. One of these organisations was the Coloured Barbers' Society. It was over fifty years old, and paid eighty dollars at the death of a member. It is said that one coloured woman organised three of these local societies that at one time were very successful.

It was among these local beneficial and secret orders of Baltimore that four of the national societies had their origin. These are the Samaritans, the Nazarites, the Galilean Fishermen, and the Seven Wise Men. The order of Galilean Fishermen, composed of men and women, was started in Baltimore in 1856, but was not legally incorporated until 1869. It is said to have more than five thousand members in the State of Maryland alone.

It is said that the beneficial and local secret orders of Philadelphia date back to the eighteenth century, and that by 1838 there were as many as one hundred of these small organisations, with 7,448 members, in the city. Ten years later there were 8,000 members, belonging to 106 societies. The plan usually followed by these societies was to collect twenty-five cents per month from each of their members with the understanding that in case of sickness members should be entitled to receive aid to the amount of $1.50 to $3.00 per week. In addition to this, sums varying from ten dollars to twenty dollars were paid upon the death of any member. A good many of these organisations have since gone out of existence, but it is said that at least four thousand Negroes in Philadelphia still belong to secret orders and collect annually something like $25,000, a part of which is paid out in sick and death benefits and a part invested. The real estate and personal property of these local organisations is said to amount to no less than $125,000. One of the oldest of these organisations is known as the Sons of St. Thomas. It was founded in 1823, and was originally confined to the members of the St. Thomas Church.

In recent years there have grown up, to take the place of the older beneficial organisations, local insurance companies. One of these, known as the Crucifixion, is connected with the Church of the Crucifixion. Still another, the Avery, is connected with the Wesley A. M. E. Zion Church. Both of these have large membership, and are said to be well conducted.*

With the organisation of the national benevolent and secret orders, large sums of money have come into the hands of the officers of these societies to be held in trust for the members of the organisations. A considerable part of this sum has found permanent investment, where it frequently yields a good return. The profits of the Masons indicate that this organisation has at least one million dollars invested. Similar reports from other organisations show that the Odd Fellows have $2,500,000 worth of property, the Pythians $500,000, the Brothers of Friendship $500,000, and the True Reformers $800,000. The other secret orders own over one-half a million dollars' worth of property, so that it has been estimated that the Negro secret societies in the United States own between $5,000,000 and $6,000,000 worth of property.

The Odd Fellows have erected in the city of

* Du Bois, "The Philadelphia Negro," p. 221 et seq.

Philadelphia a building which is reported to have cost $100,000. The Supreme Lodge of Knights of Pythias has erected in Chicago a building costing about the same amount. The Knights of Pythias in New Orleans also have erected a seven-story business block at a cost of about $100,000.

While on a visit to Pine Bluff, Arkansas, I was very agreeably surprised to find that the finest and most expensive office building in the town had been erected by the Negro Masonic order. The building was erected for the purpose of furnishing offices for Negro business and professional men, but it was so advantageously situated and was so well adapted for business purposes that it was entirely occupied by white tenants.

It often happens in a city, where there are a number of local lodges of the same order, that they coöperate and erect a building for lodge and business purposes. Such a building is the coloured Masonic Temple at Savannah, Georgia, which was erected by the local Masonic lodges of that city. This building was erected through a building and loan association. The income derived from the renting of store and lodge rooms in the building has kept up the running expenses and paid for its erection. The principal reasons why the orders are erecting buildings are to provide themselves with permanent homes and to meet the demand of coloured business and professional men for store and office rooms.

Directly and indirectly the secret societies, in addition to providing for the families of their members after death, are doing a considerable amount of charitable work. For instance, several of the orders have erected homes and orphanages in different parts of the country. The Masons are perhaps leading in this respect at the present time. They established homes for the aged members of their order in Georgia, North Carolina, Illinois, and Tennessee. The Odd Fellows, in addition to the sum paid for sick benefits and in insurance to widows and orphans, contribute annually from ten to fifteen thousand dollars to various kinds of charities. Sometimes the surplus monies of these different organisations are invested in other ways. For instance, in 1905, the Masons of Mississippi purchased a thousand acres of land in that state. In Maryland and in the District of Columbia the same organisation has organised joint stock building associations. In Massachusetts, which is the home of Negro Masonry, a monument costing $500 has been erected to Prince Hall, the first Grand Master of the order. A few years ago, also, the Massachusetts Masons published Upton's "Negro Masonry."

Perhaps the secret order having the most romantic history is the International Order of Twelve of the Knights and Daughters of Tabor, which was founded by Reverend Moses Dickson. Mr. Dickson was born in Cincinnati, Ohio, in 1824. For a number

of years he worked upon different steamboats run-
inng up and down the Ohio and Mississippi rivers
from Cincinnati. During this time he had an opportunity to see slavery in some of its most disagreeable
aspects, and as a consequence he early determined
to do something positive toward securing the freedom of the slaves. In 1844, so the story goes, he
and eleven other young men met and formed an
organisation for no less a purpose than the overthrow of slavery in the United States. After
thinking it over, however, the members decided
to take two years to study over and develope a
plan of action, and agreed to meet in St. Louis,
August 12, 1846.

During the intervening years Mr. Dickson travelled up and down the Mississippi River as far South
as New Orleans, and as far North as Iowa and Wisconsin, seeking to prepare plans for the project
he had in view. According to agreement, the
twelve young men met and organised what was
known as the Knights of Liberty. This organisation having been formed, the twelve members
separated with the understanding that they were
to travel through the South, organising local societies
in the different states through which they travelled.
Mr. Dickson, however, remained at the headquarters of the order at St. Louis.

It had been agreed among the twelve that they should
spend ten years, slowly and secretly making their

preparations, and extending the organisation of the society. At the end of this time, however, owing to the change in conditions in the North and the South, it was decided to change the plan of operation. From that time on the Knights of Liberty became actively connected with the Underground Railroad, and it was claimed that they assisted yearly thousands of slaves to escape. The methods by which the Knights of Liberty expected to accomplish their great object have never been definitely known, if, indeed, they were ever definitely formulated. When the Civil War broke out, Mr. Dickson enlisted. At the close of hostilities he settled again in Missouri, and took an active part in establishing the Lincoln Institute at Jefferson City. For a number of years he was trustee and vice-president of the Board of Trustees of that institution.

The emancipation of the slaves ended the work for which the Knights of Liberty had been formed, whereupon Mr. Dickson decided to establish a beneficial order in memory of the twelve orginial organisers of that society. As a result, the first Temple and Tabernacle of the Knights and Daughters of Tabor was established in 1871. The object of the society is to "encourage Christianity, education, morality, and temperance among the coloured people." The order is now reported to have something over fifty thousand members.

Immediately after the War, when the coloured

people were no longer hindered by restrictive legislation, a vast number of societies for mutual protection were organised. The most of these societies
were founded upon the plan of the earlier benevolent
and beneficial societies, with the purpose "of caring
for the sick and burying the dead." At first no
attention was paid to differences of age, and very
little to condition of health of members who were
insured in these organisations. Gradually, as the
societies gained in experience, they learned the
necessity of discriminating in these matters. Eventually there grew out of these mutual benefit organisations something corresponding to the insurance
companies conducted upon the mutual benefit plan
by white organisations. Many of the insurance
societies formed in this way had not the excuse of
ignorance for the bad manner in which they were
managed. Many of them, however, have done good
service and have grown in strength from year to
year. In 1907, no less than sixty-five of these organisations were known to exist in different parts of the
United States.

In the meantime, nearly all the secret orders have
added insurance to the other benefits they offer to
their members. No definite figures are at hand to
show the amount of business done by these different
insurance companies connected with the secret
orders. It is estimated, however, that in seven
years the Masonic Benefit Association of Alabama,

which is the title of the insurance department of the
Masons in that state, is reported to have paid over
$100,000 to widows and orphans of deceased mem-
bers. The Texas association reports that in ten
years it has paid $150,000 in death claims. The
Galilean Fishermen claim to have paid $48,900 in
death claims in five years. According to the statement issued by the True Reformers, that society
paid $606,000 in death claims and $1,500,000
in sick benefits in twenty years. The total
amount paid out since the organisation of the
society in sick and death benefits amounted in
1907 to $2,856,989.25.

There has been one secret and benevolent organisation of national repute organised in Arkansas. It
was known as the Mosaic Templars of America, and
was organised in 1882 by C. W. Keatts and Hon.
J. E. Bush. In twenty years this organisation paid
$175,000 for the relief of the widows and orphans of
deceased members. During this same time it paid
$51,000 to its policy holders, and in 1902 reported
a property valuation of $225,000. These figures
give a pretty good idea of the amount of money that
is collected and expended for the purposes of benev-
olence and insurance among the coloured people
in this country.

One of the most original and interesting of the
benevolent and secret orders formed in the method
I have described is what is known as The Grand

United Order of True Reformers. This organisation is the more interesting because of the singular way in which it has widened and extended its activities, until, while still retaining its fraternal and benevolent features, it has become a great business organisation.

The True Reformers, like most secret and benevolent organisations among Negroes in the Southern states, was started in a very small and obscure way, and has grown, apparently, in response to needs that are peculiar to the coloured people. The order was started in 1881 by Reverend William Washington Browne. Mr. Browne was not an educated man, and he knew very little at the time he started this organisation about the ordinary methods of conducting a business of this or any other character. He was a man of great energy, however, and grew with the organisation, so that at the time of his death he had succeeded in building up one of the strongest business organisations at that time in existence among the Negro people.

This organisation is in many respects so unusual that it was made the subject of an investigation by the United States Department of Labour, from which I am able to give some details in regard to its history. I cannot here describe in detail the different departments of this organisation nor the methods by which they are conducted, but will merely indicate the different activities in which the order is engaged and suggest the necessities out of which its different departments have grown.*

In 1882 the Grand Fountain, which was the central and controlling organisation of the whole order, established a real estate department. This grew out of the need of offices and buildings in which to carry on the business of the order. The Grand Fountain had collected a considerable amount of funds and this offered an opportunity for safe investment, while at the same time it furnished the subordinate organisations with the halls in which to hold their meetings.

The next by-product of the organisation was a depository for the funds of the Grand Fountain. I shall describe in a later chapter the circumstances under which the True Reformers' bank was organised.

Next the order felt the need of a publication by which its members, who were now scattered in different parts of the country, could be kept in touch with each other and the purposes of the organisation advertised to the general public. In 1892, therefore, the publication of *The Reformer* was begun. It was described at the time "as the headlight of the organisation, an industrial, agricultural and financial paper and economic journal of the Negro race." It was first published as a bi-monthly, but after a few months of existence it became a

---

* Bulletin of the United States Department of Labour. No. 41, pp. 807-14.

weekly paper.   In 1900, this paper had a circula-
tion of over 8,000.   In that year a job printing
department, which added considerably to the income
of the paper, was established.

The next advance of the True Reformers was along
charitable lines.   In 1893, the Grand Fountain,
through its subordinate lodges, began to collect
money for the erection of an Old Folks' Home, "for
the benefit of the old people of the entire race,
regardless of society or denomination."   In 1897,
the Grand Fountain advanced sufficient funds to
purchase the Westham Farms and the site of the
Westham Iron Furnace, six miles from Richmond,
in Henrico County.   The price paid was $14,400,
and the next year, in August, 1898, an association
was formed under the title of The Old Folks' Home
of the Grand Fountain of the United Order of True
Reformers.   In the same year a part of the Westham
Farm was laid out in town lots and a town was
started in the neighbourhood of the Old Folks' Home.
By the sale of these lots the purchase money advanced
by the Grand Fountain was repaid.

At the annual session of the Grand Fountain in
September, 1899, it was decided to apply for a new
charter which would cover all the various activities
which the order was now carrying on.   The
importance of this new charter was second only
to the charter granted eleven years before to the
True Reformers' Bank.

The purposes of the new organisation, known as the "Reformers' Mercantile and Industrial Association," as stated in the charter granted at this time, are as follows:

First, to manufacture, buy, and sell, at wholesale or retail, or both, groceries, goods, wares, implements, supplies, and articles of merchandise of any and every description, manufactured or grown, in this state or any other states or country, on its own account, and also for others on commission or otherwise; and to establish and maintain warehouses and stores at such places as may be agreed upon by the board of directors;

Second, to build and erect a hotel in the city of Richmond, Va., to lease out said hotel so erected or to conduct and carry on the hotel business therein, as shall be determined by the board of directors of said association;

Third, to conduct and carry on newspapers, book and job printing business in all its branches, and do generally all the things that pertain to a printing establishment;

Fourth, to buy and sell and improve land in the State of Virginia or elsewhere, with the right to lay off the same into lots, streets, and alleys, to improve said lands by erecting buildings thereon, maintain any structure and machinery needful for the manufacture of any kind of wood, metals, wool, cotton and other materials.

Fifth, to conduct a building and loan business and loan association.

Under this charter the association in April, 1900, opened a grocery and general merchandise store in Richmond. In March, 1901, a second store was opened in Washington, District of Columbia, and in December, 1901, a third, fourth and fifth store was opened successively in Portsmouth, Manchester, and Roanoke, Virginia. These stores seem to have been conducted on a sound basis; supplies were bought in large quantities for cash and were sold again at retail for cash. The managers of the stores made weekly reports and remittances. It is reported that these stores do an annual business of more than $100,000.

About this time the Hotel Reformer was opened at 900 North Sixth Street, Richmond, Virginia. This hotel has prospered and grown until now it has accommodations for one hundred and fifty guests. Most of the office force of the Grand Fountain make their homes in this hotel. Another enterprise of the organisation is "The Reformers' Building and Loan Association," which was incorporated for the purpose of encouraging industry, frugality, and home building, particularly among the members of the True Reformers' Association.

The headquarters of the Grand Fountain are in a large, four-story brick building, 604-608 North Second Street, Richmond, Virginia. This building contains, in addition to the various offices of the Grand Fountain, a large hall, which is sometimes used as a theatre and for other entertainments. In this same building are the offices of the True Reformers' Bank, the printing-office and the rooms of the real estate department. In 1908, this department had three farms and twenty-seven buildings of a total value of $400,000 under its control. It leases for the benefit of the order twenty-three other buildings.

As the members of the association continued to increase in numbers and the business operations continued to multiply, there was need in 1901 for an amendment to the charter to provide for further expansion of the organisation. One of the changes made in the charter at that time provided that the control of all the affiliated organisations of the order should remain in the Grand Fountain, which is the legislative body of the order, and meets annually. Another provision of the charter increased the amount of real estate that the order might hold from $25,000 to $500,000.

While the True Reformers was the first and, perhaps, the most extraordinary of the benevolent associations which have developed into coöperative business organisations it is still merely one among a number of others that have sprung up within recent years in the Southern states. While it is probably true that these organisations, owing to the inexperience of the men who started them, have not always been formed upon the best business models, it is still true that they have responded to some very definite needs of the Negro people, otherwise they could not have prospered as they have.

In the first place I think it may be safely said that these organisations have collected from the masses of the coloured people large amounts of money that would not otherwise have been saved.   In doing this they have created a considerable capital, which has been at the disposal of Negro business men.   It has enabled Negroes to erect buildings, invest in lands, and greatly increase property in the hands of members of the race.   Indirectly, these organisations have stimulated thrift and industry among the masses of the people.

One thing that has made these organisations especially attractive and valuable to the masses of the coloured people is that they have grown out of a kind of organisation for mutual helpfulness with which coloured people have long been familiar. Furthermore, they seem to be democratic in their organisation, although, as a matter of fact, I think that has seldom been true where the organisations have been successful.   At any rate, the members of the fraternal organisation have felt that they were directing and controlling, to some extent, their own investments, and that gave them an interest in the business of the organisation that they would not otherwise have felt.

The chief value of the Negro societies and benevolent organisations has been that they have been the schools in which the masses have been taught the value and the methods of coöperation.   In order to succeed these organisations have been compelled to enforce upon the masses of the people habits of

saving and of system which they would not otherwise have been able or disposed to learn. These
societies have contributed in this way, in spite of
their failings, in no small degree to the intellectual
and material development of the Negro race.

CHAPTER XXII

THE NEGRO DOCTOR AND THE NEGRO PROFESSIONAL MAN

IT WAS not until 1884, as near as I can now remember, that the first coloured physician, Dr. C. N. Dorsette, set up an office and began to practise medicine in Montgomery, Alabama. Previous to that time I do not think there was a Negro doctor, dentist or pharmacist in the state. At the present time there are more than one hundred, and the members of these three professions in Alabama maintain a flourishing state association, which in turn is connected with the National Medical Association, having representatives in ten Southern and twelve Northern states. I may add that the first woman physician who was ever granted a licence to practise medicine in the State of Alabama was a coloured woman, Dr. Sadie Dillon, a daughter of Bishop Benjamin Tanner, and a sister of H. O. Tanner, the distinguished Negro painter.

It is an indication of the progress of Negro doctors of Alabama, since Dr. Dorsette first came to the state, that there are at the present time no less than six infirmaries or hospitals which have been established since then and are largely maintained under the direction of the Negro physicians of this state. There are, for instance, the Cottage Home Infirmary, conducted by Dr. W. E. Sterrs, at Decatur; the Home Infirmary, conducted by Dr. U. G. Mason and Dr. A. M. Brown; the Selma Infirmary, conducted by Dr. L. L. Burwell, of Selma, Alabama; and the Harris Infirmary, conducted by Dr. T. N. Harris, at Mobile.   In addition to these there is the Hale's Infirmary at Montgomery, Alabama, and the Institute Hospital at Tuskegee, conducted by Dr. J. A. Kenney, who is, I may add, Secretary of the National Medical Association.

The Hale's Infirmary was given to the coloured people at Montgomery by James H. Hale and his widow, Ann Hale, at a cost of something like twenty-five thousand dollars.   When the building was first opened in 1899, Mrs. Ann Hale conducted it with her own means and what she was able to solicit from other sources.   At the present time it is supported in part by money given by the city and by donations from women's clubs, the contributions of churches and lodges of the secret orders of the city.

The rapid advancement of the Negro physician in Alabama is an indication of the progress which is taking place elsewhere throughout the South.   A few years ago almost the only Negro doctor one ever heard of in the Southern states was an individual known as "the root doctor," a kind of mendicant medicine-man, who travelled about through the country districts with a little stock of herbs and philters and a large stock of superstition, with which he traded upon the credulity of the country people. The medicines these men used were mostly harmless and the cures they performed consisted largely in convincing the people that they were going to get well, thus putting them in a way to actually recover from their ailments. They were, in fact, a kind of faith-healers, though mostly, I fear, they were merely frauds.

The "root doctor" has not entirely disappeared from the country districts of the South, but more and more the masses of the people are overcoming their instinctive distrust of hospitals and surgeons, and are learning to have faith in scientific medicine. A striking illustration of one of the ways in which this change is coming about was furnished me during a recent journey through South Carolina. At the Voorhees Industrial School, which is situated a few miles from Denmark, in the midst of a rich farming district of Central South Carolina, I observed that a large and commodious hospital had been erected. Although at the time I was there this hospital had not yet been fully equipped and put in working order, yet it suggested to me one of the unexpected ways in which an industrial school like this, situated in the open country as it is, can exercise and is exercising a civilising and uplifting influence upon the masses of the people.

Outside of the larger hospitals, like the Freedmen's Hospital in Washington, District of Columbia, the Provident Hospital in Chicago, Illinois, and the Frederick Douglass Hospital in Philadelphia, there are, in almost every city in the South, these smaller institutions to which I have referred, established by coloured physicians in order to provide for the needs of the coloured population. Although most of these institutions are poorly equipped, they have proved a great blessing to the communities in which they were established. Frequently they have been the only places in which Negroes, suffering from some unusual form of disease, could obtain anything like proper treatment. They have provided the only places in which serious surgical operations would be performed, with the assurance that the patient would be properly cared for after the operation was completed.

At first all the serious surgical operations were performed by white men but, as coloured surgeons in different parts of the country have gained in skill and in reputation, they have been invited to attend the meetings of the different state associations and to hold clinics at the different Negro infirmaries and hospitals. In these clinics the coloured physicians have had an opportunity to see major operations performed by experts and specialists of their own race and thus have gained knowledge and experience in their profession that they could not otherwise obtain. For instance, at a recent meeting of the Alabama State Association at Birmingham there were present, Dr. George C. Hall of Chicago, Dr. A. M. Curtis of Washington, and Drs. Boyd, Stewart and Roman of the Maharry Medical College of Nashville, Tennessee. All of these men have gained a national reputation, either as teachers of medicine or as surgeons.

One of the hospitals to which I have referred, the Taylor-Lane Hospital, at Orangeburg, South Carolina, was started by a coloured woman, Dr. Matilda A. Evans. Dr. Evans, aside from the fact that she was the first woman doctor in Orangeburg, and perhaps also in the State of South Carolina, has an interesting history. Her grandmother, who was Edith Willis, was kidnapped from Chester County, Pennsylvania, when she was a child, and taken to Charleston, South Carolina, where she was sold as a slave. She eventually became a cook on the plantation of Mr. John Brodie, who was a descendant of one of the old families of South Carolina. Dr. Matilda Evans was born on this plantation six years after emancipation. She was educated in the famous Schofield School at Aiken, South Carolina, and eventually studied medicine at the Woman's Medical College in Philadelphia. Before she started North, however, she stopped for a few days with a coloured family at Orangeburg. There she heard for the first time about Dr. B. W. Taylor, "Mars Ben," as the people she lived with called him. These people impressed upon her that if she ever intended to return to Orangeburg, to practise medicine, she must go to see "Mars Ben" because he would help her.

After she had completed her course at the medical college in Philadelphia, the young woman physician wrote to Dr. Taylor, and he encouraged her to return to Orangeburg and take up the profession. From the first, she says, he, as well as the other white physicians in the town, assisted her in every way. She has been unusually successful. About half of her practice in Orangeburg, I have been told, is among the white people. Among her patients are the descendants of the family to which her grandmother and mother had belonged as slaves. At the same time she is on the best of terms with all the doctors in the town, white and black, who have assisted her in establishing and maintaining the Taylor-Lane Hospital, of which she is the founder and has the entire management.

It would be a mistake to assume from what I have said, thus far, that there were no Negro physicians in the United States before the Civil War. The earliest Negro doctor to attain any degree of distinction was James Derham.

James Derham was born a slave in Philadelphia in 1767. His master taught him to read and write, and employed him in compounding medicines. After a time the young slave became so skilful that he was employed as an assistant by a new master to whom he was afterward sold. He succeeded, while he was still a young man, in purchasing his freedom and eventually removed to New Orleans, Louisiana, where he built up a lucrative practice. The celebrated Dr. Rush published an account of him in the American Museum in which he spoke in the highest terms of his character and his skill as a physician.

Another Negro doctor, who gained considerable reputation previous to the Civil War, was Dr. James McCune Smith, who, unable to obtain a technical education in the United States, went to England and eventually graduated at Glasgow. He practised in New York for twenty-five years, where he became one of the most influential men of his race. Dr. Smith was the first coloured man to establish a pharmacy in the United States.

In 1854, Dr. John V. De Grasse was admitted in due form as a member of the Massachusetts Medical Society, probably the first instance of such an honour being conferred upon a Negro in this country. When the professional schools began to receive coloured students after the close of the Civil War, a number of young men eagerly took advantage of the opportunity to equip themselves for professional careers. Howard University in Washington has graduated over a thousand students from the medical department alone and almost half that number from the department of law.

The majority of the Negro doctors, dentists and pharmacists in the South have been educated at Howard University, Washington, District of Columbia, at Meharry Medical College, Nashville, Tennessee, or at the Leonard Medical College at Raleigh, N. C. At the Leonard Medical College from the beginning, a majority of the professors have been Southern white men residing in Raleigh.

In this connection, I may add, that the Negro doctor, as soon as he shows fitness for his profession, is usually treated with every courtesy by white physicians. White doctors have everywhere encouraged the building of hospitals for coloured patients. They have shown themselves, with a few exceptions, willing and even glad to consult with Negro physicians whenever they are called upon to do so. In almost every part of the South which I have visited the Negro physician is treated with great respect by white people as well as coloured, and as a rule, I think it is true that the Negro physicians are entitled to the consideration and respect of the communities in which they live. There are comparatively few of them who have not held their own, from a moral point of view. The number of those who have gone down on account of drink, or other had habits, is comparatively small.

More and more, also, the white people of the South

are beginning to recognise that their own interests, as far as health is concerned, are intimately inter- woven with those of the coloured race. Disease draws no colour line. It is not possible that the conditions of life in that part of the city where the coloured people live should be filthy and degrading, such as tend to produce disease and crime, without these conditions sooner or later affecting the lives of those who live in other parts of the city. If the woman who does the household washing lives in a part of the city where there is consumption or small- pox, the seeds of that disease will eventually be carried into the homes of all her employers, no matter how carefully guarded they are in other respects. If the servant who prepares the food or has the care of the children spends a large part of her life among people who are unclean, and in a region that is infected with disease, it is inevitable that sooner or later she will impart that disease to the family under her care.

In the education of the people in the laws of health- ful living and in the improvement of conditions among the poorer classes the Negro doctor is able to perform a great service, not only for the people of his own race, but for all the people in the community in which he lives.

One of the agencies that has done most to build up the medical profession among the Negroes is the National Medical Association, which includes among its members some three hundred and fifty Negro physicians, surgeons and pharmacists, and reaches through correspondence some fifteen hundred others. This Association grew out of a congress of Negro physicians and surgeons that was held at the Exposition at Atlanta, in 1895. Dr. I. Garland Penn, the assistant general secretary of the Epworth League of the Methodist Episcopal Church, who was commissioner of Negro exhibits for the Atlanta Exposition, was indirectly responsible for it. He conceived the idea that, in connection with the other features of the Exposition, an attempt should be made to bring together as large a number of Negro physicians and surgeons as possible, because he believed that the meeting would not only be of advantage to the Negro physicians themselves, but also would give the world some idea of the progress Negroes were making in that branch of science.

It was Dr. R. F. Boyd, of Nashville, afterward chosen as the first president of the Association, who was largely responsible for making this congress a permanent institution. During the first years of its existence the Association met irregularly. Since 1900, however, the meetings have been held annually. One of the features of these annual meetings has been the surgical clinics held by Doctors Daniel H. Williams, George C. Hall and A. M. Curtis and others.

Dr. Daniel H. Williams and Dr. George C. Hall, of Chicago, are probably the most noted Negro surgeons in the United States. They have to their credit the performance of some of the most note-worthy operations that have been undertaken by any surgeon of any race.

The influence of the Negro doctor in the elevation of the race has extended further than the mere prac-tice of medicine. In many cases it will be found that he is a successful busines man in the community in which he lives and the owner of valuable property. In Montgomery, Alabama, for instance, the Negro doctors own and operate four drug-stores. The same is true in Birmingham and Mobile. In fact, outside of the real estate business there is probably no kind of enterprise in which Negroes have been so largely successful as in the drug business. There is hardly a city of any importance in the Southern states in which there are not Negro druggists. From such investigations as I have been able to make I have learned that, at the present time, there are no less than one hundred and thirty-six druggists in the Southern states, and, in most cases, these stores have been started, in the first instance, by or under the direction of Negro physicians.

In cases where a Negro physician has started a store in connection with his office, he will often have a wife or brother, or, after a time, a son or daughter, who is a professional pharmacist. He will place his daughter or his wife in charge of the store, while he attends to the duties of his profession. In this way he is able not only to make certain economies in the business, but also to widen the economic opportunity of the other members of the family and of the members of his race.

The progress of the Negro physician and surgeon is but an instance and an indication of the rise of the professional class among the coloured people in America. The first and largest class, since the first and most pressing need of the Negro after emancipation was education, is that of teachers. According to the census of 1900 there were 21,268 Negro teachers in schools and colleges. This was an increase of 6,168 from 1890 to 1900, or 40.8 per cent., which was more than twice as rapid as the increase of the Negro population. The increase of the white teachers for the same period was 27.7 per cent.

It is probable that in the ten years the increase has been proportionately less among the teachers than among the other professions, the professions of medicine, dentistry and pharmacy having become especially popular in recent years. Next to the teachers the ministers make up the largest group among Negroes in the professions. In 1900, the number of Negro ministers was 15,530, an increase of 3,371 from 1890 to 1900, or 27.7 per cent. During the same decade white ministers increased less rapidly, or 26.4 per cent.

In the other groups of the professional class of Negroes there were 1,734 physicians and surgeons,

212 dentists, 728 lawyers, 99 literary and scientific persons and 210 journalists.   In each of these groups there have arisen, within the short period of forty years, several men and women who, by reason of their mental and moral qualities, were an honour to their profession and an inspiration to the members of their own race, who have seen in their success a concrete example of what Negroes can do to raise themselves and make themselves of service to the world.

In the profession of teaching the work of coloured women has been, to a marked degree, one in which heroism has played a part worthy of record and remembrance.   Were I asked to select an example of the best type of the Negro woman's work for the uplift of her race since freedom began, without a moment's hesitancy my choice would be the coloured woman teacher, especially the one who has borne the burden of teaching in the rural districts of the South, where she has had to labor, for the most part, without the hope of material reward or the praise of men.

I know the names of hundreds of these devoted women, who have gone out into the country districts of the South and given their lives in a self-sacrificing and often apparently hopeless effort to lift up the masses of their own people.   Perhaps the most remarkable example of what these women have accomplished is the work of Elizabeth E. Wright, the founder of Voorhees Industrial School, at

Denmark, South Carolina. She came to us at Tuskegee, a frail young woman without means and, as it often seemed, without the physical strength to carry her through the struggle necessary to complete her course. She was compelled to give up for a time and go home until she could obtain means and strength to go on.

After being graduated at Tuskegee, she became a teacher in the little town of Denmark, South Carolina, and, at that place, before she died, succeeded in building up a school of her own, modelled on that of Tuskegee Institute. This school stands to-day as a monument to this young woman's faith and persistence. It is one of the largest and best equipped of the industrial schools for Negroes in the Southern states, and has gained a recognition and support, not only of the coloured but of the white people in the community in which it is situated. Having established the school, Elizabeth Wright literally gave her life in the effort to support and maintain it, and she lies buried on the grounds of the school which she erected with her own life.

The profession of law has enlisted from an early date a considerable number of talented coloured men and a few women. The first coloured woman lawyer was Charlotte Ray, a daughter of Charles Ray, who was at one time pastor of the famous Shiloh Presbyterian Church. She graduated from Howard University about 1872, and was still living in 1908,

I understand, though she was then something over sixty years of age.

Macon B. Allen was the first coloured attorney regularly admitted to practice in the United States. He was admitted to the bar in Maine in 1844. Robert Morris was admitted to the Boston bar in 1850, on motion of Charles Sumner, where he practised with marked success until his death in 1882. He was associated with Mr. Sumner in 1849, in the famous case before the Supreme Court of Massachusetts, to test the constitutionality of separate coloured schools in Massachusetts. John M. Langston was admitted to the Ohio bar in 1854. The first coloured man admitted to practice before the Supreme Court of the United States, was John S. Reck, of Boston, Massachusetts. He was admitted Feb. 1, 1865, on motion of Mr. Sumner.

A few of the coloured men who became Members of Congress from the Southern states had a legal training, as well as two or three who have been in the diplomatic and consular service of the United States. Among the coloured department clerks in Washington a surprising number have taken the law course at Howard University in that city. In the effort of the American Negro to widen his economic life, the lawyers of the race are finding a field for their talents which they have not hitherto had an opportunity to enter. For instance, in the building and loan associations; in the mercantile, real estate, coöperative companies and savings banks of various kinds that are now everywhere springing up, the coloured lawyer is finding a clientele far different from the young coloured men who began the study of law in the early years following the Civil War, and looked forward then to a public career, either in State or national politics as the goal of their ambition.

I have always believed that the stronger the economic and industrial foundation of the masses of the race and the more numerous those engaged in gainful occupations became, the more successful and prosperous would the professional class among the race become.

Some mention should be made of the fact that several Negro lawyers have obtained, either by election or appointment, a number of minor judicial positions in which they discharged their duties in an eminently satisfactory manner. Mifflin W. Gibbs, for instance, city judge in Little Rock, Arkansas, in 1873, was the first coloured man to be elected to such a position in the United States. George L. Ruffin was appointed a judge of a district municipal court in Massachusetts in 1883. James C. Matthews was elected a few years ago to a city judgeship, as a Democrat in the city of Albany, New York. E. M. Hewlett and R. H. Terrell were appointed by President Roosevelt as city magistrates in the District of Columbia; the latter holds his position at the present writing and is regarded as a very capable and efficient official. A few assistants to district attorneys, municipal and Federal, have been given appointments. In none of these cases have I heard of a failure.

Another profession in which Negroes have been making progress in recent years is that of journalism. The Negro journals were, in certain respects, at their best before the Civil War, during the period of the anti-slavery struggle. At that time, when Frederick Douglass was editor of *The North Star*, and all the anti-slavery leaders among the Negro race contributed more or less to the racial papers, Negro journals were, for the most part, inspired by high aims and were a source of inspiration to the masses of the coloured people in their struggle for freedom. After emancipation came, the number of these newspapers increased, but, too frequently, they became the mere organs of a party or a clique, with no higher reason for their existence than the temporary success of some political partisan or the petty spoils that fall to the lot of the Negro politician.

In recent years, however, the Negro journals, following the lead of the white journals, have become less party organs and more newspapers, seeking to report events and reflect the life and progress of the whole race. There are at present no less than two hundred Negro newspapers published in the United States. Many of them are ably edited.

One hears a great deal in both the Northern and

Southern states of the Negro politician and, inciden-
tally, of the Negro lawyer and journalist. One hears,
however, very little of the Negro physician and surgeon.   Nevertheless, of all the professions in which
the Negro is engaged, that of medicine is probably
the one in which he has attained the highest degree
of technical skill and the greatest usefulness to the
community in which he lives.   In no other direction,
I dare say, has the Negro travelled so far from the
primitive condition and civilisation of his savage
ancestors in Africa.

I was reminded of this fact the more forcibly, a
few years ago, by an incident related to me by Dr.
George C. Hall, of Chicago. In 1905, Dr. Hall was
engaged in holding a surgical clinic before the Alabama Medical, Dental and Pharmaceutical Society,
at Mobile. While there he visited the African colony
to which I have already referred, situated a few miles
out from Mobile in what is known as the African
village. He had just come from his lectures and
demonstrations in the city of Mobile, where he had
been the guest of an organisation composed of men
who were engaged in applying the latest results of
modern science to the solution of one of the most
complicated of human problems, namely, the cure
of disease. In a half-hour's ride on the street cars he
found himself in the midst of a settlement of native
Africans, who for fifty years had held themselves and
their descendants apart from the Negroes of Mobile,

and had had as little as possible to do with the white people about them.   Although they were employed as labourers in the saw-mills nearby, and cultivated the little patches of ground which they owned, they had remained, in most other respects, practically untouched by the civilisation about them.

"I could not help thinking," said Dr. Hall, in speaking of the incident, "that less than half a century ago the men with whom I had been conferring, or their ancestors and ours, were as undeveloped as these primitive people of the African village.   I never realised before the wonderful opportunities which our race has had in being thrown into contact with the science and civilisation of this modern world. Here we can see our people, practically under our own eyes, making their way, in a few years, or, at most, a few generations, from the age of stone to the age of electricity."

Few people, black or white, realise that in the Negro race, as it exists to-day in America, we have representatives of nearly every stage of civilisation, from that of the primitive African to the highest modern life and science have achieved.   This fact is at once a result and an indication of the rapidity with which he has risen.

CHAPTER VIII

THE NEGRO DISFRANCHISEMENT AND THE NEGRO IN BUSINESS

WHEN I began my work in Tuskegee in 1881 the coloured people of Alabama had just been deprived — in a way that is now familiar — of many of their political rights. There were some voting but few Negroes held office anywhere in Alabama at that time. The Negroes set great store by the political privileges that had been granted them during the Reconstruction Period, and they thought that when they lost these they had lost all.

Soon after I went into Alabama a new President, James A. Garfield, was inaugurated at Washington. A little community of coloured people not very far from Tuskegee were so impressed with the idea that the new Administration would do something to better their condition, especially in the way of strengthening their political rights, that, out of their poverty, they raised enough money to pay the expenses of one of their number to Washington, in order that he might get direct information and return and report to them what the outlook was. This incident struck me as the more pathetic because I happened to know the man who went on this errand. He was a good, honest, well-meaning fellow, but entirely lacking in knowledge of the world outside his own community. I doubt that he ever got near enough, even to the inauguration ceremonies, to see the President, and I am sure he never got inside the door of the White House. He returned to his people, at any rate, with a very gloomy report and, although it was never quite clear whom he had seen or what he had done, the people understood what it meant.

The people did not say much about their loss. They preserved outwardly, as a rule, the same good nature and cheerfulness which had always characterised them, but deep down in their hearts they had begun to feel that there was no hope for them.

This feeling of apathy and despair continued for a long time among these people in the country districts. A good many of them who owned land in the county at this time gave it up or lost it for some reason or other. Others moved away from the county and there were a great many abandoned farms. Gradually, however, the temper of the people changed. They began to see that harvests were just as good and just as bad as they had been before the changes which deprived them of their political privileges. They began to see, in short, that there was still hope for them in economic, if not in political directions.

The man who went to Washington to call on the President is still living. He is a different person now, a new man, in fact. Since that time he has purchased a farm; has built a decent, comfortable house; is educating his children, and I note that never a session of the monthly Farmer's Institute assembles at Tuskegee that this man does not come and bring some of the products from his farm to exhibit to his fellow-farmers. He is not only successful, but he is one of the happiest and most useful individuals in our county. He has learned that he can do for himself what the authorities at Washington could not do for him, and that is, make his life a success.

A large part of the work which Tuskegee Institute did in those early years, and has continued to do down to the present time, has been to show the masses of our people that in agriculture, in the industries, in commerce, and in the struggle toward economic success, there were compensations for the losses they had suffered in other directions. In doing this we did not seek to give the people the idea that political rights were not valuable or necessary, but rather to impress upon them that economic efficiency was the foundation for every kind of success.

I am pointing out these facts here in order to show how closely industrial education has been connected with the great economic advance among the masses of the Negro people during the last twenty-five years. If the effect of disfranchisment of the

Negro was to discourage and in many instances to embitter him, industrial education has done much to turn his attention to opportunities that lay open to him in other directions than in politics. It has had the effect of turning attention to the vast quantities of idle lands in many parts of the South and the West, and in many instances, has helped him take up these lands and make himself an independent farmer. It has turned attention to the opportunities in business and led him to perceive that in the South, particularly, there are opportunities for better service to his own race, which he can perform and more profitably than any one else.

The fact is, that the coloured people who went into politics directly after the war were, in most cases, what may be called the aristocracy of the race. Many of them had been practically, if not always legally, free, made so by their masters, who were at the same time their fathers, by whom they had been educated and from whom they frequently inherited considerable property. They had formed their lives and characters on the models of the aristocratic Southern people, among whom they were raised, and they believed that politics was the only sort of activity that was fit for a gentleman to engage in. The conditions which existed directly after the war offered these men the opportunity to step in and make themselves the political leaders of the masses of the people.

In the meantime, however, between the close of the war and the period to which I have just referred, there had grown up a middle class among the coloured people. This class is composed, for the most part, of men who had been slaves before the War. Some of them had been house servants and had the advantage of intimate contact with their master's family; many of them had been slaves of that class of planters sometimes referred to in the South as the "yeomanry"; others had been field hands on the big plantations. The majority had had very few opportunities before the War, except such as they obtained in practising the different trades, which were carried on about the plantations. It is from this class that the greater portion of the Negro landowners have sprung; from this class that the greater number of mechanics formerly belonged, and it was from this class that the majority of the business men of the Negro race have arisen.

A farmer, who became the owner of a large plantation of a thousand acres or more, necessarily became something of a business man. Very likely he opened a store on his plantation in order to supply the tenants on his land. That was the case, for instance, with the Reid brothers, Frank and Dow, who live in Macon County, Alabama, about twelve miles from Tuskegee at a little place called Dawkins. The father of these young men had for a long time leased and worked a large plantation of some 1,100 acres. He was enabled to send his sons to school at Tuskegee and, after their return from school, they leased 480 acres more and subsequently added to that by purchase 605 acres, making a total of 2,185 acres of land under their control.   A larger portion of this land they sublet to tenants and, as the necessities of the community they had established manifested themselves, they established successfully a store, a cotton-gin, a blacksmith shop, and a grist-mill.

Frequently, in the early days some young coloured man who had worked in a restaurant or as a waiter in a hotel, after saving a little money, would start a business for himself in a small way.   Gradually he would accumulate more capital and enlarge his business.   That was the case of my friend, John S. Trower, of Germantown, Philadelphia, who is now one of the leading caterers in the city of Philadelphia, and, also, with William E. Gross, proprietor of the Gross Catering Company, of 219 W. 134th Street, New York.   In Philadelphia, New York, Baltimore, and Washington, there are a number of noted Negro caterers who began life in the small way I have described.

Among the earlier caterers of New York was Peter Van Dyke, who owned a place at 130 Wooster Street. He became wealthy and left his children and grandchildren in good circumstances.   Another of these early caterers was Boston Crummell, father of the late Alexander Crummell, one of the first Africans to be ordained as a priest by the Episcopal Church. Boston Crummell was born in West Africa and brought to America when he was a child. It is an interesting fact that his son, Alexander Crummell, after having studied in Queen's College, Cambridge, England, went to Africa, as one of the first coloured missionaries sent out from this country to Liberia.

Thomas Downing, who kept the once famous "Downing Oyster House," was one of the early Negro caterers of New York. His son, George T. Downing, built the Sea-Girt House at Newport, Rhode Island, and was afterward a caterer in Washington, where he became a friend of Charles Sumner, Wendell Phillips, Henry Wilson, John Andrews, and others of the anti-slavery party of that time.

Charles H. Smiley, who was born at St. Catherine's, Canada, and was at one time one of the leading caterers of Chicago, began his life in Chicago as a janitor, but was employed during his spare time as a waiter at dinners and parties. Francis J. Moultry, who in 1909 was still conducting a large catering establishment at Yonkers, New York, got his training and accumulated his capital for his business career as a waiter in New York City. Mr. Moultry was at that time one of the large taxpayers of his city. He owned stock in several of the Yonkers banks and is proprietor of what is or was a few years ago the largest apartment house in Yonkers. Mr. Moultry owned valuable reality in various portions of the city and has more than once been on the bond of more than one of the county officers.

The training which many of the coloured servants received, both before and after emancipation, gave them a certain capital in the way of experience with which to go into business on their own account. Perhaps the most successful coloured hotel-keeper in the United States has been E. C. Berry of Athens, Ohio. "Hotel Berry," as I learned when I visited Ohio, has had an almost national reputation. Mr. Berry was one of the most respected citizens of the town in which he lives and so successful has he been in conducting his hotel that it is regarded by the citizens as one of the institutions of the town.

Mr. Berry was born in Oberlin, Ohio, in 1854. When he was two years old he was taken by his parents to the little town of Albany, which is about seven miles below Athens. At that time, there were a number of lines of the Underground Railway, which, starting at different points on the Ohio River, passed through Albany and Athens. At Albany there was early established what was known as the Enterprise Academy for coloured children, and it was at this Academy that Mr. Berry obtained his schooling. He first came to Athens when he was sixteen years old, and went to work in a brick-yard at the small sum of fifty cents per day, which was soon increased to one dollar and twenty-five cents. With the money that he earned in this way he helped to support the members of his family, who were still living in Albany. Eventually he secured employment in Athens in a restaurant, and it was the training he received there that enabled him later on to start a little place of his own.

Mr. Berry was successful in business from the first, and, finally, after giving the matter due consideration and talking it over with friends in the city, he made up his mind to open a hotel. It was an entirely new thing at that time to see a coloured man in the hotel business in that part of the country, and Mr. Berry knew that he was going to meet with opposition on account of his race. He determined to overcome this prejudice by making his hotel more comfortable than any other in the city, and by giving his guests more for their money than they were able to get anywhere else, not only in the city but in the state. One thing I remember which impressed me as indicating the care and thoughtful atttention which Mr. Berry gave to his guests was the fact that at night, after his guests had fallen asleep, he made it a practice to go to their rooms and gather up their clothes and take them to his wife, who would repair rents, add buttons where they were lacking, and press the garments, after which Mr. Berry would replace them. Mr. Berry's hotel, I may add, is said by Mr. Elbert Hubbard, the lecturer, who has had an opportunity to test the quality of a large number of hotels in different parts of this country, to be one of the best in the United States.

There are a number of other successful hotel men among the members of my race of whom I have made the acquaintance in different parts of the country. Joseph W. Lee, who, until he died a few years ago, kept the very popular and successful hotel at Squantum, a summer resort just outside of Boston, was one of these.

Negroes both before the War and after, entered very easily into the barber business, and there is no business, I may add, in which the Negro has met more competition from foreign immigrants. In many cities, both North and South, the Negro barber's trade is almost wholly confined, at the present time, to members of his own race. It is interesting to observe however, that this has in no way lessened the number of Negro barber shops, and the fact is an indication of the increasing economic welfare of the masses of the Negro people. In spite of the competition which I have mentioned, some of the largest and best conducted barber shops in the United States are carried on by Negroes.

As an illustration, I might mention the shop of George A. Myers, of Cleveland, Ohio, whose place of business is fitted up, not only with all conveniences that you will find in other first-class shops, but also with some that you will not find there. For instance, when I was last in his shop, he had devised an arrangement by which a customer could be connected at once by telephone with any one he wished to speak to, and that without leaving his chair. He has also provided a young woman stenographer, to whom patrons can dictate business letters if they desire, without interrupting the work of the barber.

Another business in which the Negro early found an opportunity to be of service to his people is that of undertaking. As far as they were able, the Negro people have always tried to surround the great mystery of death with appropriate and impressive ceremonies. One of the principal features of the Negro secret organisations has been the care for the sick and the burial of the dead. The demand that these organisations sought to meet has created a business opportunity, and Negro business men have largely taken advantage of it.

One of the first men to perceive the opportunity for coloured business men in this direction was Elijah Cook, a Negro undertaker of Montgomery, formerly a member of the State Legislature of Alabama. Mr. Cook was born a slave in Alabama. He was several times sold on the auction block during slavery, and at one of these sales he was separated from his brother, of whom he has never since heard. He was taught the carpenter's trade, however, and, after he had served his apprenticeship, was permitted to hire his time for $25 per month. When the Civil War broke out, Mr. Cook still paid his master's wife the stipulated sum per month and continued to do so faithfully until he was emancipated. He was a leader in founding the first coloured school in Montgomery, which was held in a basement, under a dilapidated church. He himself was one of the first scholars and, after working hard all day, was a faithful attendant of the night school.

Right after the War there was no coloured undertaker in Montgomery and frequently the corpses of the coloured people were hauled to the cemetery in rough wagons. Mr. Cook seeing this, bought a hearse and went into the undertaking business for himself. He accumulated a small fortune during the twenty years or more that he was in business, and became one of the respected citizens of Montgomery.

James C. Thomas, who, at the time I write, is said to be the richest man of African descent in New York, made a large part of his fortune in the undertaking business. Mr. Thomas came originally from Harrisburg, Texas, where he was born in 1864. In 1881, while he was employed by a steamer plying between New Orleans, Mexico, and Cuba, yellow fever broke out in New Orleans. The boat he was on came to New York to escape the quarantine. It was thus, quite by accident, that Mr. Thomas became a New Yorker.

There have been Negro undertakers in New York, I have been informed, for over 150 years. There were several Negro undertakers in New York and Brooklyn, at the time Mr. Thomas went into business, but the larger part of the trade, which should have come to the coloured undertakers, went to white men. In 1909, Mr. Thomas had one of the largest businesses of any undertaker, white or black, in the city of New York. He was, in addition, the owner of a number of valuable properties in New York City and owned stock in the Chelsea National Bank of New York.

I shall have occasion to make mention, in another connection, of the success the Negro has had as a banker, real estate dealer, and as a druggist, and in some other forms of business. As illustrating, however, the variety of enterprises into which the Negro had entered, I might mention the fact that one of the best conducted grocery stores in the city of Montgomery is run by Victor H. Tulane, who started in business in 1893 in a little building, twelve by twenty in size, with no experience and a capital of $90. Mr. Tulane, in 1909, was doing a business of forty thousand dollars a year. He has been for a number of years one of the trustees of the Tuskegee Normal and Industrial Institute.

During my visit of observation and study in the State of Mississippi in the fall of 1908, I found that the largest book-store and, I was told, the only one at that time in the city of Greenville, Mississippi, was conducted by a coloured man, Granville Carter.

Mr. Carter told me that at one time there had been as many as five book-stores in the town but he had succeeded, by close attention to business and offering his books at prices more favourable than his rivals, in outliving them all, until at the time I was there, his was the only book-store in the town. He told me that he handled the entire book business of the county and that he sold books in several of the adjoining counties. He regularly employs four helpers to assist him in the business and at Christmas time he has been compelled to increase this number to ten.

In Jackson, Mississippi, H. K. Rischer had had for nearly twenty years, at the time of my visit, a practical monopoly of the bakery business. Mr. Rischer's bakery was one of the first concerns of its kind to be established in Jackson. His business, which amounts to about $30,000 a year, gives employment to twelve persons and was first established in 1881.

While it is true, as I have already pointed out, that the disposition of the Negro people to turn their attention more and more to practical matters and to business manifested itself at about the same time that I came to Alabama and has grown with the increasing interest in industrial education, it is likewise true that only since 1897 or 1898 has there been any marked and rapid increase in the amount of business conducted by coloured people.

When the National Negro Business League met in Boston, 1900, there were but two Negro banks in the United States; at the present time there are nearly, if not quite, fifty such institutions.

In order to illustrate the improvement of the general mass of the coloured people in the South during the ten years since 1899, I shall take as an example the city of Jackson, Mississippi, where in the summer of 1898, a special study was made of the economic condition of the people. Up to 1896, Negroes who represented at that time more than half of the population, were not reckoned in the business life of the town. Few of them owned property of any kind. At the present time, the Negro population is less than half of the total population of the town, and the 8,000 Negroes who make their homes there, own, it is estimated, one-third of the area of the town, although this area represents but one-eleventh of the value of the city property. Negroes own, for instance, according to the tax records of the city, $581,580 worth of property. Over one-third of the 566 Negroes on the tax books were assessed for more than $1,000 and six of them for more than $5,000. The largest single assessment amounted to $23,800.

A careful investigation brought to light the fact that about one-half the Negro families of that town own their own homes, while more than two-thirds of the houses in which the Negroes live are in the possession of their own race. Next to the possession of property, the amount of money deposited in banks by Negroes is an evidence of their economic condition. In speaking of this matter during the summer of 1908, the president of one of the prominent white banks said that Negroes had just begun to save their money during the last ten or twelve years. He was in a position to know, for Negroes had deposited in his bank more than $25,000. Altogether Negro savings in Jackson banks amounted, at the time, to something over $200,000, more than one-third of which was in the hands of the Negro banks.

Perhaps the most successful Negro business man in Jackson, at that time, was Dr. S. D. Redmond. Dr. Redmond received his medical training at the Illinois Medical College and the Harvard Medical College. When he settled in Jackson ten years ago he had practically nothing. At the time this is written he is president of the American Trust and Savings bank, the oldest of the Negro banks in Jackson and a stockholder in three banks controlled by the white people, as well as in the electric power and light company which lights the city streets. He owns two drug-stores, one of which is situated on the chief business street of the town. He receives rent from more than one hundred houses.

There were in 1908 more than one hundred business enterprises conducted by Negroes in Jackson. Among them were the two banks already mentioned, four drug-stores, two undertaking companies, two real estate companies, Mr. Rischer's bakery, four shoemaking and repair shops, one of these doing the largest business of its kind in the town. One millinery shop, besides numerous stores, barber shops, and other smaller business concerns of various kinds. Forty-five of these, including five contracting firms, did something like $380,000 worth of business during the year 1907-1908, and gave employment to two hundred and thirty persons.

It used to be said, before much was known about Africa, that the condition of the African people had remained the same in all parts of Africa through thousands of years and nothing furnished so convincing a proof of the inability of the African to improve as the fact that during all this time he has not changed. I have already suggested, in what I have written, that an enormous change has taken place in the condition, in the feeling and in the ambitions of the coloured people in this country, since they obtained their freedom a comparatively few years ago.

The Negro came out of slavery with a feeling that work was the symbol of degradation. In nearly all the schools conducted by Negroes in the South at the present time, Negro children are learning to work. The Negro came out of slavery with almost no capital except the hard discipline and training he had received as a slave. In the years since that time, he has not only become a large land-owner, and, to a large extent, the owner of his own home, but he has become a banker and a business man.   He came out of slavery with the idea that somehow or other the Government, which freed him, was going to support and protect him, and that the great hope of his race was in politics and in the ballot.   In the last decade the Negro has settled down to the task of building his own fortune and of gaining through thrift, through industry, and through business success that which he has been denied in other directions.

Many of the men to whom I have referred in this chapter, if I had time to relate their histories, would illustrate in their own lives the changes to which I refer.   For instance, L. K. Attwood, the president of the Southern Bank, the second Negro bank in Jackson, Mississippi, was born a slave in Wilcox County, Alabama, about 150 miles from Tuskegee, in 1851.   He was sold on the block when he was eighteen months old.   His mother bought him for $300 and moved with him to Ohio. In 1874, he graduated from Lincoln University, Pennsylvania.   Two years later he was admitted to the bar in Mississippi.   He served two terms as a member of the Mississippi Legislature from Hinds County, and has held the positions of United States Commissioner and United States Deputy Revenue Collector for the Louisiana and Mississippi districts.   He is one of a group of professional coloured men who have found that business

pays better than politics.   In addition to his connection with the bank, Mr. Attwood has been actively
identified with a number of other Negro enterprises
in the town.   He has amassed considerable property
and is generally respected as a shrewd and aggressive
business man among the people of his community.

While I am on this subject, I should, perhaps, mention one other notable example of the business men
who have found a larger opportunity in business than
they did in politics.   C. F. Johnson, of Mobile, Alabama, Secretary and General Manager of the Union
Mutual Aid Association, was for many years Secretary of the Republican State Executive Committee
of Alabama.   He was for a time, also, secretary to the
Collector of Customs at the port of Mobile, but
when Mr. Cleveland was elected President he gave
up that position and took the position as elevator man
instead.   One day after he had been there for some
time the new collector, who had been appointed by
Mr. Cleveland, noticed him there and, thinking the
time had come to complete his political house-clean-
ing, dismissed him from that position.   Because the
new man whom the Collector had to take his place
did not do the work satisfactorily, he asked Mr. Johnson to return.   Johnson said he would come back
if he could have the appointment for four years, but
the Collector would not agree to that, so Johnson
went permanently out of office and into business.
He was largely responsible for the organisation of the

company of which he has been general manager and is now one of the wealthiest coloured men in the State of Alabama.

So far as I have been able to learn, no coloured man has ever been classed among the millionaires, though several men have had the reputation of being in that class.

A few years ago there was a coloured man by the name of Wiley Jones in Pine Bluff, Arkansas, who owned a street railway, a stable of trotting horses, and private trotting park. When he died it was learned for the first time that he had investments in real estate in a number of large Western cities, but his estate did not reach, as I remember, more than one hundred thousand dollars. John McKee, of Philadelphia, was reputed to be a millionaire, but his estate in Philadelphia, when he died, amounted to but $342,832. In addition to this he owned land in Atlantic County, New Jersey, which was assessed at $20,650. He also owned a tract of coal and mineral land in Kentucky, which was assessed at $70,000, which he hoped would eventually be of great value. Colonel McKee gave directions in his will that the rents and incomes of his estate should accumulate until the death of all his children and grandchildren. It was to be used to establish a college for the education of fatherless boys, white and coloured.

Perhaps the nearest approach to a coloured millionaire was Thomy Lafon, of New Orleans, who died

December 23, 1893, leaving an estate appraised at $413,000, the bulk of which was divided among the various charities of the city of New Orleans. I understand, however, that Mr. Lafon had disposed of a considerable portion of his estate in order to found various charities before his death.

Mr. Lafon was born in New Orleans, December 28, 1810, of free Negro parents. He began life as a school-teacher; then he ran for a time a small dry-goods store on Orleans Street. As he accumulated a little money he began loaning it out at advantageous rates of interest, and went from that into land speculations, which made him very wealthy. Before he died he became much attached to the late Archbishop Janssens and, under his direction, as I understand, began disposing of his fortune for philanthropic purposes. Before his death he had established an asylum for orphan boys called Lafon Asylum, and after his death he bequeathed the sum of $2,000 in cash and the revenue amounting to $275 per month of a large property at the corner of Royal and Iberville streets.

Other legacies were in favor of the Lafon Old Folks' Home, previously established, the Charity Hospital, of New Orleans, the several universities for coloured children in New Orleans and a number of charities in charge of the Catholic Church.

In this benevolent way the two largest fortunes which members of my race have yet accumulated were dispersed.

CHAPTER IX

THE NEGRO BANK AND THE MORAL UPLIFT

IN the year 1888, the statement was made upon the floor of the United States Senate that, with all the progress it had made in other directions, the Negro race had not a single bank to its credit. At the time this statement was made it was intimated that the Negro race never would support a bank; that, in short, the bank was the limit of the progress of the Negro in the direction of business.

Twenty years later, in 1908, no less than fifty-five Negro banks, large and small, had been started in the United States, and of these forty-seven were then in operation. There were eleven in Mississippi, ten in Virginia, five in Oklahoma, four in Georgia, four in Tennessee, four in North Carolina, four in Texas, two in Alabama, one in Arkansas, one in Pennsylvania, and one in Illinois.

These facts illustrate how difficult it is, in the case of a race which is coming for the first time into contact with new conditions or new opportunities, to predict from what it has done in the past what it is likely to do in the future.

In the course of my travels about the country, for

example, I am constantly meeting men who are introduced to me as "the first Negro who ever did" this thing or that thing. Sometimes the claims made for these men are more modest. In such cases I am likely to hear not that such a man is the first and only Negro who ever achieved the particular distinction mentioned, but that he is the first Negro in that particular state or community who has done so. As I have said, I meet hundreds of these men every year, and the number of them indicates to my mind that the Negro in America is making great progress. I mean that, as a race, and with reference to what they have done in the past, Negroes are probably doing more new things every year than can be said of any other race with the exception of the Japanese.

Negro banks are of various kinds and descriptions. Some of them, like the Bank of Mound Bayou, started by Charles Banks, March 8, 1904, are doing a regular commercial business. This bank is the centre of the cotton-raising community, and, during the cotton season, its clearings, through its correspondents and through other banks, have amounted to something over $200,000 per month. It had, in 1908, a paid in capital of $25,000 and resources amounting to $100,000. Other institutions, like the One Cent Savings Bank of Nashville, Tennessee, started in 1903 by J. C. Napier, are savings banks, pure and simple. Mr. Napier is one of the sub-

stantial business men of Nashville, Tennessee. He
has been four times elected a member of the City
Council, and is the owner of a handsome three-
story brick building located on one of the best
streets of that city, containing the offices of the bank,
a spacious hall, and a number of other offices. This
building is known as the Napier Court.

Quite as interesting as these banks, which have
been started on the models of similar institutions
conducted by white men, are some of the smaller
and more obscure savings and loan associations,
which have been started, frequently by untrained
men, in order to meet the necessities of peculiar
and local conditions. I have in mind such a mutual
banking association as was started by fifteen Negro
farmers in the neighbourhood of Courtland, Virginia,
the home of Nat Turner, and the scene of the
Northampton insurrection of 1831. This association was started under the leadership of Reverend O. C. Jenkins, and was formed primarily to
enable the coloured farmers in that part of the
country to assist each other in buying land and in
carrying on their farming operations. I mention
this organisation not because of its success but
because it illustrates the sort of experiments that
men, untrained in business, are making in all parts
of the South in order to improve their condition and
lift themselves up to a higher plane of living.

Before there were any banks owned by Negroes

there was the Freedmen's Bank, an institution for
Negroes, established in Washington, District of
Columbia, under the auspices of the Freedmen's
Bureau. No work was ever undertaken for the
benefit of the Freedmen more laudable in its purpose or more designed to assist a people who had
just come out of slavery to get on their feet. From
1866, when this bank was started, to 1874, when it
failed, the total amount of deposits had increased
from $305,167 to $55,000,000, and when the bank
closed its doors there was due to depositors
$3,013,670. The number of depositors to whom
this money was due was 61,131. Up to March,
1896, $1,722,548 had been re-paid to these depositors.
There still remains in the hands of the Government
$30,476.*

This bank had agents all over the South, and
coloured people were induced to deposit their earnings with it in the belief that the institution was
under the care and protection of the United States
Government. When they found that they had lost,
or been swindled out of all their little savings, they
lost faith in savings banks, and it was a long time
after this before it was possible to mention a savings
bank for Negroes without some reference being
made to the disaster of the Freedman's Bank.
The effect of this disaster was the more far-reach-

---

* "Economic Coöperation among Negro Americans." Atlanta University
Publication, No. 12, p. 135.

ing because of the wide extent of territory which the Freedmen's Bank covered through its agencies.

In March, 1888, the Legislature of Virginia granted a charter for a savings bank to the Grand Fountain of the United Order of the True Reformers. This bank was opened for business April 3, 1889, and received deposits to the amount of $1,268.69 the first day. This was the origin of the oldest and best established Negro bank in the United States. It is said that when application was made to the Virginia Legislature for a charter for this institution the matter was not treated seriously. Members of the Legislature looked upon a Negro bank as a joke, and granted the charter in a spirit of fun, never expecting to see a real Negro savings institution in operation in Virginia.

Some years ago W. P. Burrell, secretary of the True Reformers, in a report made at the Hampton Negro Conference, related an interesting anecdote in regard to the circumstances under which this bank was started. "It might be interesting to know," said Mr. Burrell, "that this bank, founded by William W. Browne, had its origin in a lynching which occurred in Charlotte County, at a point called Drake's Branch. A branch of the organisation of True Reformers had been founded at Mossingford and the fees of the members, amounting to nearly $100, had been deposited in the safe of a white man, who had thus an opportunity to see that the

Negroes of the county had some money, and that they were organising for some purpose. He decided that this was an unwise thing, and so determined to break up the organisation. This fact was reported to Mr. Browne. By a personal visit to the place, he succeeded in saving the organisation and, at the same time, had his attention called to the need of a coloured bank, where coloured people could carry on their own business. The idea of a bank was first advanced by a countryman named W. E. Grant, and immediately adopted by Mr. Browne. Thus it came to pass that, because of an unpleasant race feeling in Charlotte County, Virginia, the oldest incorporated Negro bank came into existence."

In the report to which I have referred, Mr. Burrell calls attention to the fact that, with the exception of the True Reformers' and the Nickel Savings Bank, which was started in Richmond, Virginia, in 1896, all the banks then existing in Virginia had been started since the passage of the new suffrage laws requiring Negro voters in Virginia to be property owners, or to be educated, or to be war veterans.

In the early history of the coloured banks of Virginia it has been told me that considerable difficulty was experienced because these institutions were not connected directly with the Clearing House. The result was, it is said, that the "coloured" depositors were unwilling to open accounts in "coloured" banks, since no means existed by which an exchange of checks among the "coloured" and "white" banks could take place, and the "white" banks refused to accept these checks because they could not "clear" them in the ordinary way. This policy was broken up, however, when the white merchants, who had accepted checks upon the Negro banks, threatened to withdraw their deposits unless the "white" banks made some arrangements by which checks on the "coloured" banks could be cashed. This led, finally, to the voluntary offer of one of the National Banks to act as clearing-house agents. At the present time all the "coloured" banks clear through some member of the Clearing House, for which privilege they pay a small annual tax.

Since it was started, the capital of the True Reformers' Bank has been increased from $4,000 to $100,000, all of which has been paid in. In addition to this, the bank had, on February 5, 1909, a surplus of $35,000, and undivided profits to the amount of $30,220. Since it was organised in 1881 it has held on deposit more than ten million of dollars, for the most part money collected by the True Reformers' Association from its members, and has handled a sum amounting to over eighteen million dollars, derived largely from the same sources.

After emancipation the masses of the Freedmen did not turn immediately to the getting of property and land. The first property acquired by the former slaves was their churches. Of the twenty-six thousand churches and the forty million dollars' worth of property, which these churches represent, the larger part was contributed by men and women who had little or no property of their own. It was the women who toiled over the wash-tub, and the men who worked by the day, from whose earnings for the most part this property was accumulated.

In conversation, some time ago, with a Southern white man, who is a trustee of Tuskegee Institute, he told me that a woman who had worked for a number of years in his house as a servant, contributed, year after year, half of her earnings to the support of the church to which she belonged. This man had reason to know the facts, since he was frequently called on to assist in the support of the same church, and in this way had come to know something definite about its financial affairs.

After the church, the thing that has appealed most directly to the masses of the people, has been the need of making provision for sickness, death and burial. This is the origin of the Negro benevolent and fraternal societies, of which there is a large number at the present time in the United States. It was out of these benevolent societies that the first Negro banks sprang. The names of a number of these banks indicate their origin: for instance, the

True Reformers' Bank, of Richmond, Virginia; the St. Luke's Penny Savings Bank, of the same city; the Bank of the Grand United Order of the Galilean Fishermen, of Hampton, Virginia; the Knights of Honour Savings Bank, of Greenville, Mississippi; and the Bank of the Sons and Daughters of Peace, of Newport News, Virginia. All of these banks and a number of others first came into existence as the repositories for funds of fraternal organisations.

The histories of some of these banks illustrate the manner in which the Negro has succeeded in getting hold of corporate methods of doing business and applying them to his needs. Some time in the neighbourhood of 1894 a young man by the name of L. S. Reed came to Savannah, Georgia, from Atlanta, as the agent of an industrial insurance company, conducted by white men, with an office in New York City. He was more than usually successful in selling this insurance and, because of his ability in dealing in a business way with the coloured people, he was sometimes employed by the Germania Bank to make collections. At the same time, he was engaged in selling real estate, in which he had considerable success. About 1903, taking advantage of the experience he had had as an agent for industrial insurance, he organised a company of his own, called the Union Benefit Association. Like the other associations this one was intended

to afford protection to its members in case of accident, sickness, or death.   In one respect it differed
from the older type of benefit associations: it did not
confine its membership to a single locality, but
extended its work, through the medium of agents,
all over the state of Georgia and into adjoining
states.   At the same time the monthly dues were
not the same for every individual, as they had been
in earlier forms of mutual aid associations.   Thus
the monthly dues ranged from twenty cents to two
dollars, and the sick benefits from $1.25 to $8 per
week.

The result of this more elaborate form of insurance was the accumulation of a considerable amount
of capital, the total income for a single year
amounting to as much as $25,000.   Having this
amount of funds in hand, it seemed necessary to
re-invest them in some way.   For this purpose, in
1905, a bank known as the Union Savings and
Loan Company was organised.   This bank became
the depository for the funds of the benefit association.   The character of this bank is indicated by
the fact that it had, at the beginning, 450 stockholders, and a large part of its loans were made to
its own stockholders.

A few years later the same people, under the
leadership of Mr. Reed, organised the Savannah
Mutual & Fire Insurance Co. This Company was organised at the suggestion of Professor

D. C. Suggs, of the Georgia State Industrial College. Professor Suggs is a large property owner in Greensboro, North Carolina. He has, I understand, a street named after him in that city upon which he owns most of the houses. He had become familiar, while in Greensboro, with the fire and insurance business, and saw an opportunity for coloured people succeeding in that line in Savannah.

There is, or was in 1908, another small bank in Savannah which has an interesting history. It is known as the Afro-American Union Savings, Loan & Trust Co. This company was organised by Reverend William Gray and has received most of its support from the members of his own congregation. Reverend William Gray was a coachman who turned preacher. He started a little church in a shanty on Hartridge, between Broad and Price streets, with only eleven members. He has now one of the largest congregations in the city, and his church, a brick and frame structure, cost between fifteen and twenty thousand dollars.

After he became a preacher, Mr. Gray found out that he needed education. After thinking the matter over he stated the facts to his congregation, and told them that he had decided to attend the Georgia State Industrial College at Thunderbolt, just outside Savannah. His congregation were very proud of their minister, and very proud that he had determined to go to college, so proud, in fact,

that they not only gave their support to his reso-
ultion, but decided to pay his expenses while he was
there.   Mr. Gray was already a mature man when
he started to get his education, but he was a man of
sound understanding, of great industry, and with
considerable administrative ability.   He managed,
in some way, to keep up his church work and stick
to his studies until he finally graduated.   It is said
of him in Savannah that he has always dealt fairly
and squarely with his people, both in his church
and in business, and, as the man who explained the
circumstances of his success to me said: "He owes
this reputation to the fact that he made the welfare
of his people his burden."

The first and most successful Negro bank in
Savannah in 1908 was the Wage Earners' Loan &
Investment Co.   This company was started in
1900.   It has an authorised capital of $50,000, of
which, however, only $12,663.40 was paid in up to
1908.   This company was started by a number of
well-to-do business men and some others, successful
in other ways, in Savannah.   The president, L. E.
Williams, was formerly a railway mail-clerk.   The
vice-president, W. R. Fields, was an undertaker.
The secretary-treasurer, Walter Scott, who graduated from Tuskegee Institute in 1905, was a drygoods
merchant.   One of the directors of the company, John
H. Deveaux, was collector of customs for the port of
Savannah.   Another, Sol. C. Johnson, was editor

of the Savannah *Tribune.* Among the other directors were L. M. Pollard, a mail-clerk, R. B. Brooks,
a dealer in antique furniture, and J. H. Bugg,
a physician.

In the statement issued by this company October
5, 1908, it is said that the bank began business in
1900 with $102. Its combined assets, which included
$47,836.36 in deposits, a reserve fund, and undivided
profits in the sum of $8,014.22, amounted in 1908
to $70,553.58. It is also stated that the paid up
stock has earned 12 per cent. dividends for six con-
secutive years.

A large part of the business of this bank, like
that of most other of the Negro banks, has been to
assist coloured people in buying homes. In order
to encourage the accumulation of money to buy
property, the bank agreed to accept its own stock as
cash in payment for real estate. In this way, it was
constantly selling and buying its own stock, in order
to encourage the investment of money in homes.

While, perhaps, the majority of the banks in the
Southern states are doing business largely upon
capital which has been accumulated by the fraternal societies and insurance companies, a bank was
established in Chicago, Illinois, in 1908, which has
grown out of a real estate business conducted very
largely among coloured people. The *Commerical
Chronicle* of November, 1908, records the com-
pletion of the handsome new office building by Jesse

Binga, 3633 State Street, "where he will conduct his real estate and loan business, and in addition he will shortly open a bank at the same place." This is known as the Jesse Binga Bank, and purports to do a commercial and savings banking business. Mr. Binga is one of the nine or ten coloured real estate dealers in Chicago, and one of the four or five who have been doing, during the past ten years, an extensive business among the increasing Negro population in Chicago.

A careful study of the property owned by Negroes in Chicago, in the period previous to 1902, has shown that at that date Negroes owned, according to its assessed valuation, property to the amount of $1,960,105. More than five-sixths of this property was in the hands of 604 individuals, of whom three owned real estate valued at more than $50,000 each.* A more recent investigation made by Mr. R. R. Wright, Jr., indicates that, during the past decade, Negroes have been purchasing property in Chicago at a more rapid rate than at any previous time. He estimates the present value of the real estate held by coloured people in Chicago to be $4,000,000.

The Negro bank with the most interesting history of any of these yet established is that known as the Alabama Penny Savings & Loan Co., which first opened its doors on October 15, 1890, and

---

* "Study of Negro Property Owners in Chicago," Monroe N. Work, p. 19.

received on that day $555. This sum, added to the $3,000 already paid in from the sale of stock, constituted the capital upon which this important and helpful institution began business.

In February, 1909, this bank had a paid-in capital of $25,000, with a surplus of $6,000, and deposits to the amount of $193,000. It is the owner of a handsome three-story brick building, valued at $25,000, and of real estate to the amount of $52,000.

This bank is important not merely from the success it has made, but because of the motives that inspired its organisation. Its workings clearly illustrate the deep and far-reaching influence that these savings institutions exercise upon the social conditions and the moral life of the Negro people.

Birmingham is the centre of a large labouring population. Negroes are employed very largely in the extended mining region, of which Birmingham is the centre, and in the rolling-mills by which it is surrounded. These men earn good wages, but the temptations of the city are very great. It is therefore extremely important that something should be done there to encourage them in the practice of habits of thrift and industry. The first man to clearly perceive this was Reverend W. R. Pettiford, who came to Birmingham in 1883, as pastor of the Sixteenth Street Coloured Baptist Church. It was the perception of this need that suggested to him the importance of establishing at Birmingham a Negro bank. In 1900, at the first meeting of the National Negro Business League in Boston, Mr. Pettiford told the story of this bank:

"I was riding on the electric railway in a suburb of Birmingham," he said, "where a large number of coloured people were employed. There were a number of these people on the car who had just been paid their weekly wage. I had not gone far when I was shocked by seeing a woman among the crowd on the car drinking whiskey. I spoke to her but, though I was a minister and she knew me, I found I had no influence over her. It was at that time that the thought came to me that there should be some sort of business which would take care of the money of that class of people, and that such an institution would enable me, as a minister, to instruct them in ways in which they might better dispose of their earnings. It was in the early part of the year 1890 that the first notion of establishing a bank came into my mind."

Shortly after this occurrence, Mr. W. W. Browne, who was at that time president of the True Reformers' Bank at Richmond, Virginia, visited Birmingham. Mr. Browne was an old acquaintance of Mr. Pettiford, and they discussed the project of forming a bank in Birmingham, similar to the one in Richmond. It was Mr. Browne's idea that the coloured people in Birmingham should form a branch bank of the one in Richmond, but, after talking it over, it was decided to start in Birmingham an independent institution. At the time the movement to start this bank was begun, the True Reformers' Bank, although historically not the first bank in the United States, was the only one then in existence. It seemed doubtful whether a Negro bank could be started and maintained without the advantage of a large fund collected by a fraternal organisation, and without the confidence of a large number of people to back it, such as it would have if started by a fraternal organisation instead of by individuals. But Mr. Pettiford and his associates in Birmingham decided to try the experiment.

It took about three months' agitation to get enough sentiment back of the project to give any assurance of success. After the projectors had succeeded in getting a small capital of $3,000 together it was necessary for the president and cashier to study bookkeeping under a special teacher in order to prepare themselves for the novel business experiment which they proposed to undertake. After they had collected all their resources in cash and had taken an inventory of their combined business knowledge the sum did not amount to very much. Mr. Pettiford, who was a minister, had had some business experience as Financial Agent of Selma University, of Selma, Alabama. The man who was to act as cashier, a graduate of Talladega College, had been the first coloured school-teacher of Birmingham, and was at this time a successful grocer. The vice-president had been a bartender, but he was a man who had a reputation for honesty and had the confidence of the coloured population generally.

The necessities of the business, however, were soon to increase the business knowledge of the directors of the new bank, and that in directions in which very little was to be learned from books. They found that, in starting a Negro bank on a purely business basis, they had a task before them quite different from that which confronts the average white banker. They had to make known to the coloured people what the value and use of a bank was; they had to instruct them in saving, and show them, later on, how to make investments with the money they had saved. In order to accomplish this the officers of the bank began a campaign of education. It was here that the advantage of having a preacher attached to a Negro business organisation became apparent. In order to instruct the coloured people as to the importance of saving their money and depositing it in a bank, it was necessary to preach to them the necessity of securing homes of their own, and of providing for the education of their children. In the course of their campaign, Mr. Pettiford and his associates distributed a vast number of circulars intended to educate the masses of the people on the subject of banking. They made repeated addresses in all the coloured churches in the city and in the suburbs, and they were successful in arousing interest.

After the meeting of the Business League in Boston, in 1900, Mr. Pettiford made it a custom to repeat the story of his bank to members of the League every year. I am convinced that the story of that one bank has done more than any other one thing to call into existence the fifty and more banks started since 1900.

In spite of the fact that Mr. Pettiford told his story so frequently, it was always interesting because he invariably suceeded in bringing out in his account some new fact or point of view. For instance, at the meeting of the Business League in New York, in 1905, he emphasised the fact that one of the considerations which led him and his associates to establish this bank was that it might serve to prevent the squandering not merely of wages but the little accumulation of property that the people in the Birmingham district had succeeded in making.

"During my pastorate in Birmingham," he said, "there was a family who had two children. Both of the parents died and the property left to the children was squandered. The estate was estimated at $10,000. The administrator sold to the boy, the elder of the two children, who inherited the property, old horses and carriages for his interest in the estate.   To make a bond of $20,000, as was necessary in this case, was impossible for any coloured man at that time.   When I perceived our helplessness to aid orphan children in saving the property earned by their parents, I saw that if we had a strong financial institution which could make bonds and save the property for the benefit of the heirs to whom it was left, it would greatly help the race."

As an indication of the progress which the bank had made, Mr. Pettiford said:

The next day after the opening I took my seat as president, and made the first loan in the history of our bank.   This loan was for $10 for thirty days; the interest was fifty cents.   The last loan I made in the fifteenth year of the bank's business was just before visiting the National Business League in New York City in 1905, for $14,000; time ten years.   The borrower was the Knights of Pythias of Alabama, and the money was for the erection of their magnificent three-story brick building.

One of the things which has helped to make the Alabama Penny Savings and Loan Co. and the other Negro banks succeed, under conditions and difficulties which banks of white people would not survive, is the advantage that Negro bankers have in dealing direct with Negro people.

"As a rule," said Mr. Pettiford, in one of his addresses before the Business League, "the officers of banks conducted by persons of the other race, are not well acquainted with coloured persons who apply for a loan, and, therefore, are unable, in most cases, to accommodate them. The coloured banker, however, knows his own people, and is thus enabled to extend them credit with discrimination."

"By careful and safe methods of extending credit," continued Pettiford, "our bank has assisted many persons in the establishment of small business concerns, and such persons after getting on their feet, have proved to be valuable customers. The management of our bank has all along recognised the fact that, in order to strengthen the bank, the constituency must be strengthened. For this reason, as well as to do good generally, it has been its constant aim to lose no opportunity to assist in the general uplift of the people with whom the bank has had to deal. In this effort not only has the Negro benefited, but the general welfare of the community has been subserved."

I have repeated here, in some detail, the story of the founding and working of this bank, because it illustrates better than any incident I have been able to lay my hands on, how closely the moral interests of the people are interwoven with their material and economic welfare. The savings bank teaches to save, to plan, to look ahead, to build for the future. It is, in fact, one of the most effective means of developing those latent forces in the masses of the people from which the fabric of civilisation is woven. As I have said at another time in another place: "There is no wealth in the mines or in the seas equal to that which is created by the growth and establishment in a people of habits of thrift and intelligent forethought." The importance of Mr. Pettiford's work in connection with this bank is that he, and those associated with him, have been far-seeing enough to perceive this fact and act upon it.

It happened a few years ago that an afternoon paper in Birmingham published a report to the effect that there was a run on the Alabama Penny Savings Bank, and that it was in a shaky condition. This report grew out of the fact that it was Christmas week and an unusually large number of coloured people were crowding into the bank to draw money to be used during the holidays. This report spread, and caused the officials of the bank, as well as its friends, much uneasiness, and it was, for a time, very uncertain as to what effect it was likely to have. In the meantime, a white business man, a large coal operator in the Birmingham district, heard of the report, and at once telephoned to the Negro bank that if, on account of the report which had been spread, they needed any money with which to pay depositors the next day, he would be glad to let them have all the cash that was needed. It turned out, however, that the good offices of the white friend were not needed, as there was no run on the bank.

In recent years I have had the privilege of visiting nearly every one of the communities where

Negro banks are located, and I can state without exaggeration that I have not found a single one of them that did not have the good-will and support of the white business men of the communities in which they are located. In fact, in a number of cases, the white bankers have stated that the starting of a Negro bank has increased the number of Negro depositors in the white banks, because of the general moral uplift which the influence of the coloured bank had brought about.

CHAPTER X

IN THE year 1821, one of the best known among the coloured people of Richmond, Virginia, was a Baptist preacher by the name of Lott Cary. This man had an extraordinary history. He was born a slave, about the year 1780, on a plantation thirty miles below the city of Richmond. In 1804, when he was twenty-four years of age, he was taken to the city of Richmond and employed as a common labourer in the Shockoe Tobacco Warehouse.

At this time he could neither read nor write, but one Sunday, listening to the minister in the white church which he attended read the words of Christ to Nicodemus, he was seized with the desire to learn to read. In some way or other he succeeded in carrying out the purpose he then formed. He read the Bible first but, as his mind was opened to new thoughts and ideas, he began reading every book he could lay his hands upon. His reading extended, finally, to the subject of political economy, for it is related that he was discovered one day reading Adam Smith's "Wealth of Nations." In the mean-

time, he made himself so valuable in the tobacco warehouse in which he was employed that he was given
considerable sums at different times and for different
purposes as a reward for his services. By the year
1813 he had acquired money sufficient to buy his
own liberty and that of his two children. The sum
paid was $850.

Shortly after this time the subject of colonisation
had become a subject of earnest discussion among
the coloured people, particularly of Maryland and
Virginia. Lott Cary and a brother preacher by the
name of Collin Teage, who was a saddler and
harness-maker by trade, conceived the idea of going
to Liberia to assist in founding the proposed colony
there. Although Cary was at that time in the possession of a snug little farm in the vicinity of Richmond and was earning a handsome salary of $800 a
year, he decided to give them up and go to Africa as
a missionary.

He sailed in company with Teage in January, 1821.
When the first settlement was made, the following
year, at Cape Mesurado, Lott Cary became one of
the most active agents in establishing what was,
in fact, though not in name, the first colony of the
United States. During all the difficulties and dis-
couragements of the first years of that colony he was,
next to Jehudi Ashmun, the leading spirit of the
colony. In 1826, Cary was elected to the position of
vice-agent and, after the departure of Ashmun,

continued until the time of his death the virtual head of the colony.

Cary, when asked by a brother-minister how he could think of quitting a position of so much comfort and usefulness as he at that time occupied among the coloured people of Richmond, replied: "I am an African; and in this country, however meritorious my conduct, and respectable my character, I cannot receive the credit due to either. I wish to go to a country where I shall be estimated by my merit — not by my complexion; and I feel bound to labour for my suffering race."

An interesting thing about these efforts at colonisation of Africa by American Negroes is that when the colonists reached Africa they found that they were Africans only on the outside. They were Africans in colour but not, so far as they could see, in any other respect. Two hundred and fifty years of slavery in America had converted them into Americans, at least in all their feelings and in all their traditions, just as completely as any other race which has settled on this continent. Thus Liberia has become in its laws, in its customs, and in its aspirations an American colony controlled by American Negroes.

After the settlement of Liberia and while the desire for colonisation was still strong among the free coloured people, Benjamin Lundy, the Quaker abolitionist, established a colony for Freedmen on the

Samana Peninsula on the island of Haiti in the district of what is now Santo Domingo. Among the Freedmen sent out had been slaves of David Patterson, of Grange County, North Carolina. Mr. Patterson had been converted to emancipation by Lundy's preaching and desired to emancipate his slaves, but was not able to do so until he had provided for their removal from the state.

In March, 1825, Lundy opened at Baltimore an Haitian office of emigration. He was assisted in this work by Richard Allen, the founder of the African Methodist Episcopal Church. Among the shipments from Lundy's office at that time was a colony of eighty-eight slaves, valued at $30,000, who had been emancipated by their owner, David Minge, of Charles City, Virginia. These slaves were sent to Haiti, under an arrangement with the Philanthropic Society of Haiti, which agreed to advance money for the expense of their passage with the understanding, however, that each Freedman was to repay the Society by working on its plantation for a certain length of time after his arrival. After the expiration of his apprenticeship, every Negro man, who had a family, was to receive fifteen acres of land.

Lundy continued to send colonists to Haiti under the arrangements with the Philanthropic Society for some years. In 1825, within a few weeks after his return from Haiti, he sent out a hundred and sixteen emancipated slaves and in 1829 he found it necessary to visit Haiti a second time. He took with him a small colony of Freedmen, and upon his return, announced that he had made arrangements whereby Negroes who wished to go to Haiti could obtain leases of plantations with buildings on them for seven years, the first two years free of charge, and the remaining five at a moderate rent.

In his newspaper, *The Genius of Universal Emancipation*, for November 13, 1829, there appeared an advertisement addressed "to humane and conscientious slave-holders," asking for from twenty to sixty slaves "to remove to and settle in the Republic of Haiti, where they will be forthwith invested with the rights of free men and receive constant employment and liberal wages in a healthy and pleasant section of the country." The advertisement is signed, LUNDY & GARRISON. The outbreak at Northampton shortly after this seems to have put an end to this emigration, but remnants of these colonies speaking an English dialect may be still found living on the Samana Peninsula.

Benjamin Lundy did not at this time cease his efforts to find a place of refuge for the Freedmen. He travelled through Mexico and he visited Canada, in the interest of this purpose. It was in Canada that the next settlements of Negro colonies of any size took place. Slavery had been introduced there under the French. At the request of the inhabitants a royal mandate was issued as early as 1689, permitting the holding of Indians as slaves. When Canada came under the possession of England in 1760 this form of slavery was continued and Negroes were introduced from the West Indies. But in February, 1800, the slave Robin, belonging to James Frazier, was discharged from servitude upon a writ of habeas corpus. In this case the court followed the ruling of Lord Mansfield, in the famous Somerset case, which put an end to slavery in England. The result of the case of Robin was to put an end to legalised slavery in Canada in the same way that it had been done away with in England and in Massachusetts.

Although slavery was not formally abolished by law until the act of 1833, and slaves were held to some extent in Lower Canada until that time, fugitive slaves had already begun to turn their steps in the direction of Canada in the early part of the century. A good many of these slaves found refuge among the Indians. The famous Mohawk Chief, Captain Brandt, was a holder of Negro slaves. He had large estates on Burlington Bay and Grand River. Many runaway Negroes took refuge there, were treated hospitably, and began working and living with the Indians, often adopting their customs and mode of life.

After the War of 1812, the soldiers who had served in that war brought back the news that there was a country to the north of the United States where coloured men and women were free and there was no danger of their being captured and taken back into slavery. From that time on the North Star came to have a special and peculiar interest for the discontented slaves, and many of them turned their feet northward with no other guide than its light to direct them.

In 1850, it is said that there were thirty thousand fugitives from slavery in Canada. After the passage of the Fugitive Slave Law, this number was greatly increased. In 1860, the number of coloured people in Canada was variously estimated at from 60,000 to 75,000, of which it is said 15,000 were free-born.

As a result of this influx of refugees, there grew up on the outskirts of the cities numerous communities of coloured people. In 1855, Benjamin Drew, who had visited these communities in the interest of the anti-slavery societies, published an account of the condition of the fugitives of fourteen different settlements. These were located at St. Catherine's, Toronto, Hamilton, Galt, London, Queens-Bush, Chatham, Buxton, Dawn, Windsor, Sandwich, Amherstburg, Colchester, and Gosfield, all in the province of Ontario. The most important and interesting of these colonies were the Dawn Settlement, at Dresden, the Elgin Settlement at Buxton, and the Refugees' Home near Windsor.

In 1849, the Reverend William King, a Presbyterian clergyman from Louisiana, emancipated his slaves and settled them on the tract which afterward became known as the "Elgin Settlement." His company of fifteen Freedmen formed the nucleus of the community which was called Buxton, in honour of the noted philanthropist, Thomas Fowell Buxton. This community grew rapidly and in 1850 it was incorporated as the Elgin Association. Under the direction of Mr. King, the plan was carried out which provided for the parcelling of the land into farms of fifty acres each, which were to be sold to the colonists at the government price of $2.50 per acre. A court of arbitration was established for the adjudication of disputes, and a day and Sunday school, supported by a missionary society of the Presbyterian Church of Canada, were started, in order to give the colonists the instruction they needed. Twelve years later, in 1862, when Dr. Samuel G. Howe visited this community, he found a settlement of about one thousand men, women, and children, who owned two thousand acres of land, one-third of which had been paid for, including the principal and interest.

"Buxton," said Dr. Howe, in his report, "is certainly a very interesting place. Sixteen years ago, it was a wilderness. Now good highways are laid out in all directions through the forest; and by their side, standing back thirty-three feet from the road, are about two hundred cottages, all built after the same pattern, all looking neat and comfortable. Around each one is a cleared space, of several acres, which is well cultivated. The fences are in good order, the barns seem well filled, and cattle and horses and pigs and poultry abound. There are signs of industry and thrift and comfort everywhere; signs of intemperance, idleness, of want, nowhere. There is no tavern and no groggery; but there is a chapel and a schoolhouse."

Reverend Mr. King said: "I consider this settlement has done as well as a white settlement would have done under the same circumstances."

The colony known as Refugees' Home, which was located at Windsor, Ontario, directly opposite Detroit, was started by Henry Bibb, himself a fugitive slave. Soon after the passage of the Fugitive Slave Law of 1850 he suggested the formation of "a society which should aim to purchase 30,000 acres of Government land . . . for the homeless refugees from American slavery to settle upon."

In the first year of the association's existence forty lots of twenty-five acres each were disposed of, and arrangements were made for a school and a church. Mrs. Laura S. Haviland, who opened a day school and a Sunday school there in the fall of 1852, says: "They had erected a frame house for school and meeting purposes. The settlers had built for themselves small log houses, and cleared from one to five acres each on their heavily timbered land, and raised corn and potatoes and other garden vegetables. A few put in several hundred acres of wheat and were doing well for the first year."

The oldest of these communities in Canada, and in many respects the most interesting, was the Dawn Settlement at Dresden. It was at this settlement that Josiah Henson, the original "Uncle Tom" in Harriet Beecher Stowe's story, lived and worked for many years. In the year 1842 a convention of coloured people was called to decide upon the expenditure of some $1,500 which had been collected in England by James C. Fuller, a Quaker. Reverend Hiram Wilson, a missionary, and Josiah Henson were on the committee to decide in what way this money should be expended. It was determined, upon the suggestion of Mr. Henson, to start a "manual labour school, where the children could be taught those elements of knowledge which are usually the occupations of a grammar-school; and where the boy could be taught, in addition, the practice of some mechanic art, and the girl could be instructed in those domestic arts which are the proper occupation and ornament of her sex."*

In 1852 there were, according to the first annual report of the Anti-slavery Society of Canada, sixty pupils attending this school, and settlers on the land of the institute had increased to five hundred.

* "Father Henson's Story of His Own Life," p. 169. Quoted in Siebert's "Underground Railroad," p. 206.

In the neighbourhood of the school there was a coloured population of between three and four thousand.

Josiah Henson, who was so long connected with this colony, was born a slave at Fort Tobacco, Maryland, and escaped to Canada in 1828. He became a Methodist minister and an anti-slavery lecturer of considerable influence. He made three trips to England and, on his final visit to that country, in 1876, he was entertained by Queen Victoria.

After the Civil War the interests which had brought these colonies into existence had disappeared. Many of the coloured people, particularly those who had gone out to Canada since 1850, moved back to the United States. The communities gradually dwindled away or were absorbed into neighbouring cities, on whose outskirts they had grown up. In the winter of 1895 and 1896, when I made a visit to several cities in Canada, I had an opportunity to get information from some of these fugitives. In Toronto, there was living at the time I visited the city, Dr. A. R. Abbott, who had graduated from the Toronto Medical University before or shortly after the breaking out of the Civil War in the United States. He enlisted in one of the coloured regiments and was among the first coloured men to be admitted to the Army Medical Service. After the war he returned to Toronto, where he practised his profession for many years.

It is not often one meets a coloured man acting in the capacity of mayor of a city of 200,000 inhabitants, but I met on this visit to Toronto a Negro who had occupied that position during the previous summer, while the regular mayor was absent in Europe. This man was the Honourable William P. Hubbard, president of the Toronto Board of Control, a body which, in the government of Toronto, occupies the position of the mayor's cabinet. Mr. Hubbard was born in Toronto in 1848. His parents, who were of African, Anglo-Saxon and Indian origin, came to Canada from Richmond, Virginia, in 1844. They had been, like the parents of Dr. Abbott, "free people of colour." His father, having been employed for several years as a carver in a Richmond hotel, had accumulated something like $800 before he left the South. The family settled on a little piece of land on the outskirts of the city, where his mother kept for many years a market garden, while his father worked in the city. After getting a pretty good education in the Toronto schools, young Hubbard went to work as an apprentice in a bakery shop, where he later served eight years as foreman. After that he went into the livery business with his brother, Alexander. In this business he prospered, and putting his savings into real estate, soon accumulated a small fortune. I was told at the time of my visit that Mr. Hubbard paid taxes on $36,000 worth of property. In 1894, he was elected to the position of alderman from the Tenth Ward. He held that position until he was elected, in 1899, to the position he held at the time of my visit. At this time Mr. J. C. Hamilton, who has made a study of the Negro in Canada, said: "Hubbard has about the best record of any alderman we have. I should not wonder if he would be mayor of Toronto some day."

I learned also that Mr. Hubbard had a reputation outside of Toronto and throughout the Province of Ontario, for he has been elected, during previous years, president of the Ontario Municipal Association.

I referred, in an earlier chapter, to the town and colony of Mound Bayou, which is situated in the centre of the Yazoo Mississippi Delta, about midway between Vicksburg and Memphis. This colony which, as I have said, was founded by Isaiah T. Montgomery, who had been a slave of Joseph Davis, the brother of the president of the Confederacy, was started about 1890. I frequently have heard Mr. Montgomery tell the story of the way in which he succeeded in arousing the interest of the first settlers in this project. When he first went there the country was a perfect wilderness; it was not believed that white men could live in that region, and that was one reason that it was decided to try the experiment of settling a colony of coloured people there. Mr. Montgomery finally succeeded in inducing a party of coloured men to come down and look over the country. A South-bound train dropped them off at a saw-mill in the midst of the woods one morning, and they walked several miles up the railroad track to the site that Mr. Montgomery had selected for the town.

"We had been pretty silent on the way up the track," said Mr. Montgomery, "for we were in the midst of a perfect wilderness. After we reached the point where I desired to locate, I turned and pointed in the direction of the woods and said to the men: 'You see what this country is, but you should remember this whole state was once like this. Your fathers cleared it, cultivated it, and made it what it now is. They did this for the white man. Now, the question is, can we do the same thing for ourselves?'

"Well," continued Mr. Montgomery, "some of them saw the point, and with these men we started in and began cutting down the timber, and making it into railway ties. Then we built the saw-mill and, by that time, the town was fairly started."

I visited the town of Mound Bayou in the fall of 1908. I found a little village, with between five hundred and a thousand inhabitants, which was the centre of a community of perhaps four or five thousand people, among whom there was not a single white man. There were twenty or thirty little country stores, three cotton gins, a bank, which at the time had resources amounting to $100,000, and I

was told had paid 10 per cent. dividend on its stock
of $25,000.   The town looked raw, but it looked like
the real thing.   I learned that it had been growing
slowly but steadily.   During the whole period of its
existence an earnest effort was being made to build
up the schools, and to adapt the teaching in them to
the actual needs of the people.

During my visit I made an address to the people of
that colony.   As there was no hall sufficiently large
enough to accommodate the crowds that had
assembled, I spoke from a platform erected upon the
foundation of a new cotton-seed oil mill which was
being erected at the cost of $40,000, a sum collected
among the coloured people in different parts of the
State of Mississippi.   The interesting thing to me
was that I found there a sober, earnest, orderly
community of coloured people, who had the respect
of all their neighbours, including the sheriff of the
county, and were going forward in the solution of
their problem, along the lines of orderly industrial
progress.

Mound Bayou is, so far as I know, the oldest
exclusively Negro community established since the
War.   There is, however, a flourishing little town
in Oklahoma called Boley, which was started in
1903.   There is a story told in regard to Boley,
which, even if it is not true in all its details, illustrates
the temper of the coloured people and their relations
to the white people in that region.   Early in the

spring of 1903, so the story goes, a number of gentlemen were discussing, at the neighbouring city of
Weleetka, the inevitable race question. The point
at issue was the capability of the Negro for self-
government. One of the gentlemen, who happened to be connected with the Fort Smith Railway,
maintained that the Negro had never been given a
fair chance; that if Negroes had been given a white
man's chance they would have proved themselves
as capable of self-government as any other people of
the same degree of culture and education. The other
gentlemen naturally asserted the contrary, and the
result of this argument was, to state it briefly, Boley.

Just at this time a number of town sites were being
laid out along the railway which connects Guthrie,
Oklahoma, with Fort Smith, Arkansas. In order
to put the capability of the Negro for self-government
to test, there was established in August, 1903, seventy-
two miles east of Guthrie, the site of a Negro town.
It was called Boley after the man who built that section of the railway, and it was widely advertised as a
town which was to be exclusively under the control
of Negroes.

One thing that, perhaps, made this town attractive
to coloured people was the fact that there are a
number of communities in Oklahoma which rigidly
exclude Negroes from settlement. On the other
hand, there has grown up in other parts of Oklahoma, communities, like the little town of Taft,

which, although not settled exclusively by Negroes, are sometimes referred to as "Negro towns," because of the large proportion of the Negroes in the population.

A large proportion of the settlers of Boley were farmers from Texas, Arkansas and Mississippi. The proprietor of the largest cotton-gin was, in 1907, C. W. Perry, who came from Marshall, Texas. Perry had worked in the railway machine shops for a number of years and had gained enough of the trade of a machinist to be able to set up his own cotton-gin and the machinery connected with it. E. L. Lugrande, one of the principal stockholders in the second bank in Boley, came to this new country, like many others, to get land. He had owned 418 acres of land in Denton County, which he had purchased some years before at a price of four and five dollars an acre. In recent years land has gone up in price and Mr. Lugrande was able to sell his property for something like fifty dollars an acre. He came to Boley and purchased a large tract of land just outside the town. Now a large part of this acreage is in the centre of the town. Mr. Lugrande is representative of the better class of Negro farmers who, for several years past, have been steadily moving into the new lands in the West.

I might add, in conclusion, that from all I have been able to learn Boley, which, like Mound Bayou, is entirely controlled by Negroes, is one of the most peaceful towns in that part of Oklahoma. When I was at Topeka, Kansas, in 1907, I was told that not a single citizen of Boley had been arrested for two years.

I have spoken of the settlements of Negroes in Liberia, in Canada, and in the different parts of the United States in the same connection, because they seem to me to represent the same wholesome desire of members of my race to do something for which they will be respected, not merely as individuals but as a race; to achieve something in their own way and in their own right, which would be a worthy contribution to American civilisation.

The story told by one of the most successful citizens of Boley, for example, illustrates the motives which have inspired the building of this bustling and progressive little Negro city. This man had been a railway brakeman, was well respected by his employers, owned a little home of his own, and had a bank account. When it was learned that he was selling his property in Texas in order to emigrate to Oklahoma a number of the prominent white citizens of the community called upon him and asked him why he was going to leave. "We know you," they said, "and you know us. We are behind you and will protect you."

"Well," he replied, "I have always had an ambition to do something for myself. I do not always want to be led; I want to do a little leading."

Whatever one may be disposed to think of this segregation of the white and black races which one sees going on, to a greater or lesser extent, in every section of the country, it is certain that there is a temporary advantage to the Negro race in the building up of these "race towns." They enable the masses of the people to find a freer expression to their native energies and ambitions than they are able to find elsewhere, and, at the same time, give them an opportunity to gain that experience in coöperation, self-direction, and self-control, which it is hard for them to get in the same degree elsewhere.

In the year 1905 I had occasion to visit Winston-Salem, in North Carolina, to speak in a public meeting in the interest of the Slater industrial and State Normal School, at that place. This school had been established some years before by Mr. S. G. Atkins, who is now Secretary of Education in the A. M. E. Zion Church. He had been a teacher in the public schools in Winston. In 1892 he moved to some high ground outside the city and built himself a home. A few years later he started a little Industrial School at this place. As time went on the school increased in size and importance and a little community grew up around it.

After the school had been established, Mr. R. J. Reynolds, of the Reynolds Tobacco Company, gave Mr. Atkins $4,500 to assist him in building out there a hospital for coloured people. Mr.

Reynolds was a large employer of coloured labour in the tobacco factory, and he assisted in establishing this hospital in order to made some adequate provision for his own employees in case of sickness. The thing that impressed me at the time about this little community was the fine location chosen for it and the number of thrifty little cottages which I saw growing up, nearly all of which, I learned, had been paid for by the people who lived in them.

This was the first time, I think, that my attention had been specially drawn to a number of quiet, clean, thrifty little Negro communities that are growing up everywhere in the South at the present day, frequently in the neighbourhood of some school. Particularly has this been true in the last ten years, since Negro banks and building and loan associations have sprung up to encourage the people in all parts of the South, as well as in some of the Northern cities, to purchase their own homes. Since my visit to Winston-Salem in 1905 the coloured people in that city have, I understand, prospered greatly. This is due, to some extent, to the fact that since the organisation of the Tobacco Trust they have had steady employment in the tobacco factories, but it is also due in a large part to the assistance and encouragement the coloured people have received from the white people of that city, particularly from the descendants of the Moravians of Salem.

In May, 1907, the Forsythe Savings and Trust Co.

was organised at Winston-Salem.   This bank, which
was organised largely for the purpose of assisting
coloured people in securing homes, reported in
December, 1908, that it had transacted a volume of
business from the time it was organised which
amounted to $302,738.86.   In close connection with
this bank there was organised the Twin City Reality
Company, of which Mr. S. G. Atkins was president,
and Andrew Jackson Brown vice-president.

Mr. Brown is an interesting character.   He came
from Lynchburg to Winston to work in the tobacco
factory.   After he was forty years old, his home having been broken up by the death of his wife, he
decided to go to school.   He made his home in the
little community, Columbia Heights, which had
sprung up around Mr. Atkins's school.   He had been
the chief agent of the True Reformers' Association
in the region before this time, and he supported himself mainly in this way while he was in school.   He
was a man of simple manners and sturdy honesty,
and has become, I have been told, a very positive
constructive force in his community.

What I have described as taking place in Winston-
Salem has been going on, in much the same way, in
every other part of the country where any considerable
portion of the population belongs to the Negro race.
In some places, like Baltimore, Philadelphia, and
New York, whole avenues for considerable distances
have been taken up by coloured people who have

moved out of the slums, in which the masses of the Negro people are usually to be found during the first years of their life in the cities. In these new districts they have been building comfortable and frequently handsome houses.

Perhaps I cannot better describe the change that has taken place, in this and other parts of the South, than in the words of a Southern white man who has watched the changes I have referred to, and has been able to appreciate their significance. Writing in the *Century* Magazine for June, 1906, Harry Stillwell Edwards, speaking of this matter, says:

Thirty years ago, when I was a boy in Georgia's central city, one part of the suburbs given over to Negroes contained an aggregation of unfurnished, ill-kept, rented cabins, the occupants untidy and, for the most part, shiftless. Such a thing as virtue among the female members was in but few instances conceded. Girls from this section roamed the streets at night, and vice was met with on every corner. Recently, in company with a friend, who was interested in a family residing in the same community, I visited it. I found many families occupying their own homes, flowers growing in the yards and on the porches, curtains at the windows, and an air of homelike serenity overflowing the entire district. In the house we entered, the floors were carpeted, the white walls were hung with pictures, the mantels and the tables held bric-à-brac. In one room was a parlour organ, in another a sewing-machine, and in another a piano, where a girl sat at practice.

In conversation with the people of the house and neighbourhood we heard good ideas expressed in excellent language and discovered that every one with whom we came in contact was possessed of sufficient education to read and write, while many were much further advanced.

Just one generation lies between the two conditions set forth, and the change may be said to indicate the urban Negro's mental and material progress throughout the whole South. Of those of us who see only gloom ahead for the Negro, the question may fairly be asked: Where else in the world is there a people developing so rapidly?

In the course of my journeys about the country I have had an opportunity to go into many Negro homes in all parts of the United States, where I have found, not merely the comforts, but some of the elegancies of life. Books, pictures, fine table-linen, furniture, carpets, and not infrequently mementoes of travel in many parts of this country and of Europe. What interests me more than anything else, however, is to see the number of them who are collecting books, histories, pictures, and all kinds of material concerning their own race or of work by members of their own race, showing evidences of its progress.

Aside from Chicago, Philadelphia is the only city, so far as I know, in which a systematic and careful study has been made of the condition of the Negro population. In 1897, Professor W. E. B. Du Bois estimated that Negroes owned $5,000,000 in that city. A more recent investigation made by Richard R. Wright, Jr., indicates that the number of home owners has increased 71 per cent. since 1900. In 1907 he stated that within twenty months seven real estate companies had been organised among Negroes in Philadelphia. One of these had succeeded in providing homes for twenty-five Negroes within a year.

Probably the most important influence in assisting coloured people to obtain homes in Philadelphia has been the Berean Building and Loan Association, established in connection with the Berean Presbyterian Church, which is one of the three coloured Presbyterian churches in Philadelphia. According to a report published in 1906, this association has purchased one hundred and forty-five homes for its members, valued at $304,500 and has paid back matured stock to the value of more than $80,000. The Berean is the largest and the oldest of seven building and loan associations of Philadelphia.

So far as I know there is no city in the United States where the coloured people own so many comfortable and attractive homes in proportion to the population, as in the city of Baltimore. In what is known as the Druid Hill district of the city, there are, perhaps, fifteen thousand coloured people. For fifteen blocks along Druid Hill Avenue nearly every house is occupied or owned by coloured people. In the latter part of the ninties Dr. R. M. Hall, who is one of the oldest coloured physicians and one of the wealthiest coloured men in Baltimore, moved into 1019 Druid Hill Avenue. He was almost the first coloured man to make his home upon that street. Since that time the white people who lived there have moved out into the suburbs and the coloured people have moved in to take their places. I have been told that fully 50 per cent. of the coloured people on Druid Hill Avenue own their homes, though, so far as I know, no systematic investigation has been made of the facts. This part of the city has had for a number of years its own coloured representative, Harry S. Cummings, in the city council. This district which Mr. Cummings represented in the city council in 1908 was that, I have been told, in which, forty-five years before, his parents had been held as slaves.

CHAPTER XI

NEGRO POETRY, MUSIC, AND ART

THERE is an African folk-tale which tells of a mighty hunter who one day went into the forest in search of big game. He was unsuccessful in his quest, and sat down to rest. Meanwhile he heard some strange and pleasing noises, coming from a dense thicket. As he sat spellbound, a party of forest spirits came dancing into view, and the hunter discovered it was they who were making the sounds he had heard. The spirits disappeared, and the hunter returned to his home, when, after considerable effort, he found that he was able to imitate the sounds which he had heard. In this way, it is said, the black man gained the gift of song.

The Bantus of South Africa say that African music at the present time is not what it used to be in the old days. There was a time, they say, before the coming of the white man, when musicians had power to charm the beasts from the forest and the birds from the trees. Be this as it may, we find at the present day that singing is a universal practice among the Africans in every part of the Dark

Continent. The porters, carrying their loads along the narrow forest paths, sing of the loved ones in their far-away homes. In the evening the people of the villages gather around the fire and sing for hours. These songs refer to war, to hunting, and to the spirits that dwell in the deep woods. In them all the wild and primitive life of the people is reflected and interpreted.

When the Negro slaves were carried from Africa to America they brought with them this gift of song. Nothing else which the native African possessed, not even his sunny disposition, his ready sympathy or his ability to adapt himself to new and strange conditions, has been more useful to him in his life in America than this. When all other avenues of expression were closed to him, and when, sometimes, his burden seemed too great for him to bear, the African found a comfort and a solace in these simple and beautiful songs, which are the spontaneous utterance of his heart.

Nothing tells more truly what the Negro's life in slavery was, than the songs in which he succeeded, sometimes, in expressing his deepest thoughts and feelings. What, for example, could express more eloquently the feelings of despair which sometimes overtook the slave than these simple and expressive words:

O Lord, O my Lord! O my good Lord!
Keep me from sinking down.

The songs which the Negro sang in slavery, however, were by no means always sad. There were many joyous occasions upon which the natural happy and cheerful nature of the Negro found expression in songs of a light and cheerful character. There is a difference, however, between the music of Africa and that of her transplanted children. There is a new note in the music which had its origin on the Southern plantations, and in this new note the sorrow and the suffering which came from serving in a strange land finds expression.

The new songs are those in which the slave speaks, not merely thé sorrow that he feels, but also the new hope which the Christian religion has lighted in his bosom. The African slave accepted the teachings of the Christian religion more eagerly than he did anything else his master had to teach him. He seemed to feel instinctively that there was something in the teachings of the Bible which he needed. He accepted the story that the Bible told him literally, and, in the songs he composed under its influence, he has given some wonderfully graphic and vivid pictures of the persons and places of which the Bible speaks, as he understood them. Grotesque as some of these pictures may seem, they are merely the vivid and literal interpretation of what he heard, and all of them are conceived in the spirit of the deepest reverence.

Neither the words nor the melodies of these songs

originated after the manner in which music is ordinarily composed nowadays. In fact, these songs are not the music of any one individual. They were composed under the excitement of a religious meeting. Some black bard, under the inspiration of the moment, flung out a musical theme which was taken up by the whole company, and words and music were thus spontaneously composed upon the spot. These songs, still sung with the old-time fervour in the little country churches throughout the South, were created in the same way in which the students of literature and language tell us that the early Scotch and English ballads were composed, by crowds of men and women singing together.

Thomas Wentworth Higginson was, I believe, one of the first, if not the first man to make a study of this music of the slaves. While he was in charge of a black regiment at Port Royal, South Carolina, he had abundant opportunity to hear these songs, as they were sung by the Negroes, who had been freshly recruited from the plantations in that region. In his interesting book, "Army Life in a Black Regiment," he has given a very vivid and a very accurate description of this music. Among other things he says:

I had been a faithful student of the Scottish ballads, and had always envied Sir Walter Scott the delight of tracing them out among their own heather, and of writing them down piecemeal from the lips of ancient crones. It was a strange enjoyment, therefore, to be suddenly brought into the midst of a kindred world of

unwritten songs, as simple and indigenous as the Border Min-
strelsy, more uniformly plaintive, almost always more quaint,
and often as essentially poetic. . . . Almost all their songs
were thoroughly religious in their tones, however quaint their
expression, and were in a minor key, both as to words and music.
The attitude is always the same, and as a commentary on the life
of the race, is infinitely pathetic. Nothing but patience for this
life — nothing but triumph in the next.

One of the songs which Mr. Higginson quotes,
and which he regards as one of the most expressive
songs that he heard while he was in the South, is
the following:

> I know moon rise, I know star rise,
>   Lay dis body down,
> I'll walk in de graveyard,
>   To lay dis body down.
>
> I'll lie in de grave and stretch out my arms,
>   Lay dis body down,
> I'll go to de Judgment in de evenin' of de day,
>   When I lay dis body down.
> And my soul and your soul will meet in de day,
>   When I lay dis body down.

"Never, it seems to me," says Mr. Higginson,
"since man first lived and suffered, was his infinite
longing for peace uttered more plaintively than in
that line, 'I'll lie in de grave and stretch out my
arms.'"

Another and more familiar one of the plantation
hymns which Mr. Higginson quotes is the following:

> O wrestlin' Jacob! Jacob!
> Day's a-breakin';
>   I will not let you go!

O wrestlin Jacob! Jacob!
Day's a-breakin'
 He will not let me go!
O! I hold my brudder
Wid a tremblin' han'!
 I would not let him go!
I hold my sister
Wid a tremblin' han'!
 I would not let her go!

There is something in this slave music that touches the common heart of man. Everywhere that it has been heard this music has awakened a responsive chord in the minds and hearts of those who heard it. Antonin Dvorak, the eminent Bohemian composer, who lived for several years in this country, in his admirable symphony, "Out of the New World," used several themes taken from these Negro folk songs. S. Coleridge Taylor, the well-known coloured English composer, has used this music for many of his best known piano compositions. Edward Everett Hale once said it was the only American music.

Not only is the music of these songs strangely touching and beautiful, but the songs themselves contain many striking and significant expressions, as Mr. Higginson has pointed out, which indicate a native talent in the masses of the people for poetic expression. For example, one of these songs in referring to the Judgment Day, describes it as the time "when the stars begin to fall." Another **of**

these songs suggests the terrors of the last Judgment, in the refrain, "O Rocks, fall on me."

There was a time, directly after the War, when
the coloured people, particularly those who had
a little education, tried to get away from and forget these old slave songs.   If they sang them still,
it was about the home and not in public.   It was
not until after years, when other people began to
learn and take an interest in these songs, that these
people began to understand the inspiration and the
quality that was in them.   It is an indication of
the change that has gone on among the Negro people
in recent years that more and more they are beginning to take pride in these folk-songs of the race,
and are seeking to preserve them and the mem-
ories that they evoke.

As an illustration of what I have said, I cannot
do better than quote the lines of James W. Johnson,
a Negro poet and writer of popular songs, which
suggest, better than anything I have heard or read,
what seems to me the true significance of this music.
In the *Century* Magazine for November, 1908, the following poem was published, addressed to the unknown
singers who first sang these heart songs of my race:

O BLACK AND UNKNOWN BARDS!

O black and unknown bards of long ago,
   How came your lips to touch the sacred fire?
How, in your darkness, did you come to know
   The power and beauty of the minstrel's lyre?

Who first from midst his bonds lifted his eyes?
  Who first from out the still watch, lone and long,
Feeling the ancient faith of prophets rise
  Within his dark-kept soul, burst into song?

There is a wide, wide wonder in it all,
  That from degraded rest and servile toil,
The fiery spirit of the seer should call
  These simple children of the sun and soil.
O black singers, gone, forgot, unfamed,
  You — you alone, of all the long, long line
Of those who've sung untaught, unknown, unnamed,
  Have stretched out upward, seeking the divine.

You sang not deeds of heroes or of kings:
  No chant of bloody war, nor exulting pæan
Of arms-won triumphs; but your humble strings
  You touched in chords with music empyrean.
You sang far better than you knew, the songs
  That for your listeners' hungry hearts sufficed
Still live — but more than this to you belongs:
  You sang a race from wood and stone to Christ.

I have already referred to the fact that Thomas
Wentworth Higginson was the first, so far as I know,
to take note of this slave music and make a serious
study of it. The first man who seems to have realised that this music would touch the popular heart,
if it could be made known, was George L. White,
the man who was responsible for the success of the
Jubilee Singers of Fisk University, Nashville, Tennessee. It was the Fisk Jubilee Singers who first
made the Negro folk-music popular in America
and in Europe. They not only made this music
popular, but upon their return from their second

concert tour, in 1874, they brought back ninety thousand dollars as their contribution to Fisk University.

Perhaps one thing that made the singing of these songs more effective was that the singers themselves had, in many cases, been slaves, or were directly descended from slave parents, and they felt the music they sang more deeply than others who have tried to sing it since. One of the most interesting of these singers was Ella Sheppard, who was born in Nashville, in 1851. Ella Sheppard's father ran a livery stable in Nashville before the War. He had succeeded in purchasing his own freedom for $1,800, and was hoping to be able to purchase that of his wife and family, when suddenly he was separated from them by the fact that his wife's master removed from Nashville to Mississippi. Mr. Sheppard heard very little from his wife and child after this until one day a white man, who had been in Mississippi on business, returned and told him that his little girl was dying from neglect. He added that, as the child was sickly, possibly her father would be able to purchase her for a small sum. Mr. Sheppard started to Mississippi, purchased his child for $350, and brought her back to Nashville. Shortly after this he attempted to purchase his wife, but for some reason or other, after the sale had nearly been completed, her master refused to sell her and she did not succeed in gaining her freedom until the Civil War finally emancipated her.

Before freedom came, Mr. Sheppard failed in business and was compelled to move secretly to Cincinnati to prevent his creditors seizing his children for debt. There Ella Sheppard gained a little education in what was known as the Seventh Street Coloured School. When she was thirteen years old she commenced taking lessons in music from a German music teacher. About this time her father died and she was compelled, as she says, to go to work, for herself "in right good earnest." Fortunately, she made the acquaintance of Mr. J. P. Ball, of Cincinnati, who adopted her and gave her a thorough musical education, with the understanding that she was to repay him at some future time.

"I took twelve lessons," she says, "in vocal music of Madame Rivi. I was the only coloured pupil, and was not allowed to tell who my teacher was. More than that, I went up the back way to reach my teacher and received my lesson in the back room upstairs from nine to a quarter of ten at night."

After teaching school for a time, Ella Sheppard entered Fisk University, where, by teaching music and sewing at odd moments, or when she was confined to her bed, as she frequently was by illness, she managed to make her way through the University until she joined the first campaign of the Jubilee Singers through the Northern states. Ella Sheppard is still living in Nashville. She is now the wife of Reverend George W. Moore, who is the field superintendent of the church work of the American Missionary Association, and one of the most distinguished men of his race. Mr. Moore was, for a number of years, pastor of the Lincoln Memorial Church in Washington, District of Columbia. In all the work which this church attempted to do for the masses of the coloured people in Washington, Mr. Moore was greatly assisted by the labours and counsel of his wife.

Another distinguished member of the Jubilee Singers' Band, as it was called, was Jennie Jackson, who afterward became the wife of Professor DeHart, until recently teacher in the public schools of Cincinnati. Jennie Jackson was born free, but her grandfather was a slave and body-servant of General Andrew Jackson. During the War and afterward her mother supported the family by washing and ironing. It was by assisting her mother in this work that Jennie Jackson earned enough money to make her way through school, until, her voice having attracted the attention of her teachers, she became a member of the Jubilee Singers, whose fortunes she shared until the end of their campaign.

Maggie Porter was another of the singers who distinguished herself. She was born in 1853, at Lebanon, Tennessee. Her master was Henry

Frazier, and the owner of some two hundred slaves. Her mother was a house servant, and Maggie was brought up in the household of her master. In January, 1866, when the Fisk School was first opened, Maggie Porter was one of the three hundred pupils who gathered, during the first week, in the old hospital barracks. She was one of the first of the pupils at the Fisk School to enlist as a teacher in the country districts. She taught in different parts of Tennessee until Mr. White, who knew of her natural musical talent, sent for her to take the part of Queen Esther in the cantata that the students of Fisk University were preparing to give. She was so successful in this part that she became a member of the first band of Jubilee Singers that went out from Fisk in the following fall of 1871. After the disbandment of the Jubilee Singers Maggie Porter travelled for a number of years as a concert singer in various parts of the United States. Her name at present is Maggie Porter Cole. She is living with her husband in Detroit, where she has a beautiful home, and is making her life of great service to her people.

Of the other singers of whom I have been able to get some recent record, I recall the name of Thomas Rutling, who is now a teacher of English language and literature in a school at Geneva, Switzerland. He was the son of a runaway slave, and was born while his mother was hiding out in the woods in Wilson County, Tennessee.

There was, as I have said, a peculiar pathos about the old slave songs that invariably touched the hearts of those who heard them. Through these songs the slaves found a means of telling what was in their hearts when almost every other means of expressing their thoughts and feelings was denied them. For this reason, if for no other, they will always remain a sacred heritage of the Negro race.

The creation of music so original, by a people so wholly lacking in musical education, indicates a natural taste and talent for music in the Negro race which, perhaps, has not been equalled by any other primitive people. This native talent has manifested itself not only in the songs, spontaneously produced by the slaves on the plantation, but by the ease with which Negro musicians have been able to execute and interpret the music of all other peoples.

The most noted example of this native talent for music in a member of the Negro race is Thomas Greene Bethune, who was better known under the name of "Blind Tom." Blind Tom was born near Columbus, Georgia, May 25, 1849, and died July 3, 1908. He was blind from birth, and while deficient in some other directions, he manifested from infancy an extraordinary fondness for musical sounds. He is said to have exhibited his musical talent before he was two years old.

It is said that he showed, from the first, great interest in every kind of musical sound, "from the soft breathing of the flute to the harsh gratings of the corn-sheller." He also showed a remarkable power for judging the lapse of time. There was a clock in his master's house that struck the hour. Every hour in the day, just before this clock made the sharp click preparatory to striking, Tom would be there and remain until the hour was struck, and it was evident that he took the greatest delight in the musical tones which the clock gave forth. Frequently in the evening the young ladies of his master's family would sit on the steps and sing. At such times Tom would invariably, if he were allowed to do so, come to the house and sing with them. One evening one of the young ladies said to her father: "Pa, Tom sings beautifully, and he don't have to learn any tune, for as soon as we sing he sings right along with us." Then she added: "He sings fine seconds to anything we sing."

When Tom was about four years of age his master purchased a piano and brought it to the house. The first note from this new instrument brought Tom into the house. He was permitted to indulge his curiosity by running his fingers over the keys. As long as anyone would play on this piano Tom was content to stay out in the yard, where he would dance and caper to the music, but as soon as the music ceased he would try to get to the instrument in order to continue the sweet sounds in which he took such delight.

One night when the parlour door had been left open, Tom escaped from his mother and crept into the parlour. Early in the morning the young ladies of the household were awakened by hearing some one playing upon the piano. The music continued to reach their ears from time to time, until at the usual hour they arose and went into the parlour where, to their astonishment, they saw Tom playing the piano in what seemed to them a remarkable way. Notwithstanding this was his first attempt to play this instrument, they noted that he played with both hands, and used black as well as white keys.

After a time Tom was allowed free access to the piano and commenced to play everything he heard. After he had mastered all the music that he heard any one play, he commenced composing for himself. He would sit at the piano for hours playing over pieces he had heard, then he would go out, run and jump about the yard for a little while and, after returning, play something of his own. If any one asked him what he was playing, he replied that it was something that the wind said to him, or "what the birds said to me," "what the trees said to me," or what something else said to him. Speaking of the natural sense for music which this strangely

gifted Negro boy displayed, the biographer of Blind
Tom says:

There was but one thing that seemed to give Tom as much pleas-
ure as the sound of the piano.   Between a wing and the body of
the dwelling there is a hall, on the roof of which the rain falls from
the roof to the dwelling, and runs thence down a gutter.   There
was in this water something so enchanting to Tom, that from his
early childhood to the time he left home, whenever it rained,
whether by night or day, he would go into the passage and remain
as long as the rain continued.   When he was less than five years
of age, having been there during a severe thunderstorm, he went
to the piano and played what is now known as his "Rain Storm"
and said it was what the rain, the wind, and the thunder said to
him.*

When Tom was eight years of age he was permitted to appear in a regular concert in the city of
Columbus, at which a German, the leading musician
of the town, was present.   The next day this man
was asked to undertake Tom's musical education.
He replied: "No, sir, I can't teach him anything;
he knows more of music than any of us know or
can learn.   All that can be done for him is to let him
hear fine playing.   He will work it all out by himself after a while, but he will do it sooner by hearing
fine music."

This man was correct.   Tom did work it all out
by himself after a while, and became one of the most
noted musicians in the world.   He gave concerts in
every important city of the United States, and in all
the principal cities of Europe.   It was said of him,

* J. M. Trotter. "Music and Some Highly Musical People," p. 146.

as showing the remarkable power which he possessed, that he could stand with his back to a piano and let any number of chords be struck simultaneously, thereupon he would instantly be able to tell every note sounded, showing that his memory retained all the notes distinctly, and in such a manner that he was able to discriminate between every sound made.

In 1867 Blind Tom gave a concert in Glasgow, Scotland. The following morning the Glasgow *Herald*, in its account of his performance, made the following interesting statement, which gives a very accurate estimate of Tom's musical talent at this time:

Mozart, when a mere child, was noted for the delicacy of his ear and for his ability to produce music on a first hearing; but Burney, in his History of Music, records no instance at all coming up to this Negro boy for attainments in phonetics, and his power of retention and reproduction of sound. He plays first a number of difficult passages from the best composers; and then any one is invited to come forward and perform any piece he likes, the more difficult the more acceptable, and if original the more preferable. Tom immediately sits down at the piano, and produces verbatim et literatim the whole of what he has just heard. To show that it is not at all necessary that he should be acquainted with any piece beforehand to produce it, he invited any one to strike any number of notes simultaneously with the hand or with both hands; and immediately, as we heard him do yesterday, he repeats at length, and without the slightest hesitation, the whole of the letters with all their inflections representing the notes. Nor are his wondrous powers confined to the piano, on which he can produce imitations of various instruments and play two different tunes — one in common time and a second in triple — while he sings a third, but he can, with the voice, produce with the utmost accuracy any note which his audience may suggest.

Some of the most interesting music, produced by the Negro slaves, was handed down from the days when the French and Spanish had possession of Louisiana. All these songs, many of which have been preserved through the writings of George W. Cable, were composed in the Creole dialect of Louisiana.

From the free Negroes of Louisiana there sprang up, during slavery days, a number of musicians and artists who distinguished themselves in foreign countries to which they removed, because of the prejudice which existed against coloured people. Among them was Eugène Warburg, who went to Italy and distinguished himself as a sculptor. Another was Victor Séjour, who went to Paris and gained distinction as a poet and composer of tragedy. Another by the name of Dubuclet was a physician and musician of Bordeaux, France. The Lambert family, consisting of seven persons, were noted as musicians. Richard Lambert, the father, was a teacher of music, Lucien Lambert, a son, after much hard study, became a composer of music. He left New Orleans, however, and went to France, where he continued his studies. Later he went to Brazil, where he engaged in the manufacture of pianos. Among his compositions are: "La Juive," "Le

Départ du Conscript," "Les Ombres Aimées," "Le Niagara."

Another brother, Sidney Lambert, stimulated by the example and fame of his father and brother, made himself a name as a pianist and a composer of music. He wrote a method for the piano of such merit that he received a decoration in recognition of his work from the King of Portugal. At last accounts he was a professor of music in Paris. Edmund Dèdè, who was born in New Orleans, in 1829, learned while a youth to play a number of instruments. He was a cigar maker by trade and, being of good habits and thrifty, accumulated enough money to pay his passage to France. Here he took up a special study of music and finally became director of the Orchestra of L'Alcazar, in Bordeaux, France.

The late J. M. Trotter, of Boston, himself a Negro of unusual intelligence, has written a history of the Negroes who distinguished themselves in music in the period from 1850 to 1880. In this history he mentions more than fifty Negroes who achieved distinction in some form of music, either as singers, performers on musical instruments, or composers. One of the most famous of these was Elizabeth Taylor Greenfield, who was known as the "Black Swan." She was born in Natchez, Mississippi, in 1809. When about a year old she was brought to Philadelphia by an exemplary

Quaker lady, Mrs. Greenfield, by whom she was carefully reared. One evening, while visiting at the house of a neighbour, the daughter of the house, who knew something of her ability, invited her to sing. Every one present was astonished at the power and richness of her voice, and it was thereupon agreed that she should receive music lessons.

These lessons were carried on at first without the knowledge of Mrs. Greenfield, because, according to the discipline of the Friends, music, like every other art, was a forbidden occupation. When the good lady learned that Elizabeth was taking music lessons, she summoned her to her presence. Elizabeth came, trembling, and prepared for a severe reprimand.

"Elizabeth," said she, "is it true thee is learning music and can play upon the guitar?"

"It is true," Elizabeth reluctantly confessed.

"Go and get thy guitar and let me hear thee sing."

The girl obeyed, and when she had finished was astonished to hear her kind friend say: "Elizabeth, whatever thee wants thee shall have."

From that time on Mrs. Greenfield assisted her in every way to make herself proficient in the profession of music, which she had chosen to follow.

When her benefactress died, the young coloured girl was thrown upon her own resources. Remembering some friends in Western New York, who had been very kind to her, she resolved to visit them.

Her chance singing upon a boat, which was crossing Lake Seneca, gained her new friends and opened a way for her to come prominently before the public.

In 1851 she gained a reputation by her singing before the Buffalo Musical Society. From that time on she was known as the "Black Swan," and invitations to sing in concerts came to her from cities in all parts of the North. In 1853 she gave a concert in Exeter Hall, London, England, where she made a great success.

Among other distinguished singers of this period were the Luca family, father and three sons, of Cleveland, Ohio. The father was born in Milford, Connecticut, in 1805. He was a shoemaker by trade. He became a chorister in one of the Congregational churches of New Haven, and his choir was considered one of the best in the city. The children inherited their father's talent, and in the fifties travelled about the Northern states, giving musical entertainments.

Among the more recent singers, perhaps the most distinguished is Madame Sissieretta Jones. She was born in Portsmouth, Virginia, in 1870. Her father was pastor of the local Methodist Church. When still a young woman her parents moved to Providence, Rhode Island, where her voice soon attracted public attention. After making a number of public appearances in Providence, she was invited to go to New York and sing at Wallack's Theatre. Her success was so great that she was immediately engaged to tour South America and the West Indies. In 1886 she sang with great success in Madison Square Garden. She has sung with success in all the principal cities of Europe, and during recent years has had her own company, known as the Black Patti Troubadours, at the head of which she has appeared in every important city in the United States.

Except as a singer in concerts or as a musician, almost the only opportunity that the Negro has had until recently to appear upon the stage has been as a minstrel. The first Negro minstrels were white men, and they sang songs and cracked jokes that were invented by white men in imitation of the songs and jokes of the Negroes, with which the Southern people had become familiar during slavery days. Immediately after the War, however, there was a company of coloured minstrels organised, known as the "Georgia Minstrels." These minstrels became famous and were succeeded by others. Out of these minstrels there grew later a kind of Negro comedy, in which there was some attempt to depict the characters and tell the story of Negro life. The man who made this transition from the old Negro minstrels to the more modern Negro comedy was Ernest Hogan, who died in the spring of 1909, in New York, and was buried from the church of St. Benedict the Moor, an honoured and respected member of his profession.

The success of Ernest Hogan has made it possible for other Negro comedians to gain a foothold in the better class of the theatres, and create a more worthy kind of Negro comedy. Among the more talented of these players are Bert Williams, George Walker, and his wife, Aida Overton Walker, Bob Cole, and J. Rosamond Johnson.

Year by year the character of the pieces produced by these men has improved in quality, both as to the music and as to the manner and style of presentation. At the present.time I have heard it said that there are few musical comedies on the American stage that equal those that are produced by some of the players to whom I have referred.

Little by little these players, and the men who have written their songs and music, have managed to bring into connection with the rather rough humour of these comedies, music and songs of a much higher order than are usually heard in this kind of entertainment. Among the men who write the music and these songs are some men like James W. Johnson, whose poetry I have already quoted, and Harry T. Burleigh, a concert singer of more than ordinary cultivation and refinement. The songs which these young men have written are not only among the most popular songs of the day, but some of them must be counted among the very few which have real and permanent value. There is a note in the best of them which is entirely distinctive.

The most noted figure among Negroes who have appeared upon the stage was Ira Aldridge. He was born near Baltimore in 1804. In 1826 he met Edmund Kean, with whom he travelled for several years. He accompanied Keene to Europe, and when, finally, he expressed to him a desire to become an actor himself, the distinguished tragedian encouraged him in that ambition. Ira Aldridge made his first appearance as Othello at Covent Garden, London, April 10,. 1839. Keene took the part of Iago, and from that time on the success of the coloured actor was assured.

In 1852 Ira Aldridge appeared in Germany, where his success was so great that the King of Prussia conferred a decoration upon him and sent him an autograph letter, expressing his appreciation of his performance. The coloured actor afterward received the Cross of Leopold from the Emperor of Russia. He played in all parts of Europe, and finally died at Lodz, Poland, just as he was preparing to come to America to fulfil an engagement.

In recent years the number of coloured performers upon the stage has multiplied rapidly. At the present time one of the regular features of the coloured newspaper is a theatrical column, which is devoted entirely to chronicling the doings of the coloured theatrical performers. So successful have these performers been that, in a number of cities, theatres owned and conducted by coloured people have been started expressly for the use of coloured companies. Theatres were owned and operated by coloured people in 1909 in Chicago, Illinois; New Orleans, Louisiana; Jackson, Mississippi; Memphis, Tennessee; Atlanta, Georgia; Columbus, Ohio; Jacksonville, Florida; Yazoo City, Mississippi; Baton Rouge and Plaquemine, Louisiana.

The ability which the Negro has shown to express his feelings in the form of music is also shown, in a lesser degree, in expressing himself in poetry and in other forms of art. The natural disposition of the native African to express himself poetically has been frequently noted by students of African life. The traveller Schweinfurth noted among the peoples of Central Africa a number of striking expressions. For example, one tribe referred to a leaf as "an ear of the tree," and in speaking of a man's chest, called it "the capital of the veins." In many parts of the black man's Africa there are professional singers who practise the art of improvising songs upon almost any topic that may be assigned to them.

I have myself frequently noticed the striking expressions that are sometimes used by the people in the country districts, when they wish to make any particular impressive statement. For instance, in talking with an old farmer in the vicinity of my home at Tuskegee, I happened to give expression to some opinion or idea that struck him with peculiar force when he exclaimed: "Mr. Washington, you said a thousand words in one." At another time there was a coloured preacher who had a church which was near a plantation school and settlement that had been started by some of the teachers at Tuskegee. Some one asked this preacher if the school had made any change in conditions in that neighbourhood since it had been established. He raised his hands and exclaimed: "I'll tell you in a word. When this school started it was midnight; now it is dawn." Upon another occasion, when one of these men was describing his religious experience, how he "came through," as the expression is, he used these words: "All of a sudden a star busted in my breast and I was mighty happy in the Lord."

This same natural gift of expression, which is frequently possessed by some of the rude and unlettered people of my race, has been frequently noted by other persons. A typical example of this is Harriet Tubman's description of the Battle of Gettysburg, which Professor Albert Bushnell Hart has noted in his "History of Slavery and Abolition." He heard this description from Harriet Tubman's own lips as she was describing some of her experiences during the Civil War. One sentence from that description was as follows: "And then we saw the lightning, and that was the guns; and then we heard the rainfall, and that was the drops of blood falling; and when we came to get in the crops, it was dead men that we reaped."

It is this same natural ability for picturesque expression which makes the Negro a natural orator. Even the disposition of the Negro to pick up and repeat high-sounding words and expressions is but another indication of his sense for impressive language.

I have noted, also, that where Negro college students do not excel their fellows of the white race in other branches of study, they frequently come off first in oratorical contests. For example, in 1907, a Zulu, who some years before came from Africa to America to get an education, carried off the oratorical honours at Columbia University. The name of this orator was Pixley Isaka Seme. When I last heard from Mr. Seme he was a student at Jesus College, Oxford, where he, with a number of other African students, was studying preparatory to going back to South Africa to enter the colonial civil service.

One of the most striking illustrations of the natural poetic talent in a member of the Negro race is in the verses of Phillis Wheatley. It requires a considerable amount of natural talent for any person to master a strange language and to learn to express himself poetically in it. It would seem that this must be particularly difficult for one coming from a condition and a life as remote and as different from that of a civilised European people as that of the primitive African. Nevertheless, the Negro has shown his ability to accomplish this feat.

One day in the year 1761, Mrs. John Wheatley, of Boston, went into the city slave market to purchase a Negro servant girl. She selected as suitable for her purpose a child between seven and eight years of age who had but recently come from Africa, and was hardly able to speak a word of English. The little girl was taken home and soon showed such marked intelligence that her mistress's daughter determined to teach her to read. Within sixteen months she had so far mastered the English language that she could read with ease and apparent understanding the most difficult passages of the Scriptures. She acquired the art of writing, it is said, almost wholly by her own exertion and industry. The great interest that she showed in learning to read and write, and the eagerness with which she read the books that were supplied to her, were so unusual at that time that it attracted general attention.

After a time she began to write verses. She was about fourteen years old when she wrote the first verses that attracted any particular attention. From this time until she was nineteen years of age she seems to have written all the poems which she gave to the world. They were published in London, in 1773, and dedicated to the Countess of Huntingdon, who had been her friend and patron. A letter of recommendation, signed by the Governor, Lieutenant-governor and several other respectable persons of Boston, was printed by the publishers as a sort of introduction to this little volume. This letter of recommendation was as follows:

To THE PUBLIC:

As it has been repeatedly suggested to the publisher, by persons who have seen the manuscript, that numbers would be ready to suspect they were not really the writings of Phillis, he has procured the following attestation from the most respectable characters in Boston that none might have the least ground for disputing the original:

"We whose names are underwritten, do assure the world, that the poems specified in the following pages were (as we verily believe) written by Phillis, a young Negro girl, who was but a few years since brought, an uncultivated barbarian, from Africa, and has ever since been, and now is, under the disadvantage of serving as a slave in a family in this town. She has been examined by some of the best judges and is thought qualified to write them."

Phillis Wheatley addressed a poem to General Washington, which seemed to have pleased him very much. In a letter to Joseph Reed, dated February 10, 1776, from Cambridge, General Washington made the following reference to this poem:

I recollect nothing else worth giving you the trouble of, unless you can be amused by reading a letter and poem addressed to me by Miss Phillis Wheatley. In searching over a parcel of papers the other day, in order to destroy such as were useless, I brought it to light again. At first, with a view of doing justice to her poetical genius, I had a great mind to publish the poem; but not knowing whether it might not be considered rather as a mark of my own vanity, than as a compliment to her, I laid it aside, till I came across it again in the manner just mentioned.

This kindly reference of George Washington to the Negro slave girl poet and the uniform kindness and courtesy with which he is known to have treated black men and women in every station in life has gone far to endear the memory of the Father of our Country to the coloured people of the United States.

Phillis Wheatley died December 5, 1784, when she was thirty-four years of age. She was one of the first women, white or black, to attain literary distinction in this country. I have frequently noticed, in travelling in different sections of the country, that many of the literary organisations and women's clubs among the members of my race bear the name of Phillis Wheatley, showing how well her name is still remembered among the masses of the Negro people.

Another slave poet whose name is remembered, but whose history is shrouded in mystery, is George M. Horton, of Chatham County, North Carolina. Horton could not write, but his poems were taken down by some white man and were regarded as of such importance that they were printed in a small volume in 1829.

Frequently I have run across the names of Negroes

from the West Indies or elsewhere who have written poetry in the Spanish or French languages. Now and then I have received a volume of poems in some language that I was not able to read, which were written by some Negro poet in some part of the world. The great national poet of Russia, Alexander Sergeievich Pushkin, although of noble family, inherited African blood from his mother.

The history of Alexander Dumas, who was born of a Negro mother in one of the West Indian islands belonging to France, is familiar.

One of the most charming writers of verse in America at the present day, William Stanley Braithwaite, of Boston, is a young coloured man who was born in the West Indies. He is the author of several books of verse, one of them entitled "Lyrics of Love and Life," published in 1904. He is a frequent contributor to the magazines.

I should mention here, also, the name of Charles W. Chesnutt, the novelist, who makes his home in Cleveland, Ohio. Mr. Chesnutt, although he was born in the North, is descended from free coloured people of North Carolina. Shortly after the War his parents returned to the South, where Mr. Chesnutt was for some time a school-teacher. It was while thus occupied that he obtained that acquaintance with the South upon which his stories are founded. Among them are: "The Conjure Woman," "The House Behind the Cedars," "The

Wife of His Youth," and "The Marrow of Tradi-tion." This latter is said to be the best description of the Wilmington riot and the events that led up to and produced it that has yet been written. Mr. Chesnutt's last story of Southern life is called "The Colonel's Dream," and describes the efforts of a Southerner who had gone North and become wealthy to return to his native village and build up its resources and make it prosperous.

But the poetry to which I have referred was written for the most part at a time when the masses of the Negro people could not read. It was the work of men who were, to a large extent, out of touch with the masses of the Negro people. The poems they wrote were not in the language which the masses of the people spoke, sometimes not even in a language which they could understand, and did not in any sense express or interpret the life of the Negro people.

Almost the first representative poet of my race was Paul Laurence Dunbar. Of Dunbar, William Dean Howells, to whom he owed to some extent his success, said that Dunbar was the only man of pure African blood and of American civilisation "to feel the Negro esthetically and express it lyrically." And that the Negro race "had attained civilisation in him." Mr. Howells believed that Dunbar more than any other Negro had gained for the Negro a permanent position in English literature.

Paul Laurence Dunbar was born in Dayton, Ohio, in 1872. His parents had been slaves. He received a high school education, but before his education was completed, while he was still working as an elevator boy, he began to write verses. He succeeded after a hard struggle in gaining recognition for his poetry, and became a frequent contributor to the leading magazines of the country. He was, likewise, a successful reader of his own verse. He published a number of volumes of poetry and of prose. To the time of his death, February 9, 1906, he seemed to be gaining in intellectual power and in popularity.

Shortly before he died, when it had become clear, even to his naturally hopeful mind, that he had not long to live, he wrote the following verses which are so full of pathos and express so clearly at once the strength and the weakness, as he felt them, not only of himself, but perhaps also of his race, that I quote them here:

> Because I had loved so deeply,
>   Because I had loved so long,
> God in His great compassion
>   Gave me the gift of song.
>
> Because I have loved so vainly,
>   And sung with such faltering breath,
> The Master in infinite mercy
>   Offers the boon of Death.

It has always seemed strange to me that Dunbar, who was born in a Northern state, and knew so little from actual experience of the life of the Negro in the South, could have been able to interpret that life so sincerely, so sympathetically, and so beautifully. No doubt the most that he knew about the life of the Negro before and after the War he gathered from the lips of his devoted mother, who had been a slave and had known and felt it all. There were no bitterness and no harsh notes in Dunbar's music. Perhaps this also is due to the fact that he saw the condition of his race sympathetically, through his mother's eyes. His songs have been of great service not only to his own race, but to the rest of the world. He was in a sense a direct descendant of the old slave singers. He expressed intelligently and poetically the deeper feelings and thoughts of the masses of the Negro people, so that the world could understand them. He was, in fact, the poet laureate of the Negro race.

From among the Negroes in the United States there have come from time to time not merely singers, but artists. One of the most noted of these, and the earliest to gain reputation, was Edmonia Lewis, who was born of Negro and Indian parentage in the State of New York, in 1845. During a visit to Boston she chanced to see a statue of Benjamin Franklin. She stood transfixed before it. Perhaps it was the latent genius within her which was stirred, for after looking at it with deep emotion she said: "I, too, can make a stone man."

It was William Lloyd Garrison to whom she turned for advice, who gave her encouragement to study sculpture. She first attracted attention by exhibiting in Boston, in 1865, a bust of Colonel Robert Gould Shaw. The same year she went to Rome to study and has resided there permanently since 1867. She has created a number of works of merit, the most noted of which are, "The Death of Cleopatra," which was exhibited at the Centennial Exhibition at Philadelphia, in 1876; "Asleep," "Marriage of Hiawatha," "Madonna with the Infant Christ," and the "Freedwoman." She has made a number of portrait busts in terra cotta, among which are those of Longfellow, Charles Sumner, John Brown, and Abraham Lincoln. The bust of Abraham Lincoln is in the public library at San José, California.

A younger sculptress, who has recently attracted attention, is Meta Vaux Warrick. She was born in Philadelphia, and gained her first lesson in modelling clay flowers in the public kindergarten. Afterward she secured a free scholarship in the Pennsylvania School of Industrial Art. Her first piece of original work in clay was the head of Medusa. In 1899 Miss Warrick went to study in Paris. She finally succeeded in attracting the attention of the famous French sculptor, Rodin, who is said to have given her his approval in these words: "My child, you are a sculptress. You have the sense of form." One

of her best pieces of work was made for the Jamestown Tercentennial, and represented the advancement of the Negro since he landed at Jamestown,
in 1619.

The Negro artist who has gained greatest fame,
however, is Henry O. Tanner, son of Bishop Benjamin T. Tanner, of the A. M. E. Church.   After
studying for a time in the Pennsylvania Academy of
Fine Arts, he opened a photograph gallery in
Atlanta, Georgia.   This venture was unsuccessful,
however, and the next year he taught freehand
drawing in Clark University, in the same city.   His
ambition, however, was to go to Paris and study
under one of the living masters of art.   By the
assistance of friends he was finally able to gratify
this desire.   His first picture to receive official recognition was entitled, "Daniel in the Lions' Den,"
which received honourable mention in the Paris
Salon of 1896.   The next year his "Lazarus
Rising from the Dead," received the third medal,
and was purchased by the French Government
for its collection of modern art in the Luxembourg
gallery:

From that time until this Mr. Tanner has produced something every year, and every year the
painting which he exhibited has been better
than that of the previous year.   In December,
1908, a comprehensive exhibition of his paintings
was made in New York City.   At the time the

art critic of the New York *Herald* said of Mr.
Tanner and his art:

Works of Mr. Henry Tanner, a distinguished American artist,
long resident in Paris, who has been honoured abroad, are shown
in a comprehensive exhibition for the first time at the American
Art Galleries. All are religious paintings and reveal, as in flights
of poetic fancy, the story of the "Prince of Peace." The thirty-
three canvases form a veritable epic, and unfold the life of Christ
from the Nativity to Golgotha, and then picture events that followed the Resurrection.

Mr. Tanner is a son of a bishop, and from his earliest years the
inspiring traditions of the Old Testament and the New have been
to him realities. With the development of his genius came the
wish to show his conception of the ideals which to him had been
realities from a child. Yet his point of view is not that of a religion-
ist, but that of the true artist. He has sensed events, removed by
the lapse of nineteen centuries, and has depicted them with such
sincerity and feeling that the personages seem to live and breathe.
Such qualities as these enabled him to make a deep impression in
Paris, and two of his canvasses were purchased by the French
Government for the Luxembourg.

The largest painting in the present exhibition was received with
the warmest praise and occupied a prominent place in the last Paris
Salon. It is entitled "Behold, the Bridegroom Cometh," and its
theme is the familiar parable of the wise and foolish virgins.
The painting, with its numerous figures of life size, occupies
an entire panel of one of the lower galleries. The Master of
Ceremonies is in the act of giving his summons and the
maidens are forming themselves into the procession which is to
go forth and meet their Lord. The masterly composition, the
Oriental richness yet softness of the colouring, the instinctive
command of detail have drawn the various elements together
into a convincing picture.

Among notable canvases are several which, on account of the
ideality of their conception and beauty of their tone, will at once
draw to them the notice of the observer. They are, "Christ at

the Home of Mary and Martha," "Christ and Nicodemus," "The Return of the Holy Women," "On the Road to Emmaus" and "He Vanished Out of Their Sight."

What impresses me most about Mr. Tanner's paintings is the vividness, the sincerity and, I may say, literalness with which he has depicted the incidents of the Bible story. He paints all these things, it seems to me, with something of the spirit in which these same incidents are pictured in the old plantation hymns, vividly, as I have said, literally, and with a deep religious feeling for the significance of the things that he paints.

CHAPTER XII

D URING his travels in Africa Mungo Park, the famous African explorer, came one day to Sego, the capitol of the Kingdom of Bambara, which is situated on the Niger River. Information was carried to the king of that country that a white man wished to see him. The king in reply sent one of his men to inform the explorer that he could not be received until his business was known. He was advised to find lodgings for the night in a neighbouring village. To his great surprise, Park found no one would admit him. After searching for a long time he finally sat down, worn out, under the shade of a tree, where he remained for a whole day without food.

As night came on the wind arose and a heavy storm threatened. To the other dangers of the situation was added the fear that he might be devoured by the numerous wild beasts that roamed about in that region. Just as he was preparing to climb into a tree, however, a woman passed by and perceiving his weary and dejected appearance, spoke to him and inquired why he was there. On receiving his explanation she told him to follow her to her house. Here he was given food and a mat was spread on which he lay down to sleep. The women of the house were meanwhile employed in spinning cotton and, as they worked, they lightened and enlivened their labour by songs. One of these songs was extemporised in honour of their guest. Park described this music, in the story of his travels, as sweet and plaintive. The words were:

> The wind roared and the rain fell.
> The poor white man, faint and weary,
> Came and sat under our tree;
> He has no mother to bring him milk,
> No wife to grind his corn.
>
> Let us pity the white man,
> No mother has he to bring him milk,
> No wife to grind his corn.

This incident has been often quoted. Sometimes it has been referred to as an illustration of the easy and spontaneous way in which the African people are accustomed to express their thoughts and feelings in song. To my mind, however, it seems rather an illustration of that natural human sympathy which is characteristic of the women of most races, but particularly so of Negro women, whether in Africa or elsewhere.

Whatever may be said about the thoughts and the failings of Negro women, no one, so far as I know, has ever denied to them this gift of sympathy. Most people have recognised this quality but nowhere is the kindness and helpfulness of Negro women better known and appreciated than among the white people of the Southern states. The simple-hearted devotion of the Negro slave women to their masters and their masters' families was one of the redeeming features of Negro slavery in the South.

The devotion the slaves sometimes showed to their masters did not fail to inspire a corresponding affection in the members of the master's family. I know of scarcely anything more beautiful than the tributes I have heard Southern white men and women pay to those old coloured mammies, who nursed them as children, shared their childish joys and sorrows and clung to them through life with an affection that no change of time or of circumstance could diminish.

Southern literature is full of stories which illustrate the strength of this mutual affection, which bound the young master or the young mistress to his or her faithful Negro servant. When all other ties which bound the races together in the South have snapped assunder, this tie of affection has held fast.

I remember reading a few years ago, shortly after the Altanta riots, a story written by a young Southern white man entitled, "Ma'm Linda." The central theme of this story was the affection of a young white woman for her coloured "mammy." This affection was strong enough to resist and finally overcome attachments that divided the community in which these two persons are supposed to have lived. It put an end to an exciting episode which would otherwise have terminated in a most hideous mob murder.

As an illustration of this devotion of some of the slave women to their masters and masters' families, the following incident, which took place in Washington, District of Columbia, in 1833, is in many ways typical. A Southern gentleman and his family were stopping at a Washington hotel when he began a conversation with some persons who were opposed to slavery. After they had discussed the question at some length the slave-holder said to them: "Here is our servant; she is a slave, and you are at liberty to persuade her to remain here if you can." The anti-slavery people sought out the young woman and informed her that having been brought by her master into the free states she was, by the law of the land, a free woman.

The young woman promptly replied that this could not be so. They talked the matter over thoroughly and made every effort to show her that she was free under the existing laws, but she shook her head, saying that a legal decision did not touch her case, "for you see," she said, "I promised my mistress that I would go back with the children."

An attempt was then made to induce her to break her promise. It was pointed out that a promise made while she was not free could not be binding, but the young slave woman refused to look upon it in that light.

At length one of the abolitionists said: "Is it possible that you do not wish to be free?"

"Was there ever a slave that did not wish to be free?" the girl replied. "I long for liberty. I will get out of slavery, if I can, the day after I return, but I must go back because I have promised."

Among those slaves who became free, either through the kindness of their owners or as a result of their own individual efforts, the number of Negro women is large. Olmsted, in his "Cotton Kingdom," records an instance of a woman who had obtained her freedom in Virginia, but, being in fear that she might be reënslaved, fled to Philadelphia. Here for a time she almost starved. One day a little girl, who saw her begging on the streets, told her that her mother wanted some one to do her washing. When the poor woman applied for this work she was at first refused, because her prospective employer was afraid to trust valuable clothing to so unfortunate appearing a creature. The coloured woman begged earnestly for the chance to do this work and finally suggested, if there was any fear she would not return the clothes, that she should be locked in a room until the work was completed. She pleaded so earnestly that she was allowed to do this work, and in this way began her life in Philadelphia.

Ten years afterward a white man from her old home in Virginia happened to be in the city. The coloured woman recognised him and was over-joyed to see some one from her old home. She invited him to come to her house. He did so and found it a handsomely furnished three-story building. From the window she pointed out three other houses in the vicinity which she owned and rented. In order that her children might be educated she had employed for them a private instructor. This story illustrates the manner in which many other Negro women set to work, after emancipation, to build homes for themselves and their children.

To the twenty-five million dollars, which it is estimated the free Negroes accumulated before the Civil War, the thrift and industry of Negro women contributed no small amount. Likewise, in the remarkable amount of property accumulated and in the home-building which has gone forward for the last forty years, the women of the Negro race have ever been foremost.

I have seldom found an instance where a man of my race has accumulated property, that his wife has not only urged that a home be bought but has like-wise aided, by extra work, in buying it. In the struggle for homes and for a substantial family life the women of no race have shown a greater devotion and more constant self-denial than have the Negro women since the masses of the race have become free. They have engaged in all forms of personal and domestic service, to supplement the small wages of their husbands, in order that their children might be fed, clothed, kept in a school and something laid aside to pay on a home that more than likely is being purchased through some building and loan association. These women have frequently had almost no learning in books and but little idea of the settled and traditional regard of mankind for the sacredness of the home and family ties. When they began to lay the foundation of the Negro family life they were simply following the dictates of their own hearts, and the natural instincts which their ancestors had brought from Africa. For, contrary to the general notion, it will be found that family life, where native institutions have not been broken down through contact with the white race, is highly developed among the native Africans.

Some idea of the part that the Negro women are taking in the economic development of the race may be gained by considering how large a place they hold in the field of industry. The statistics show that coloured women, as wage-earners, do more than their full share of the work of the race. According to the census of 1900, for every thousand coloured women or girls, ten years of age and over, four hundred and seven were reported as bread-winners. In the case of white women, on the contrary, the corresponding number was one hundred and fifty. This means that about two coloured women out of five and one white woman out of six work for wages. Of the total number of Negroes engaged in gainful occupations in 1900, nearly one-third were women. The proportion of coloured women to the whole number of Negroes employed in various groups of occupations was as follows: in agriculture 27.1 per cent., in the professions 32.9 per cent., in domestic and personal service 51.5 per cent., in trade and transportation 1.9 per cent., and in manufacturing and mechanical pursuits 12 per cent.

In the professional class there were 262 women who followed the stage as a career; 164 were ministers, 7 dentists, 11 journalists, 10 lawyers, 25 were engaged in literary and scientific work, 86 were artists and teachers of art, 160 physicians, 1,185 musicians and teachers of music, and 13,525 were school-teachers. In the 140 groups of occupations, concerning which statistics are given in the census, coloured women are represented in 133. The remaining groups were of such a character that men alone could be employed in them.

It is, perhaps, in the matter of educating their children that Negro women have made their greatest sacrifices. I have referred to the freed woman in Philadelphia, who employed private teachers for her children. Thousands of Negro women at the present day are working in the kitchen, over the washtub, or in the field in order that their children may have the advantages of an education.

A considerable number of Negro women have distinguished themselves as teachers of their people. The fourth school established in the District of Columbia for coloured children was started by Mrs. Anne Maria Hall. This school was opened in 1810. The Costin sisters, Louisa and Martha, from 1823 to 1839, did much to improve the character of the education of coloured children in the District of Columbia. Fannie Jackson Coppin, wife of Bishop Levi J. Coppin, of the African Methodist Episcopal Church, was one of the best known of the women coloured teachers in the United States. She was born a slave in Washington, District of Columbia, in 1837, and was purchased by her aunt. She graduated with honours from Oberlin College and began to teach in 1865. From 1869 to 1899 she was principal of the Institute for Coloured Youth in Philadelphia. The present principal of that school, Hugh M. Browne, was her pupil.

The first coloured school-teacher in the public schools of Philadelphia was Cordelia A. Jennings, who for a number of years maintained a private institution for coloured children in the city. In 1864, her school having reached an enrollment of one hundred and fifty, Miss Jennings decided to apply for recognition and support as a public school. Under the regulations that prevailed at that time she was entitled to do this. The request aroused considerable discussion, but was finally granted, and Miss Jennings's school became part of the public school system, with its former teacher as principal.

After forty-five years, this school is still in existence. During this time it has had but two principals; the present incumbent being Miss Caroline R. Le Count, who has under her as teachers a number of those who had previously been her pupils. It is now well known under the name of the Catto school, named after Octavius V. Catto, a coloured schoolmaster, who was killed in the election riot in October, 1871.

Miss Jennings was born in Poughkeepsie, New York, in 1843. She graduated from the Institution of Coloured Youth in Philadelphia. After leaving Philadelphia, she helped to establish at Louisville, Kentucky, in 1886, the first coloured high school in that state. While there she became the wife of Reverend Joseph S. Attwell. Mr. Attwell, who was born in Barbadoes, British West Indies, in 1831, had come to America about 1864, to collect funds to assist a number of his countrymen to emigrate to Liberia. He succeeded in collecting about twenty thousand dollars, and thus became instrumental in founding the settlement known as Crozerville, on the Liberian coast.

After the close of the War, Mr. Attwell went South as agent of the Episcopal Church. He established mission churches in several cities in Kentucky, founded a mission church in Petersburg,

Virginia, and was for several years rector of St. Stephen's Church, Savannah, Georgia. He finally became rector of St. Philip's Church, where he died in 1881. St. Philip's Church, New York, is said to be the richest coloured church in the United States. It bears, in this respect, somewhat the same relationship to the other coloured churches that Trinity Church, New York — from which, in fact, it is an offshoot — does to the white churches of the city.

During all this time Mrs. Attwell was active as a teacher or as a worker in other directions, for the benefit of her race. She was principal of the parochial school, at Petersburg, and principal of the West Broad Street School, at Savannah, and after her husband's death, in 1881, she worked as a professional trained nurse. Mrs. Attwell was, for a time, matron of the Home for Aged and Infirm Coloured Persons in Philadelphia, and was afterward in charge of the Industrial Home for Working Women, at Germantown, Pennsylvania. At present, 1909, she is living with her son, Ernest T. Attwell, who is Business Agent of the Tuskegee Institute.

Mrs. Attwell's mother, Mrs. Mary McFarland Jennings, was herself a school-teacher. When, in the summer of 1909, I made an extended trip of observation through the Southern part of Virginia, I passed through Kenbridge, Lunenburg County, where Mrs. Jennings was born, and where, after the War, she conducted a school for many years for Freedmen. For four years after the close of the War, Mrs. Jennings carried on this school at her own expense and without salary. In 1869, however, through the intervention of her son-in-law, Mr. Joseph S. Attwell, the support of the school was taken over by the Domestic Missionary Society of the Protestant Episcopal Church. The school was closed in 1894, but at the time of my visit to Kenbridge, citizens of the county and former pupils of the school had purchased land and were preparing to erect a building for a memorial school to be established there in memory of Mrs. Jennings and her work.

Lucy C. Laney, a graduate of Atlanta University, has done an interesting and important work in education in Georgia. She was for a time principal of a public school in Savannah. In 1886, however, she resigned this position and went to Augusta, Georgia, in order to establish in that city an industrial school. Although she started this school almost unaided, making herself responsible for the support of the teachers and the expense of the institution, somehow or other the school has grown steadily from the time it was started. It has since then received a liberal support from the Presbyterian Church and is now the chief school supported by this denomination south of North Carolina.

In this connection I want to mention the noble work for the care and education of orphans and neglected children, which has been carried on for many years by Dinah Pace at Covington, Georgia. This is known as the Reed Home and School. After years of struggle Miss Pace has been able to build up at Covington, largely through the assistance of her own pupils and teachers, an industrial school and orphans' home which is valued at the present time at about ten thousand dollars. Another of the early schools established in the way I have described is the Industrial School at Manassas, Virginia, which was started by a coloured woman by the name of Jennie Dean, and is now in charge of Mr. Leslie P. Hill and his wife, both of whom were formerly teachers in the institute.

I feel certain that, if I had space to do so, I could name hundreds of other women who are doing, in different parts of the South, a work similar to that I have already mentioned. The names of these women are frequently scarcely known outside of the communities in which they live and labour, but the value of the service they have rendered is greater than can ever be fully measured or known.

In speaking of the coloured women who have distinguished themselves as teachers, I should not fail to mention the name of Maria L. Baldwin, a coloured woman who is principal of one of the best graded schools of Cambridge, Massachusetts, in which she has under her care not less than 600 white children. Miss Baldwin is one of the best known women of her race in New England and is frequently called upon to address teachers' associations in different parts of New England. At Hampton Institute, Hampton, Virginia, and at the Institute for Coloured Youth at Cheyney, Pa., her summer-school classes have had a large and enthusiastic attendance.

Negro women have not only been, to a very large extent, the teachers of their race, both before and since the War, but several of them played important parts in the antebellum struggle for freedom. I have already referred, in another part of this volume, to the story of Harriet Tubman. Another woman, who did much to change sentiment in the United States in regard to slavery, was Sojourner Truth, one of the most original and best known of anti-slavery characters.

Sojourner Truth was born about 1775. She was brought as a child with her parents from Africa and sold as a slave in the State of New York. She has described this incident in her own picturesque language.

"Ye see," she once said, "we was all brought over from Africa, father an' mother an' I with a lot more of us. We was sold up an' down, an' hither an' yon; an' I can 'member, when I was a little thing, not bigger than this," pointing to her grandson, "how my ole mammy would sit out o' doors in the evenin', an' look up at the stars an' groan. She'd groan an' groan, an' says I to her: 'Mammy, what makes you groan so?' An' she'd say, 'Matter enough, chile! I'm groanin' to think o' my poor children: they don't know where I be, an' I don't know where they be; they looks up at the stars an' I looks up at the stars, but I can't tell where they be.'"

Sojourner Truth was called Isabella by her parents. Her parents' names were James and Betsy. They were owned by Colonel Ardinburgh, who lived in Hurley, Ulster County, New York. At nine years of age Isabella was sold to John Nealy, of the same county, for $100. She thought that her sale in some way was connected with a flock of sheep. At any rate, it was the beginning of her trials, for her former master belonged to the class of people called Low Dutch, and she had not learned the English language and no one in the family except Mr. Nealy, her new master, understood the Dutch language. This led to frequent misunderstandings and punishments for Isabella. Her mother had said to her when she was very small, that when she should grow up and be sold away from all of her old friends and had great troubles, that she was to go to God and he would help her.

"An' says I to her, 'Who is God, anyhow, mammy?' An' says she, 'Why chile, you jes look up dar! its him dat made all dem.'"

At the Nealys' she had many occasions to remember the words of her mother. Once she was ordered to go to the barn, where she found her master with a bundle of rods waiting for her. She was stripped to her waist and given the most cruel beating she ever received, and she never knew why she was so cruelly whipped. Often afterward she would say: "When I hear 'em tell of whippin' women on the bare flesh it makes my flesh crawl an' my very hair rise on my head. Oh, my God, what a way is this of treatin' human bein's!" And then she said, "I thought about what my old mammy had told me about God, an' I thought I had gone into trouble sure enough, an' I wanted to find God, an' I heerd somebody tell a story about a man that met God on the threshing floor, an' I thought, good an' well, I will have a threshing floor.

"So I went down in the lot an' I thresh down a place real hard, an' I used to go down there every day an' pray an' cry with all my might, a-praying to the Lord to make my massa an' missus better."

The Lord, however, did not answer her prayer and so she said, "Why, God, maybe you can't." She then proposed to the Lord that if He would help her to get away she would be good. "But if You don't help me I really don't think I can be."

Then she said the Lord told her to get up about three o'clock in the morning and travel. In the course of the day she came to the house of some

Quakers, who treated her very kindly, and after supper they took her into a room in which there was a bed and told her to sleep there. But instead of sleeping in the bed she slept under it, and in the morning, when they came to ask her if she hadn't been asleep, she said, "Yes, I never slep' better."

"Why, you haven't been in the bed at all," they exclaimed.

"Laws, you didn' think of sech a thing as my sleepin' in dat ar bed, did you?" she replied. "I never heerd o' sech a thing in my life."

The immediate cause of Sojourner's running away from her master was that, by an act of the New York Legislature, passed in 1817, all slaves forty years of age were to be liberated at once, children on reaching their majority, and the others, in 1827. Sojourner would have been free on July 4, 1827, but her master, in consideration of her long years of faithful service, had promised to give her free papers a year in advance of the time which the law had set. He backed out of this agreement, however, on the plea that during the year her hand had been disabled; and, therefore, she had not performed as much work as he had expected.

The next year, after the law had made her free, Sojourner's former master came to her and invited her to come back and see his family. When she reached her master's house, she found, to her great sorrow, that her son, who was a small boy, although free according to law, had been carried off by the daughter of her former mistress to Alabama. Sojourner vowed that she would have the child back. She was told to present her case to the Grand Jury. She had never heard this word, Grand Jury, before, and thought it meant some sort of a very important individual. She went to town, therefore, when the court was in session.

"An' I stood 'round the court-house," she said, "an' when dey was comin' out I walked right up to de grandest one I could see and I says to him, 'Sir, be you a Grand Jury?'"

The Grand Jury took up her case, and, in the course of time, her child was restored to her. Then an incident took place which illustrates how easily a Negro woman forgives and forgets, as soon as her sympathies are touched.

When she found that her child had been unlawfully taken to Alabama, Sojourner prayed, in the bitterness of her despair, that the Lord would render unto her mistress double for all the trouble and sorrow she had been instrumental in bringing upon her former slave. Shortly after this Sojourner happened to be at the home of her former master when a letter was received, saying that the daughter in Alabama had been murdered by her husband, while he was in a drunken frenzy. Sojourner, feeling that her prayer had been answered, now repented having called upon the Lord to revenge her injury. Her account of what then took place has been reported as follows:

Then says I, "O Lord, I didn' mean all that. You took me up too quick." Well, I went in an' tended that poor critter all night. She was out of her mind cryin' an' callin' for her daughter an' I held her poor ol' head on my arm an' I watched her as if she had been my baby, an' I watched by her an' took care of her an' she died in my arms, poor thing.

A few years after this Sojourner felt called of God to labour for the salvation of souls, and the good of her own people. It was at this time she decided to change her name. She has described how this was done:

My name was Isabella; but when I lef' the house of bondage I lef' everythin' behind. Wan't goin' to keep nothin' of Egypt on me. An' so I went to the Lord an' asked him to give me a new name. An the Lord gave me Sojourner, because I was to travel up an' down the land, showin' the people their sins an' bein' a sign unto 'em. Afterward I told the Lord I wanted 'nother name, cause everybody else had two names, an' the Lord gave me Truth, because I was to declare the truth to the people.

Sojourner could neither read nor write, but she soon became widely known in the North, and was a prominent figure at anti-slavery meetings. One day she was speaking at one of these meetings when a man interrupted her and said: "Old woman, do you think that your talk about slavery does any good? Do you suppose that people care about what you say? Why, I don't care any more for your talk than I do for the bite of a flea."

"Perhaps not," she answered, "but, the Lord willin', an' I will keep you scratchin'."

About this time an insect known as the weevil appeared in different parts of the country and destroyed a large part of the wheat crop. Sojourner, taking this for her text, made the following point on the Constitution:

Children, I talks to God, an' God talks to me. Dis mornin' I was walkin' out, an' I got ober de fence into de field. I saw de wheat a-holdin' up its head, lookin' very big. I goes up an' takes hold ob it. You believe it, dare was no wheat dare? I says, 'God (speaking the name reverently), 'what is de matter wid dis wheat?' an he says to me, 'Sojourner, dare is a little weasel in it.' Now I hears talkin' about de Constitution, an' de rights ob man. I comes up an' I takes hole ob dis Constitution. It looks mighty big, an' I feels for my rights, but dar ain't any dar. Den I says, 'God, what ails dis Constitution?' He says to me, 'Sojourner, dar is a little weasel in it.'

On another occasion Parker Pillsbury, in speaking at an abolition meeting one Sunday afternoon, criticised the attitude of churches in regard to slavery. Just then a furious thunderstorm came up, and a young Methodist minister arose and interrupted the speaker, saying, among other things, that he was fearful God's judgment was about to fall on him for daring to sit and hear such blasphemy; he said it almost made his hair rise in terror.

"Chile," said Sojourner in a voice that was heard above the rain and thunder, "don't be skeered; you're not goin' to be hurt. I don' spect God ever hearn tell on you."

On another occasion Sojourner Truth was at a woman's rights convention, in which the ministers of the town turned out and took issue against the ladies. Public sentiment was turned against them, and for a time the women sat in despair. Suddenly Sojourner voluntarily stepped to the front and made a speech which won a complete victory for the women. This speech contains so much unlettered eloquence that it seems to me worth repeating here. As reported, this is what she said:

"Well, chil'en, what's all dis here talkin' about? Dat man ober dar say dat womens needs to be helped into carriages, and lifted ober ditches, an' to have de bes' place everywhar. Nobody eber helped me into carriages, or ober mud puddles, or gives me any bes' place (and raising herself to her full height and her voice to a pitch like rolling thunder, she asked), an' ar'n't I a woman? Look at me! Look at my arm!" And she bared her right arm to the shoulder, showing her tremendous muscular power. "I have plowed, an' planted, an' gathered into barns, an' no man could head me — an' ar'n't I a woman? I could work as much an' eat as much as a man, when I could git it, an' bear de lash as well — an' ar'n't I a woman? I have borne thirteen children, an' seen 'em mos' all sold off into slavery, an' when I cried out with a mother's grief, none but Jesus heard, an' ar'n't I a woman? Den dey talks 'bout dis ting in de head; what dis dey call it?" ("Intellect," whispered some one near.) "Dat's it, honey. What's dat got to do with woman's rights or niggers' rights? If my cup won't hold but a pint an' yourn holds a quart would n't ye be mean not to let me have my little half-measure full?" Thereupon she pointed her finger and directed a keen glance at the minister who had made the argument.

"Den dat little man in black dar, he say woman can't have as much rights as man, cause Christ wa'n' a woman. Whar did your Christ come from? From God and a woman. Man had nothing to do with him. If de fust woman God ever made could turn the world upside down, all 'lone, dese togedder ought to be able to turn it back an' git it right side up agin, an' now dey is askin' to do it, de men better let 'em."

Wendell Phillips said that he never knew but one human being who had the power to bear down a whole audience by a few simple words, and that person was Sojourner Truth. As a case in point, he relates how once, at a public meeting in Boston, Frederick Douglass was one of the chief speakers. Douglass described the wrongs of the Negro, and, as he proceeded, grew more and more excited until he ended by saying that there was no hope of justice from the whites, no possible hope except in their own right arms. It must come to blood. They must fight for themselves or it would never be done.

Sitting on the very front seat, facing the platform, was Sojourner Truth and, in the hush of deep feeling, as Douglass sat down, she rose and uttered these words:

"Frederick, is God dead?"

The effect was electrical, and thrilled through the house, changing, as by a flash, the whole feeling of the audience.

Mr. Story, the sculptor, has attempted to preserve the spirit of Sojourner Truth and the impression she made upon him, in his statue called the Lybian Sybil. After a sojourn of more than one hundred years on this earth, during which she always proclaimed the truth, Sojourner Truth passed to her reward November 26, 1883.

I have ventured to describe the doings and sayings of this remarkable woman at some length, because the pithy sayings she uttered, and the sympathy with suffering that she showed, are typical of a large class of Negro slave women.

Another woman, of a very different type, who distinguished herself during slavery days, was Frances Ellen Watkins. Born in Baltimore, Maryland, in 1825, she went to school to her uncle, Reverend William Watkins, who taught a school in Baltimore for freed coloured children. About 1851 she moved to Ohio and began teaching. A little later she taught at Little York, Pennsylvania. It was here that she became acquainted with the workings of the Underground Railway.

A law had been enacted in Maryland preventing free people of colour from entering that state, on pain of being imprisoned and sold into slavery. A free coloured man, however, who had unwittingly violated this statute, had been sold into Georgia, but had escaped by secreting himself behind a wheel-house of a northbound steamship. Before he reached freedom, however, he was discovered and sent back to slavery. This incident, which came directly under her notice, made a great impression upon the young coloured school-teacher, and it was this that finally determined her to devote her life to the cause of anti-slavery.

After she came to Philadelphia, Miss Watkins made her home at the station of the Underground Railway. Here she had abundant opportunity to see the passengers and hear their tales of hardship and suffering. She began her career as a public lecturer in 1854, and, for a year and a half, spoke in the Eastern states. In 1856 she visited Canada and lectured in Toronto. From 1856 to 1859 her work was mainly in Pennsylvania, New Jersey, New York and Ohio.

Not only did she give of her time, but of her limited means to the cause of freedom. William Still, in his Underground Railway, gives a number of instances where she gave him financial aid. In one case she wrote: "Yesterday I sent you thirty dollars; my offering is not very large, but if you need more send me word."

In the fall of 1860 she was married in the city of Cincinnati to Fenton Harper. She gave up her public work until the death of her husband, May 23, 1864. She had by this time become known as an anti-slavery writer in both prose and poetry. After the close of the War she came South, and began to work for the uplifting of her people in the states of South Carolina, Georgia, Alabama and Mississippi.

To the present generation of coloured people

Mrs. Harper is known principally as a writer. She has published a number of books of poetry. Her best known prose work is "Iola Leroy, or the Shadows Uplifted." On returning from her work in the South she became a lecturer and writer on temperance, and for some time had charge of the W. C. T. U. among the coloured people. She now makes her home in Philadelphia.

Another somewhat remarkable character is Amanda Smith, the evangelist. She was born a slave at Long Green, Maryland, January 23, 1837. Her father wanted to free himself and his family, so he worked at night, making brooms and husk mats, and burning lime. During harvest time he would work in the grain fields until one and two o'clock in the morning. In this way he first purchased himself and then set himself to the task of buying his wife and five children. After he had succeeded in this, he moved his family to Pennsylvania.

Amanda taught herself to read by cutting out large letters from the newspapers, laying them on the window sill, and getting her mother to make them into words. When she was eight years old, she attended a private school for six weeks. Five miles from her home there was a white school, to which the few coloured children in the neighbourhood were allowed to go. They were, however, placed at a disadvantage, for all the white children had their full lessons first and then, if any time was left, the coloured children had a chance. It often happened, therefore, that after Amanda had walked the five miles through the deep snow she would get but one lesson, and that would be while the white children were taking down their dinner pails and putting on their wraps. In this way she received three months' schooling, and this was the end of her education in the schoolroom.

Amanda joined the Methodist Episcopal Church, and it was in the great camp-meetings of this church in the seventies, that her power as an evangelist was first manifested. In a little book, "Amanda Smith's Own Story," an extended sketch of her evangelistic labours are given. In this work she laboured not only in this country, but also in India, in Africa, in England and Scotland. Bishop J. M. Thoburn, of the Methodist Episcopal Church, gives the following concerning her:

During the summer of 1876, while attending a camp-meeting at Epworth Heights, near Cincinnati, my attention was drawn to a coloured lady dressed in a very plain garb (which reminded me somewhat of that worn by the Friends in former days), who was engaged in expounding a Bible lesson to a small audience.

I was told that the speaker was Mrs. Amanda Smith, and that she was a woman of remarkable gifts, who had been greatly blessed in various parts of the country.

The meetings of the day had not been very successful, and a spirit of depression rested upon many of the leaders. A heavy rain had fallen and we were kneeling somewhat uncomfortably in the straw which surrounded the preacher's stand. A number had prayed and I myself was sharing the general feeling of depression, when I was suddenly startled by the voice of song. I lifted my head, and at a short distance, probably not more than two yards from me, I saw the coloured sister of the morning kneeling in an upright position, with her hands spread out and her face aglow.

She had suddenly broken out with a triumphant song, and while I was startled by the change in the order of the meeting, I was at once absorbed with interest in the song and the singer. Something like a hallowed glow seemed to rest upon the dark face before me, and I felt in a second that she was possessed of a rare degree of spiritual power.

That invisible something that we are accustomed to call power, and which is not possessed by any Christian believer except as one of the fruits of the indwelling spirit of God, was hers in a marked degree. From that time onward I regarded her as a gifted worker in the Lord's vineyard, but I had still to learn that the endowment of the spirit had given her more than the one gift of spiritual power.

A few years after my return to India, in 1876, I was delighted to hear that this chosen and approved worker of the Master had decided to visit this country. She arrived in 1879, and after a short stay in Bombay, came over to the eastern side of the empire, and assisted us for some time in Calcutta. She also returned two years later, and again rendered us valuable assistance. The novelty of a coloured woman from America, who had in her childhood been a slave, appearing before an audience in Calcutta, was sufficient to attract attention, but this alone would not account for the popularity which she enjoyed throughout her whole stay in our city.

She was fiercely attacked by the narrow-minded persons in our daily papers and elsewhere, but opposition only seemed to add to her power. During the seventeen years that I have lived in Calcutta, I have known many famous strangers to visit the city, some of whom attracted large audiences, but I have never known anyone who could draw and hold so large an audience as Mrs. Smith.

She assisted me both in the church and in open-air meetings, and never failed to display the peculiar tact for which she is remarkable. I shall never forget one meeting which we were holding in the open square, in the very heart of the city. It was at a time of no little excitement, and some Christian preachers had been roughly handled in the same square a few evenings before. I had just spoken myself when I noticed a great crowd of men and boys, who had succeeded in breaking up a missionary's audience on the other side of the square, rushing toward us with loud cries and threatening gestures.

If left to myself I should have tried to gain the box on which the speakers stood, in order to command the crowd, but at the critical moment our good Sister Smith knelt on the grass and began to pray. As the crowd rushed up to the spot, and saw her with her beaming face upturned to the evening sky, pouring out her soul in prayer, they became perfectly still, and stood as if transfixed to the spot! Not even a whisper disturbed the solemn silence and, when she had finished, we had as orderly a meeting as if we had been within the four walls of a church.

During Mrs. Smith's stay in Calcutta, she had opportunities for seeing a good deal of the native community. Here, again, I was struck with her extraordinary power of discernment. We have in Calcutta a class of reformed Hindoos called Brahmos. They are, as a class, a very worthy body of men, and at that time were led by the distinguished Keshub Chunder Sen.

Every distinguished visitor who comes to Calcutta is sure to seek the acquaintance of some of these Brahmos, and to study, more or less, the reformed system which they profess and teach. I have often wondered that so few, even of our ablest visitors, seem able to comprehend the real character either of the men or of their new system. Mrs. Smith very quickly found access to some of them, and beyond any other stranger whom I have ever known to visit Calcutta, she formed a wonderfully accurate estimate of the character, both of the men and their religious teaching.

She saw almost at a glance all that was strange and all that was weak in the men and their system. This penetrating power of discernment which she possesses in so large a degree impressed me more and more the longer I knew her. Profound scholars and religious teachers of philosophical bent seemed positively inferior to her in the task of discovering the practical value of men and systems which had attracted the attention of the world!

I have already spoken of her clearness of perception and power of stating the undimmed truth of the Gospel of Christ. Through association with her, I learned many valuable lessons from her lips, and once before an American audience, when Dr. W. F. Warren was exhorting young preachers to be willing to learn from their own hearers, even though many of the hearers might be comparatively illiterate, I ventured to second this exhortation by telling the audience that I had learned more that had been of actual value to me as a preacher of Christian truth from Amanda Smith than from any other one person I had ever met.

Amanda Smith has now largely given up her evangelistic labours and conducts the Amanda Smith Orphans' Home for Coloured Children, at Harvey, a suburb of Chicago, Illinois.

One of the ablest and best known women lecturers before the public at the present time is Mary Church Terrell. Her opportunities and training have been exceptional. She was born in Tennessee, a daughter of well-to-do parents, graduated with honours from Oberlin College in 1884, and finally spent two years in European study and travel. She was for a time a teacher of ancient and modern languages at Wilberforce University, and later, in the high school for coloured children in Washington, District of Columbia. At the International Congress of Women in Berlin, Germany, in 1904, it is said that Mrs. Terrell had the unique distinction of delivering one speech in excellent German and another in equally good French. Mrs. Terrell has been prominent in the work of the National Association of Coloured Women, of which she several times has been president.

Another woman who has gained some public distinction is Mrs. Lucy Thurman, of Jackson, Michigan, who succeeded Mrs. Francis E. W. Harper in charge of the work of the W. C. T. U. among the coloured people.

The most important work done by coloured women for coloured women has been through the coloured women's club movement. As early as 1890 there were coloured women's clubs in nearly every large city where there was any considerable coloured population. The best known of these are, perhaps, the Phillis Wheatley Club, of New Orleans, of which Mrs. Sylvania Williams is the head, and the Woman's Era Club, of Boston, which was founded by Mrs. Josephine St. Pierre Ruffin. In addition to these clubs there were in existence at the date of which I have mentioned, the Ellen Watkins Harper Club, of Jefferson City, Missouri; the Loyal Union Club, of Brooklyn, New York; the Ida B. Wells Club, of Chicago, Illinois; the Sojourner Truth Club, of Providence, Rhode Island; and, quite as influential as any other, the Woman's League, of Washington, District of Columbia.

The first National Conference of Coloured Women was held in Boston in the latter part of July, in 1895. The person more responsible than any one else for the first national meeting of coloured women was Mrs. Josephine St. Pierre Ruffin, the founder and first president of the Woman's Era Club, of Boston.

Mrs. Ruffin was born in Boston, in 1844. Her father, John St. Pierre, had the blood of three races in his veins — namely, French, Indian, and African. Her mother was an English woman, a native of Cornwall, England. As a girl Mrs. Ruffin attended the public schools of Salem, Massachusetts, and later studied at a private school in New York. While still a girl in school she married George Ruffin, of Richmond, Virginia. I have already referred, in an earlier chapter, to the position which Mr. Ruffin made for himself in Massachusetts.

Mrs. Ruffin early became interested in the advancement and welfare of coloured women. During the period of the "Kansas Exodus," in 1879, she called together the women of her neighbourhood, in the West End of Boston, and organised the Kansas Relief Association. In the work that this association undertook Mrs. Ruffin was greatly aided by the counsel of William Lloyd Garrison, and other prominent anti-slavery people. A large amount of clothing, old and new, and a considerable sum of money were collected and forwarded to the Kansas refugees.

The success of this work of philanthropy lead to Mrs. Ruffin's connection with the Associated Charities which, at that time, was just being organised in Boston. For the next eleven years she acted as a local visitor for this organisation. She also became a member of the Country Week Society, devoting herself to the difficult task of finding places in the country for coloured children.

The work that Mrs. Ruffin did in this, and other directions, brought her in contact with many of the best and most cultivated women of New England. She became a member of the Massachusetts Moral Education Association, and of the School Suffrage Association, of Massachusetts; was for a number of years one of the members of the executive board of both these organisations. Later she became prominent in the Woman's Educational and Industrial Union, of Boston.

The work Mrs. Ruffin did in these various organisations did not cause her to lose interest in the work she had begun to do for the members of her own race. On the contrary, the experience she obtained served to make her more useful in all that coloured women were at this time attempting to do for themselves.

The Woman's Era Club, of which, as I have said, Mrs. Ruffin was founder, became one of the most influential of coloured women's clubs in America. In the interest of this organisation a paper, *The Woman's Era*, was started, and Mrs. Ruffin was for years its editor. It was as editor of this paper that she first gained a national reputation. It was through this paper that, in 1894, she advocated the holding of a National Conference of Women's Clubs.

The immediate cause of holding this conference,

however, was the publication, by an editor in Missouri, of an open letter to Mrs. Florence Belgarnie, of England, who had manifested interest in the American Negro. In this letter the editor declared that the coloured women of America had no sense of virtue and were altogether without character. As a result of the agitation begun at this time, about one hundred women representing about twenty-five clubs, from ten different states, gathered in Boston, July 29, 1895. As a result of this meeting it was determined to establish a permanent organisation. The first officers of the association were: Mrs. Booker T. Washington, of Tuskegee, Alabama; Mrs. U. A. Ridley, of Brookline, Massachusetts; secretary, Mrs. Libbie C. Anthony, of Jefferson City, Missouri; treasurer, and Mrs. Victoria E. Matthews, of New York, chairman of the executive committee.

For the organisation of the National Federation of Coloured Women's Clubs, Mrs. Ruffin was largely responsible. Through the paper, of which she was editor, she has exercised influence on the coloured women throughout the United States. Under her influence the Woman's Era Club had a large part in enlarging what is known as Mrs. Sharpe's Home School in Liberia, Africa. When the American Mt. Coffee School Association was formed in January, 1903, to aid this work, Edward Everett Hale was elected president and Mrs. Ruffin vice-president. She is still active in all good work for the coloured women of her race, not only in New England but throughout the United States.

Since the organisation of the National Federation of Coloured Clubs the number of these clubs has greatly multiplied. In many cases they have been organised into State Federations.

As an illustration of the sort of work that these women's clubs do in some of the Southern states, I may cite the case of the Alabama Federation, of which I happen to know more than of some of the other organisations. A few years ago this Alabama Federation of Coloured Women's Clubs established a reformatory for boys which is located at Mt. Meigs, Alabama. During the year 1908, over forty boys were received at this reformatory from the police court of Montgomery and Birmingham. During that year the clubs raised something like $2,283.73, a large part of which was expended in paying for and maintaining the reformatory at Mt. Meigs, to which I have referred.

The work of the women's club at Tuskegee is typical of what many of the other clubs are doing. The work of this club is carried on through the following departments: current literature, music, prison work, open-air meetings, settlement work, and temperance work. At the present time this club is carrying on a Sunday-school in a neglected part of the Tuskegee town. Sunday meetings are held in the town jail, more than twenty mothers' meetings have been organised among the farmers' wives in the country districts surrounding the town. These mothers' meetings are maintained under the supervision of the club. A woman's rest room, for the benefit of farmers' wives, who usually come into town on Saturday in large numbers, is maintained in town. The club has recently taken care of the family of a man who has been sent to prison for life. It is paying for the education of a boy and girl of whom it has had charge since they were small children. The Tuskegee Town Reading Room, Library, and Night School, which are now carried on by the Tuskegee Institute, were first established by the Tuskegee Woman's Club.

These facts show, it seems to me, that Negro women, in spite of criticism, are going forward quietly and unostentatiously doing those things which develop that character and moral sense in the members of the race in which it is sometimes said that Negro women are lacking.

CHAPTER XIII

THE SOCIAL AND MISSION WORK OF THE NEGRO CHURCH

THE first mission of the Negro Church was started in 1824, in the Black Republic of Hàiti. This was only eight years after the first general conference of the African Methodist Church was held at Philadelphia. Bishop Allen, the first bishop of the African Methodist Church, was associated about this time with Benjamin Lundy, the Quaker abolitionist, in the effort to colonise free coloured people on free soil, outside the limits of the United States, in Mexico, Canada, and Haiti. The Black Republic, where a few years before Negroes had established an independent government, seemed a proper place to establish a branch of the Independent African Church. Thus it came about that in close connection with the colony started by Benjamin Lundy, the mission work of the African Methodist Church was begun.

This Church has, in the meantime, extended its influence over several of the other West India Islands, chiefly in those regions which have not yet been reached to any extent by missions of the other

Protestant churches. The society reports fifteen missionaries in the Windward Islands, three in Cuba, and twenty stations in British Guiana, with five thousand adherents.

About the same time that the African Methodist Church was seeking to extend its work and influence to the Republic of Haiti, Lott Cary, the noted slave preacher of Richmond, Virginia, was the head of a little local missionary association, started by the Negro Baptists of Richmond, Virginia.

The Negro churches of Richmond seem to have been stirred at that time by the general excitement aroused by the colonisation movement, and this mission society was founded by the Negro Baptists at this time in the hope of sending out a missionary from its own number to Africa.

As a matter of fact, Lott Cary, who went out to Liberia in 1821 with the second shipload of colonists from America, became the first Negro missionary to that country. The mission work of the Baptist Church owing to its congregational organisation, has never been so systematic or so vigorously carried on as that of the African Methodist Society, which has maintained a strong central organisation. It is, nevertheless, worth noting that the first Negro missionary to Africa was of that denomination and the name and memory of Lott Cary are still preserved to-day among the Negro Baptists in this country, through the work of the Lott Cary Missionary Society.

At the present time, the African Methodist Church has mission stations in Sierra Leone, Lagos, and Liberia on the west coast of Africa. It also has churches scattered all over South Africa, as far north as Rhodesia. It supports at the present time more than three hundred preachers and has 11,000 members among the native Africans.

The rapid growth in numbers and influence, during recent years, of the African Methodist Church in South Africa has been due to the withdrawal, in 1894 and 1895, of a number of the native members of the Wesleyan Methodist Church in the Transvaal, in order to form an independent Ethiopian Church. The seceders afterward united with, and became a part of, the African Methodist Episcopal Church of the United States.

Whatever may have been the occasion for this independent movement, the real causes for it seem to be similar to those which have gradually brought about a separation of the races, in their church life, in this country. While there are some disadvantages in this arrangement, and these disadvantages may be greater in South Africa than they have been in the United States, there are reasons, more potent than those which appear on the surface, that have brought this separation about and made it perhaps inevitable. It seems rather curious to Americans that the secession of a few of the native churches should have caused so much alarm in

South Africa. In this country, whenever the Negro takes it into his head to go off by himself, the white people usually give him every encouragement. It is a little hard to understand why a similar movement in South Africa should make a commotion. Perhaps, as has been asserted, the time was not ripe for such a separation. I am inclined to believe, however, that if it is wisely dealt with, the so-called Ethiopian Movement, which has been the source of so much apprehension to the British Government in South Africa, should work to the advantage of both races in Africa, just as the separate church movement has done, on the whole, it seems to me, in the United States.

In my opinion, there is no other place in which the Negro race can to better advantage begin to learn the lessons of self-direction and self-control than in the Negro Church. I say this for the reason that, in spite of the fact that other interests have from time to time found shelter there, the chief aim of the Negro Church, as of other branches of the Christian Church, has been to teach its members the funamental things of life and create in them a desire and enthusiasm for a higher and better existence here and hereafter.

More than that, the struggle of the masses of the people to support these churches and to purify their own social life, making it clean and wholesome, is itself a kind of moral discipline and one that Negroes need quite as much as other people. In fact, I doubt if there is any other way in which the lessons that Christianity is seeking everywhere to enforce, could be brought home to the masses of the Negro people in so thorough-going a way as through their own societies, controlled and directed by the members of their own race.

Aside from those missionaries sent out to Africa by the African Methodist Episcopal Church, some of the most enterprising and successful missionaries sent out to Africa by the white churches have been Negroes. Some of the most distinguished of these men, also, have been native Africans. There was, for instance, Samuel Crowther, who was rescued when a boy from a slave-ship; taken to Sierra Leone, where he was educated in Fourath Bay College, and in 1864, consecrated in Canterbury Cathedral, England, the first native Bishop of Africa. In the same year he received the title of Doctor of Divinity from the University of Oxford, and afterward became a member of the Royal Geographical Society, because of the contributions he made to the knowledge of the geography of Africa. He helped to translate the Bible into the Yoruba language, and his studies in the Nupe and Ibo languages are said to have shown unusual ability.

The story of Daniel Flickinger Wilberforce, another and a later of these African missionaries, reads like a romance. Daniel Flickinger was a companion of George Thompson in Africa. He aided in establishing the United Brethren Mission on the west coast of Africa, and made six voyages through that continent. During his first visit to Africa, in 1855, while at Good Hope Station, Mendi Mission, on the eastern banks of Sherboro Island, he employed a native to watch him at night. While this native was so employed, his wife gave birth to a child, which he named Wilberforce, and then, in honour of the visiting missionary, he added the name Daniel Flickinger.

Sixteen years later, in 1871, while his boxes were being loaded and unloaded at the American mission rooms in New York, Dr. Flickinger noticed a young Negro employed about the offices of the Missionary Association, who seemed to take an unusual interest in the names upon the boxes which he was assisting to load and unload. It turned out that the name of this boy was Daniel Flickinger Wilberforce, and the reason he was so interested in the boxes was that he had been able to decipher a portion of his own name upon them. It appeared that the boy had been sent over from Africa as a servant to one of the missionaries who was returning home ill. Dr. Flickinger became so interested in the young man that he determined to give him an education. He was sent to Dr. Flickinger's office in Dayton, Ohio, with an express-tag around his neck. Seven years later he returned to Africa as a preacher, teacher and physician. He had succeeded in completing his education in the primary school in four years, from there he went into the Dayton High School, where he graduated at the head of his class, having completed the course in three years. In the meantime he had been given instruction in medicine and in theology, so that he went out to Africa a fully equipped missionary.

While young Wilberforce was studying in the high school, Paul Laurence Dunbar, who was born in Dayton, Ohio, was a boy playing about the streets. Daniel Flickinger Wilberforce left Dayton in 1878, and returned as a missionary to his own people, where he has since lived and worked.

One of the most successful of the missionaries of Africa to-day is W. H. Sheppard, who was a student in my day at Hampton Institute, and later at the Stillman Institute at Tuscaloosa, Alabama. He went out to the Kongo in 1896 with Reverend Samuel N. Lapsley, of Alabama, as a missionary of the Southern Presbyterian Church. Mr. Lapsley chose a station to establish his mission at Luebo, far in the interior of Africa, and Mr. Sheppard remained and worked with him there until Mr. Lapsley's death. After this the work of the mission was continued, with great success by Mr. Sheppard, in association with Mr. William Morrison. Mr. Sheppard has returned to America several times since then, and spoken throughout the South in the interest of his work in Africa.   Everywhere I hear him referred to with the greatest respect, and even affection.

I have spoken thus far of the work that the Negro churches are doing for missions in Africa and elsewhere. The amount of money raised for this purpose is small compared to that which is contributed every year by the Negro churches for the purpose of education. Unfortunately, no detailed study has ever been made, so far as I know, which gives any adequate notion of the money that is actually contributed by Negroes through all the religious organisations to which they belong, to their own education.

The Negro Baptists, for example, have never published a complete list of the schools conducted by their different churches and church organisations. In the Year Book for 1907, one hundred and ten schools were reported as owned by Negro Baptists. There were 16 in Louisiana, 13 in North Carolina, 11 in Mississippi, 9 in Kentucky, 8 in Arkansas, 6 in Texas, 5 in Virginia, 5 in South Carolina, 5 in Florida, 4 in Georgia, 3 in Tennessee, 3 in West Virginia, 2 in Illinois, 2 in Oklahoma, 1 in Kansas, 1 in Missouri, 1 in Ohio, 1 in Maryland, 1 in Indiana, and 5 in Africa. Besides those mentioned in the Year Book there are, I have been told, several others in Louisiana, Virginia, and North Carolina, so that all together there are no less than 120 schools owned entirely by Negro Baptists.

During the year 1907, these schools employed 613 teachers, and gave instruction to 18,644 students. During this year also the Baptist churches reported collections for educational purposes amounting to $97,032.75. This did not include the amounts raised in Maryland, Tennessee, Texas, and Virginia, churches in those states for some reason or other making no report.

Educational work of the Negro Baptist churches was at first largely carried on under the control of the American Baptist Home Mission Society, which is managed by white people. In recent years, however, there has been a movement among Negro Baptists to do their educational work independently.

One of the first things that was done after the Negro Baptists had decided to carry on their Sunday-school and educational work independently of the white Baptist churches, was to establish a printing plant in order to publish books and pamphlets needed in Sunday-school and church work. In 1896, Reverend R. H. Boyd established the National Baptist Publishing Company. Mr. Boyd had been a preacher in Texas, and his only experience as a publisher was a brief one, in association with a white man, from which he emerged, as he says, with much valuable experience, but with a financial loss of five hundred dollars.

The new publishing business was started with almost no capital, and under the most discouraging circumstances. Nevertheless, the enterprise has prospered steadily until, at the present time, the value of the stock equipment and property of the concern is worth, according to an inventory made by Bradstreet's Agency, not less than $350,000.

The building in which the company is located occupies half a block in the business portion of Nashville, Tennessee. According to a statement made at the National Negro Business League at Louisville, Kentucky, in 1909, the Company circulated, during the previous year, not less than 12,000,000 issues of the different periodicals that it published. During the same year the Company paid its employees $165,000 for labour.

Notwithstanding that many Negro Baptists have become independent, the Baptist Home Mission Society (white) is every year receiving an increasingly large number of contributions for the schools they maintain from the Negro themselves. Of the twenty-three schools under the direction of this society, for instance, fourteen are owned by Negroes themselves. The report of the educational work of the society for the year 1907-08 shows that the receipts for that year from all sources, including the fees paid by students, were $269,795.78. Of this amount $10,782.36 was contributed by white churches and individuals, while $27,724.42 was contributed by Negro churches and individuals.

The educational work of the African Methodist

Episcopal Church began in 1844, with the purchase of 120 acres of land in Ohio for the Union
Seminary, which was opened in 1847. In 1856,
the A. M. E. Church united with the Methodist
Episcopal Church (North) in establishing Wilberforce University. In 1863, this University became
the sole property of the A. M. E. Church. At the
present time this denomination maintains twenty
schools and colleges, one or more in each of the
Southern states, two in Africa, and one in the West
Indies. These schools and colleges employ 202
teachers and have something like 5,700 pupils.

The third Sunday in September is set aside in
all of the A. M. E. churches as Educational Day.
On this day a general collection is taken in all the
churches for educational purposes. The amount
collected in 1907 was $51,000. In addition to this,
every member of the church is taxed eight cents per
year for the general educational fund. I have not
been able to learn the amount of money collected
in this way, but the quadrennial reports show that
these schools collect from all sources, including the
fees paid by students, something like $150,000 a
year.

The A. M. E. Zion Church carries on educational
work in twelve institutions, four of which are colleges,
one a theological seminary and seven secondary
schools. These schools have 150 teachers and more
than 3,000 pupils. During the year 1907, these

schools raised from all sources something over $100,000.

In 1906 I had an opportunity to be present and take part in the twenty-fifth anniversary exercises of Livingstone College at Salisbury, North Carolina. This college was established and has been maintained by the A. M. E. Zion Church. The leading spirits in establishing it were the present Senior Bishop, Right Reverend J. W. Hood, and the late Dr. Joseph C. Price, who was its first president, and did the most to put the college on its feet and make it known to the world.

Joseph Price was a remarkable man. He was, in the first place, like Lott Cary, Alexander Crummell, and Henry Highland Garnet, a man of unmixed African blood. He was a remarkable orator, and when only twenty-seven years of age, he was sent as a delegate of the A. M. E. Zion Church to the Ecumenical Council in London. While he was there, through the eloquence with which he described the condition of education in the South, he succeeded in raising ten thousand dollars, which was used in purchasing the grounds upon which Livingstone College now stands, and in erecting some of the buildings.

During the days that the anniversary celebration lasted, something like $8,000 in cash and pledges was secured for the benefit of the college. I was interested to see the way in which this money was secured. When the hour for taking the subscriptions arrived, you would see, perhaps, a coloured bishop rise and announce his subscription for something like fifty dollars. Then a coloured woman would stand up and announce that she would give ten dollars. Then others would announce more modest sums. Altogether the amounts of the different contributions ranged, as I remember, from twenty-five cents to a thousand dollars. The man who gave a thousand dollars would not permit his name to be known, but it is now an open secret that this generous gift was contributed by Dr. W. H. Goler, the Negro president of the college.

The Coloured Methodist Church, which was organised among the coloured people who, after the Civil War, still clung to the Southern branch of the Methodist Church (South), has done, according to the number of its members, quite as much as any other coloured religious organisation for the education of the Negro race. This denomination controls six educational institutions, among them Lane College, at Jackson, Tennessee, founded by Bishop Isaac Lane, and the Mississippi Theological and Industrial College, founded by Bishop Elias Cottrell, of Holly Springs, Mississippi.

The interesting thing about Bishop Cottrell's school is that it was started as a result of the veto by Governor Vardaman of the appropriation for the State Normal School, which was formerly located at Holly Springs. When that school went out of existence, as a result of this action of the Governor, the Negroes of Mississippi, under Bishop Cottrell's leadership, determined that they would build a school of their own to replace it. They succeeded in raising in the short period of three years something like $65,000, and erected two handsome modern buildings. At the last meeting of the National Negro Business League in Louisville, Kentucky, Bishop Cottrell said that within the last eight years, the Coloured Methodist Church had raised, within the State of Mississippi alone, over $100,000, of which all but $35,000 had been collected in small contributions from the Negro people themselves.

The African Union Methodist Protestant Church, which has less than 6,000 members, has been able, in spite of its small membership, to support three schools — one at Baltimore, Maryland, one at Franklin, Pennsylvania, and a third at Holland, Virginia.

Besides the contribution of Negroes to Negro education, made through their own Negro organisations, the coloured people have contributed largely to education through the Freedmen's Aid Society of the Methodist Episcopal Church (North); the Freedmen's Board of the American Missionary Association, the Church Institute for Negroes of the Episcopal Church, and through the Catholic Church.

No record has been published of the amount of money contributed by Negroes to the support of schools conducted by the Catholic Church, but the total amount must have been considerable. For instance, in 1829, when the St. Francis Academy was founded in Baltimore by Negro sisters of the Catholic Church in the West Indies, these sisters gave all that they had in the way of furniture and real estate to this institution. Nancy Addison left this institution $15,000 and a Haitian, by the name of Louis Bode, left the institution $30,000. The contributions of Colonel John McKee, of Philadelphia, and Mr. Thomy Lafon, of New Orleans, made to the Catholic schools and benevolent institutions, amounted, at a low estimate, to something like a million dollars.

The contributions, made through the churches, do not include those that are constantly made by coloured people to local and independent institutions, which are not connected with any church organisation. For example, Tuskegee Institute receives annually a number of small contributions from the coloured people of the country, and from its former students. The largest sum received in this way was the legacy of Mrs. Mary E. Shaw, a coloured woman of New York City, which amounted to $38,000.

Among the other notable contributions which have been made from time to time to Negro educa-

tion by Negro philanthropists, I might mention
that of a coloured man by the name of George
Washington, a former slave, of Jerseyville, Illinois,
who is said to have left $15,000 to Negro education.
Mr. Thomy Lafon gave Straight University, of
New Orleans, $6,000.   It is known that Bishop D.
A. Payne, the founder of Wilberforce, gave at different times and in different amounts, several thousand
dollars to that institution.   Mr. Wheeling Gant
gave $5,000 to Wilberforce.   Bishop J. B. Camp-
bell gave $1,000, Bishop and Mrs. J. A. Shorter
gave $2,000, and Henry and Sarah Gordon gave
$2,100 toward the endowment of this same school.

Recently Mr. French Gray gave land, said to be
valued at $2,000, to the Dooley Normal and Indus-
trial School in Alabama.   Bishop Isaac Lane has
given at various times considerable more than a
thousand dollars to the college bearing his name
at Jackson, Tennessee.   Fisk University received
from Mrs. Lucinda Bedford, of Nashville, Tennessee, $1,000, and John and James Barrows, of the
same city, gave $500 to the same institution.   Joshua
Park gave $6,000 to the State College of Delaware,
George, Agnes and Molly Walker gave $1,000 to
Straight University, New Orleans.

After the Kentucky Legislature, in 1904, passed
a law which made it illegal for white and black
students to attend the same school, Berea College,
which had been conducted as a mixed school for

both races since 1865, was closed to Negroes. After the case had been finally settled in the highest courts, a campaign of education was started under the direction of Reverend James Bond, the coloured trustee of the college, to raise money to found a school for coloured students to take its place. In about twelve months, $50,000 was raised in the state of Kentucky. Of this sum, $20,000 was pledged by the coloured people of Kentucky.

Considering the small amount of money that Negroes have thus far accumulated, and the hard struggle that they have had to get it, the facts that I have mentioned indicate that Negroes appreciate the value of education for their race and are willing to contribute generously to its support.*

While the chief work of the Negro church has been and still is among the people of the small towns and the country districts, where the bulk of the Negro population is located, in recent years a serious effort has been made by some of the larger city churches to deal with some of the comparatively new problems of the city Negro. I have already mentioned the work of the First Congregational Church, under H. H. Proctor, in Atlanta, and of the Berean Presbyterian Church, of Philadelphia. In addition to the Berean Building and Loan Asso-

* "Self-Help in Negro Education," Publications of Committee of Twelve, R. R. Wright, Jr.

ciation, to which I have referred, the Church started, in 1884, a free kindergarten, which it still maintains. Then in 1889 the Berean Manual Training and Industrial School was started, which gives instruction in carpentry, upholstering, millinery, practical electricity, plain sewing and dressmaking, stenography, cooking, waiting and tailoring. Two years before this, in 1897, a bureau of mutual help was established in order to find employment, particularly in domestic service, for the large numbers of coloured people who are constantly coming to Philadelphia from the South.

Another organisation, the Berean Trades Association, seeks to aid Negro tradesmen and other skilled workmen to find employment in the trades. In addition to these the church has charge of the Berean Seaside Home, a seaside resort for respectable coloured persons, near Asbury Park, New Jersey. In 1900 the Berean Educational Conference was started, and in 1904 there was added to this the Berean Seaside Conference. All of these institutions, though started and maintained by this Church, are each independent of the other, and are patronised by thousands of persons who are neither members of the congregation of the Berean Church, nor of the Presbyterian denomination.

In addition to these institutional churches there have grown up in connection with the large city churches, literary societies and organisations for mutual improvement, which meet Sunday afternoon to read papers or discuss general topics. These societies help to furnish wholesome recreation for young men and women, and sometimes they do something more than this. For example, there was organised in Savannah, Georgia, in 1905, what was known as the Men's Sunday Club. At that time there was very little effort made to close the saloons in Savannah on Sunday; a law against minors entering these places was not enforced, at least with respect to the coloured youths. Thousands of coloured people spent their Sundays at a park in the suburbs of the city, which had been erected for the special use of the coloured people, and which was infested by a number of disreputable characters who made it a dangerous place for young men and girls to go.

The Young Men's Sunday Club, which was composed of some of the better educated and more serious young men of the city, determined to do something to counteract the evil influences of this resort. By means of this club hundreds of young men and women were kept off the streets, and were induced to come to the meetings of this society, where they heard interesting discussions, not merely of literary subjects, but topics of vital interest to the coloured people of the city. One of the things that the club attempted to do was to inculcate a respect for law and order, and make the coloured people realise the fact that it was especially important for them, who so frequently needed the protection of the law, to see to it that they themselves obeyed it.

One of the chief temptations to the coloured young men and women of Savannah were dance halls, run in connection with saloons in those sections of the city in which the majority of the coloured people lived. The Men's Club was instrumental in having these dance halls abolished by law. After the law had been passed a committee of the club was appointed to see that it was enforced.

After a time there was organised, in connection with the Men's Club, a woman's auxiliary, which, in turn, organised a number of mothers' clubs in various sections of the city.

In these mothers' meetings an effort was made not only to interest mothers in keeping their children off the streets, and away from the association of criminals, but also to teach the proper care of children and inculcate some of the simple rules of the hygiene of the home.

Another organisation which is now doing an important and valuable work for Negroes is the coloured Y. M. C. A. Under another name the work of this organisation has been carried on since before the Civil War, although no definite organisation was formed until 1879, when the first international secretary to take charge of the work among the coloured people was appointed.

From 1879 to 1890 this work was carried on under the direction of Henry E. Brown. In 1890, the first coloured international secretary, Mr. W. A. Hunton, was appointed to do this work. In 1898 another secretary, Dr. J. E. Moorland, was appointed to assist Mr. Hunton.

These two men now have under their supervision one hundred and ten associations. Seventy-three of these are student associations, and thirty-seven of them are city associations. Sixteen of these associations employ general secretaries and twelve of them conduct night schools. The total membership in these associations now exceeds 9,000 men. Twelve associations own real estate to the value of $80,000.

One of the most interesting of these associations is that which was formed at Buxton, Iowa. This town is made up almost wholly of Negro miners. Of the population of five thousand, 93 per cent. are black and 7 per cent. white. It has no regular city government, since all the property in the town belongs to the Consolidated Coal Company, in which these men are employed.

This mining company is therefore enabled to exercise a benevolent despotism, so far as maintaining order in the community is concerned, and no disreputable characters are allowed to remain there. In the company's plan of government the Y. M. C. A., which was conducted for some time, and very successfully, under the direction of Lewis E. Johnson, a young coloured man, who is now secretary of the Y. M. C. A. in Washington, District of Columbia, has played an important part.

The mining company at Buxton erected a $20,000 Y. M. C. A. building, which was provided with a library, and served as a social centre for the 1,500 coloured employees of the company, which make up the bulk of the population. By furnishing innocent recreation for the miners during the time that they were idle, by encouraging them to read, save their money, and by giving them religious instruction, it was found possible to maintain something approaching perfect order in this little town, without the necessity of banishing any large number of the employees of the company for misbehaviour.

Perhaps the greatest achievement, in a material way, of the coloured Y. M. C. A., has been the undertaking to erect a $100,000 building in Washington, District of Columbia. Washington has the largest coloured population of any city in the United States, and in this city the problems of city life present themselves in a most difficult form. It is, therefore, peculiarly appropriate that in the nation's capital, where so large a number of coloured people live, the work of the Y. M. C. A. should be conducted on a scale adequate to the need.

In the fall of 1906 Mr. John D. Rockefeller offered to give $25,000 toward the erection of a permanent home for the coloured Y. M. C. A. in Washington, provided a similar sum could be collected from among the coloured people of the city. From April 7 to May 7, 1908, a campaign was carried on among the coloured residents of Washington, and $30,535 in subscriptions was secured. Since that time this amount has considerably increased, and it is hoped eventually to raise enough money to insure the erection of a $100,000 building, for which plans have already been drawn.

Aside from the direct influence which the coloured Young Men's Christian Association has been able to exert upon its members, these local organisations have frequently exercised an important indirect influence for good in the community. For example, I learned, during the meeting of the National Negro Business League, in Louisville, in August, 1909, that the Young Men's Christian Association had been largely instrumental in securing, for the coloured people of Louisville, the magnificent library they now possess, erected in 1908 by the generosity of Mr. Andrew Carnegie. This library, which is a regular branch of the Louisville Public Library, is probably the most complete and best equipped library for coloured people in the South. The total cost, including the books, was something like $42,000. Thomas F. Blue, who was formerly Secretary of the Coloured Young Men's Christian Association, is the librarian in charge.

The work of the coloured Y. M. C. A. began in the colleges. It is gradually reaching out, however, to the larger cities and, to some extent, into the smaller towns. As this work extends steadily it is getting a larger hold upon the masses of the coloured people, and is forming a nucleus for work of social service in the cities, the places where that work is most needed. In this way the Y. M. C. A. is supplementing the mission and social work of the Negro Church.

CHAPTER XIV

LAW AND ORDER AND THE NEGRO

NOT infrequently I hear it said that, since the overthrow of the Reconstruction governments, and particularly since the passage of the disenfranchisement laws, the Negro has lost his place in Southern politics. This depends, to some extent, on what one means by politics. Negroes still vote in all the Southern states, though the number of Negro voters has been very greatly curtailed in some states, and particularly in those which suffered most from the vices and mismanagement of the Reconstruction governments. Negroes still hold offices under the Federal Government, and the proportion of Negroes in the civil service of the United States is constantly increasing.

Aside from the number of votes cast, however, and the number of offices which these votes controlled, Negroes probably exercise a greater influence on public order and public policy in the Southern states to-day than they ever did before. Directly and indirectly, through their churches and through their schools; through their doctors of medicine, lawyers, and business men; through their lodges, banks, corporations, clubs, law and order leagues, etc., Negroes are exercising a very large and a very positive influence upon the lives of the communities in which they live. As an illustration of what I mean I want to relate, as briefly as I am able, the story of the coloured Law and Order League, of Baltimore, Maryland.

In the city of Baltimore there is one of the largest and most populous coloured neighbourhoods in any city in the world. I have already referred to this neighbourhood as one which possibly contains more homes and better homes, owned and occupied by coloured people, than any other similar district in any of the large cities of the country.

This district extends along Druid Hill Avenue from Utah Street to North Avenue, and with the adjacent streets covers an area a mile and a half long, by from one-sixteenth to one-half a mile wide. The upper part of this district is given up to the better class of residences, usually three-story brick buildings, fronting directly on the street, and is comparatively free from saloons or other nuisances. A few years ago this region was inhabited by some of the best white families in the city, but as the city has grown these people have moved out into the suburbs, and the coloured people have come in to take their places.

The lower end of Druid Hill Avenue is a district of quite a different character. In a section seven blocks long and two blocks wide there were, a few years ago, before the coloured Law and Order League began its work, no less than forty-two saloons. What made this situation the more disagreeable, and even dangerous, was the fact that these saloons were located in close proximity to most of the Negro churches and Negro schools in that district. For example, there were, all in close proximity to the saloons I have mentioned, fifteen churches, twelve schools, one home for old people, one home for friendless children, the Coloured Young Men's Christian Association, and the Coloured Young Women's Christian Association. In addition to the forty-two saloons there were, in this same region, numerous dance-houses, billiard-halls, and club-rooms, where gambling was openly carried on, which frequently became places of assignation for girls and young women.

The better class of coloured people on Druid Hill Avenue had long looked with concern on the condition of things that existed in the lower part of the district. But it is not an easy thing for Negroes to take the initiative in matters of this kind. For one thing, Southern white people, as a rule, do not expect it of them, and it is true of the race as it is of an individual, that you rarely get from them anything more or better than you expect. Another thing that, perhaps, made the coloured people hesitate was the fact that a large proportion of the saloons in the district, more than half, although they were supported by Negroes, were kept by white people. Besides that, these places seemed to have had a sort of police protection, which, because it was long established, would be hard to break up. It was, perhaps, true also, that in Baltimore, as in some other cities, saloons and dens of vice which were not allowed to exist in other parts of the city, were permitted to take refuge in the districts where the masses of the coloured people lived. For this reason many people have been led to assume that respectable and industrious Negroes do not have the same objection to the presence of vice among them that other people have.

It was the Atlanta riot, I have been told, that set the better class of coloured people to thinking, and led them finally to the conviction that this reform movement must be undertaken by themselves. In October, 1906, a meeting was called by Reverend John Hurst, one of the most progressive of Baltimore's coloured ministers. At this meeting there were present W. Ashbie Hawkins, one of the leading coloured lawyers of the city; Dr. Howard E. Young, a druggist; Dr. Whitfield Winsey, a physician who had practised for thirty years among the coloured people; Dr. Thomas S. Hawkins, one of the younger coloured physicians of the city; Heber E. Wharton, vice-principal of one of the coloured public schools; Harry T. Pratt, a grade supervisor in the public schools; Dr. J. H. N. Waring, principal of the Coloured High School; Reverend E. F. Eggleston, pastor of the Grace Presbyterian Church, and Reverend J. Albert Johnson, who shortly afterward became a bishop of the A. M. E. Church.

At this first meeting it was decided to make a careful study of the actual conditions among the coloured people in the city. The committee divided themselves into sub-committees. One of these made a study of the sanitary conditions; another investigated the moral influence surrounding the schools.

One of the facts which the committee learned from a study of a map furnished by the health office, was that a narrow street, called Biddle Alley, running off from Druid Hill Avenue, was the "tuberculosis centre" of the state. This meant that in that particular region there were more deaths from tuberculosis than at any other point in the whole State of Maryland. One line from the report of the Association for the Improvement of the Condition of the Poor, indicates at least one cause for this condition. The report stated that of the two hundred and fifteen houses in Biddle Alley seventy-one had leaky roofs.

In these narrow alleys, however, tons of washing were gathered every week from the best homes in the city, to be laundered by the Negro washerwomen who lived in this district. This condition is, of course, not different from what may be found in almost any other Southern city, but it makes clear the danger that threatens the more well-to-do portion of the population, when the people, who work for them and are dependent upon them, are thus neglected and allowed to live in filthy, unwholesome, and immoral surroundings.

As the committee progressed in its investigation and sought to lay its plans to improve the conditions that they had discovered, they were made to feel their dependence upon the white people of the city and their inability to accomplish anything unless they secured their support. Liquor boards had been accustomed to ignore the protests of the coloured churches. Police boards were not inclined to consider their complaints. There seems to have been a general feeling that coloured people were either themselves so criminal, or so disposed to shield and protect criminals of their own race, that their protests against lawlessness and law-breaking were not to be taken seriously. It became absolutely necessary, therefore, that the committee should secure the support of the influential white people of the city, if they hoped to be successful in the campaign they had planned.

The next move, therefore, was to appoint a sub-committee to secure the active interest of leading white men. This committee visited the late Daniel C. Gilman, ex-president of Johns Hopkins University;

Mr. Douglas H. Wylie, at that time president of the
Chamber of Commerce; Mr. Eugene Levering, presi-
dent of the Commercial National Bank; Bishop
Paret, head of the Episcopal Church in the Balti-
more Diocese; Mr. Joseph Packard, at that time
president of the Board of School Commissioners;
Mr. Robert H. Smith, a leading lawyer; Mr. John
C. Rose, United States District Attorney, who subse-
quently acted as legal advisor for the committee;
Mr. Isaac Cate, a retired capitalist; Mr. John M.
Glenn, secretary of the Sage Foundation; Judge
Alfred S. Niles, of the Supreme Court of Maryland,
and Mr. W. Hall Harris, city postmaster.

All of these men, as soon as the matter was fairly
presented to them, showed the heartiest interest in
the plans and purposes of the committee. The
members of the committee found, however, that
there were certain questions, which continually
occurred, to which they felt compelled to find a
definite answer. For instance, one of the questions
that was frequently asked was whether or not the
saloons and dives, which they wanted suppressed,
and the conditions of immorality surrounding them,
were not due for the most part to the idleness and
laziness of the coloured people. A study of the
statistics compiled by the U. S. Census Bureau
showed, however, that a larger percentage not only of
the coloured women, but of the coloured men of
Maryland, were at work than is true of the whites.

The committee were frequently asked in regard to the home life of the coloured people. In reply to this inquiry the committee pointed out that, while the conditions in Negro homes are, in many cases, not what they should be, nevertheless the rapid increase in the ownership of homes, particularly in the Druid Hill District, indicated that there was an upward movement in this direction, and this is true not only in the cities, but in the country districts as well. The statistics of the United States Census Bureau show, for instance, that the coloured farmers of the State own 57 per cent. of the farm lands they till.

Another question frequently asked of members of the committee concerned the effect of education upon the Negro. One of the men, I was informed, who was most helpful to the committee in its work, did not believe that the education paid the state what it cost, or was of any particular value to the Negro himself. In reply to this question the committee was able to show that the Coloured High School, which has been in existence more than twenty-five years, in all its history had furnished but one inmate for a jail or penitentiary. The committee was able to show, not only that this school had not made criminals of its students, but that, on the contrary, its former students and graduates were nearly all of them engaged in occupations in which they were more useful to the community than they otherwise could have been.

In order to illustrate the value of the education of the Negro to the community at large the committee cited the history of a Negro criminal, Ike Winder by name, who had murdered a toll-gate keeper in Baltimore County. To arrest, try, imprison and execute Ike Winder cost the state $2,000 more than it cost to educate one of the graduates of the Coloured High School. Assuming that Ike Winder, if he had been graduated from the high school, would have done as well as the other graduates, the state lost, not only the money expended in convicting and executing him, but it lost the economic value of an educated citizen. The committee estimated that the average earnings of an ignorant Negro in the state of Maryland were not much more than fifteen dollars a month, while the average earnings of an educated Negro averaged about seventy-five dollars a month.

The full and frank discussion of these questions between the members of the committee and representative white citizens whom they visited showed that there was a basis for coöperation between the best whites and the best blacks of the city. The result was the formation of a joint plan of action in which both races might unite their efforts. It was decided, among other things, to appoint an advisory committee of the whites to act in conjunction with a similar committee of the coloured people.

The first thing attempted was the organisation of a larger and more representative body of coloured men to be known as the Law and Order League. The purpose of this Law and Order League was, first of all, to create a public spirit among the masses of the coloured people which could be positively opposed to all forms of vice, immorality and crime, such as is fostered by the low saloon and dive. Petitions were drawn up and sent to the Liquor Board and the Police Board for the purpose of securing a better enforcement of the law and, if possible, a suppression of some of the more notorious saloons in the district. A series of meetings were held at Grace Presbyterian Church, at which the coloured ministers, doctors, lawyers, and business men all took part. In this way a campaign was begun to give Baltimore's coloured children a real chance in life.

A law and order league was formed and a petition to the Liquor Licence Board was drawn up. A bill was drawn up for presentation to the Legislature to prevent the sale of liquor in certain sections of Baltimore.

Finally, it was decided, in order to arouse sentiment in favour of the work of the League among the white people, to take measures to present their case to the ministers of both races. Members of the committee appeared before the Association of Presbyterian, Congregational, and Reformed Church ministers, before the Ministerial Union, the Methodist Ministers' Association, before the African Methodist Episcopal Ministers' Association and the Coloured Ministerial Union. One of the ministers, who was most helpful to the committee, I was informed, was an ex-Confederate chaplain, and three or four of the other white men who took an active interest in the work were Confederate soldiers.

After the petition, drawn up by the Law and Order League, had been approved by the Advisory Committee of white men, it was presented to the Board of Liquor Licence Commissioners. Perhaps because of the source from which the petition came, it created considerable comment in the newspapers. The Baltimore *Sun*, in commenting upon it, said:

The Liquor Licence Board's action upon the petition of many good citizens for a reduction of the number of licences for saloons at certain points in northwest Baltimore is awaited with much interest by that portion of the public which is concerned in the good order of that section of the city. It is a section which has not in the past had the best reputation for freedom from acts of violence and disorder on the part of Negro roughs and bad characters, and this is believed to be connected with the fact that in a comparatively small area there are as many as forty-five saloons, of which eight are conducted by Negroes. As a considerable portion of the Negro population of the city has its habitat there, it is interesting to note that the most urgent advocates of a reduction of the number of the saloons are the Coloured Law and Order League, with many coloured ministers, teachers and lawyers. . . . The white element of the northwestern section is also concerned to have eliminated, as far as possible, the danger to peace and order created by the objectionable places in its neighbourhood. It is clearly up to the Liquor Licence Board to exercise, in the public interest, the wide discretion it possesses. When saloons are excessively numerous and a menace to good people, licences may and should be withdrawn till the quota for each neighbourhood is within reasonable limits.

An interesting feature of the struggle was the petition sent in by property-holders on McCulloh Street. McCulloh Street immediately adjoins Druid Hill on the north, and marks the boundary between the white and the coloured districts. The people in this street bitterly resented the "invasion" of Druid Hill Avenue by the blacks. Their action in coming to the support of the Law and Order League was consequently a great and welcome surprise.

One of the points brought out in the discussion before the Board of Liquor Licence Commissioners was that the presence of so large a number of saloons in this neighbourhood had depreciated the value of the property in some cases as much as 100 per cent. There was a disposition at first to charge this depreciation in value to the presence of coloured people. It was asserted that coloured people always lowered the value of property. This charge was easily disproved by showing that on the upper end of Druid Hill Avenue, in the neighbourhood into which the better class of coloured people were moving, property was actually selling at higher prices than it had reached when it was inhabited wholly by whites. One of the first coloured men to buy property in the upper Druid Hill District bought a house in a row in which prices have advanced over 60 per cent. It is said that houses in this neighbourhood rent and sell for from 20 to 50 per cent. higher than prevailed when the neighbourhood was white.

The testimony offered by the coloured people, by the men who owned the saloons and by the police, was so conflicting that the Liquor Licence Commissioners determined to make a personal inspection. They found eleven saloons openly violating the law, and determined that these eleven should not be re-licensed. The next day the Baltimore *News* gave the following account of the results of the inspection made by the Licence Commission:

The Board of Liquor Licence Commissioners deserve, and will receive, public commendation for their refusal yesterday to grant eleven saloon licences which the Law and Order League protested against. The saloons are situated on Druid Hill Avenue, Pennsylvania Avenue and adjacent streets, and have been the subject of grave complaint. President Howard and his associates could not signalise the close of their term of office better than by setting such an example to the incoming Liquor Licence Commissioners.

There is one development in connection with the hearings in these cases which calls for more than passing notice, and that is the testimony of the police as to the character of the saloons. It is a remarkable thing that with so many respectable people in a neighbourhood complaining about these saloons, the police — who should be most familiar with conditions — could find nothing wrong about them. Worse than this, in the case of saloons so plainly objectionable that the Liquor Licence Commissioners, on personal inspection, discover reason enough for refusing licences, policemen are found blandly swearing that they are decent, orderly places.

The report of the Liquor Licence Commissioners is a serious

indictment of the credibility of policemen as witnesses in hearings of this character, and suggests the need of a searching investigation to ascertain why the police are ignorant of conditions in the neighbourhood in question, which are shown to be shockingly bad.

The rejection of the application of the eleven saloons for renewal of their liquor licences was immediately followed by renewed applications under other names. But the Law and Order League had the support of all the best white and coloured people in the city, and the licences were not renewed.

I have described the work of the Baltimore Law and Order League* at some length because it illustrates the way in which the better element in both races are quietly getting together, in many parts of the South, in order to bring about an improvement in conditions which are dangerous to both races. Similar efforts in other directions and on a smaller scale are being made in many of the smaller cities in the Southern states. Even where these movements have not been wholly successful, the effort of the two races to get together in the way I have described seems to me a hopeful sign, and one on which we cannot place too much emphasis.

In regard to the political influence of the Negro, I might say, also, that close observation in every state in the South convinces me that while the Negro does not go through the form of casting the ballot

---

*A more complete account of the " Work of the Coloured Law and Order League," will be found in the publication of the Committee of Twelve, by James H. N. Waring, under that title.

in order to express his political influence to the extent that the white man does, in every Southern community there is a group of property-holding men, and often women, of high character, who do always exert political influence in the matters that concern the protection and progress of their race. Sometimes this influence is exerted individually, sometimes in groups, but it is felt nevertheless. I know any number of Negroes in the South whose influence is so strong because of their character that their wish or word expressed to a local or state official will go almost as far as the word of any white man will go. There is a kind of influence that the man exerts who is prosperous, intelligent and possesses high character, a kind of influence that is intangible and hard to define, but which no law can deprive him of.

I do not mean to suggest that the sort of personal influence I have described is in any way a substitute for the ballot, or can be expected to take its place. It ought to be clearly recognised that, in a republican form of government, if any group of people is left permanently without the franchise it is placed at a serious disadvantage. I do not object to restrictions being placed upon the use of the ballot, but if any portion of the population is prevented from taking part in the government by reason of these restrictions, they should have held out before them the incentive of securing the ballot in proportion as they grow in property-holding, intelligence, and character.

I have already referred, in another part of this book, to the town of Mound Bayou, Mississippi. This town, with the colony of which it is the centre, is one of the few places in this country in which the government is carried on entirely by Negroes. A few years ago I made a special study of this town, and I was very much impressed with a statement which I heard frequently repeated that Mound Bayou was one of the most orderly communities in the Yazoo Delta.

The records of the mayor's court show that, as Delta towns go, Mound Bayou is a remarkably quiet and sober place. There have been but two homicides in twenty years. Both of these were committed by strangers — men who drifted into the community in the early days before the local self-government and the traditions of the town had been established. One of the men killed was Benjamin T. Green, who was the partner of Isaiah T. Montgomery in the early days of the town. The man who committed this crime was afterward identified as a fugitive from justice, who was wanted for some desperate crime committed in the vicinity of Mobile. The murder was the result of a trivial altercation in regard to a box of tacks.

During the whole twenty years of the town's existence, only three persons have been sent to the Circuit Court for trial. Two of these were men convicted of theft. Since the town obtained its charter in 1898, there have been, up to February, 1907, but 163 criminal cases tried in the town. Of these, fifty were committed by strangers or by men who had come into town from the surrounding community. Twenty-eight cases were either never tried or were of so trivial a nature that no fine was imposed. Sixty-four were cases of disturbing the peace.

It is interesting to read the records of the mayor's court. They are an index to the life of the village, and reflect the changing current of public opinion in regard to the moral discipline and order of the town.

In July, 1902, the records show that fourteen persons were arrested and fined for failure to pay the street tax. Every citizen of the town is required to do three dollars' worth of work on the streets every year. Some had neglected to pay this labour tax, and allowed the streets to fall into a condition of neglect. As a result of a discussion of the matter in the town council, a number of the delinquents were arrested and compelled to pay fines amounting to $3.30, and costs amounting to $1.40 each.

Again, in 1904, a man was arrested for gambling. He had established what is known in sporting parlance as a "crap" game, and on Saturday nights a number of young men of the village were accustomed to gather at his place to gamble. He was repeatedly warned, and finally the town marshal and some of the more substantial citizens made a raid upon the place and arrested fifteen persons. The cases were dismissed after each man had paid a fine of two dollars. A year later, another man was arrested for running a "blind tiger," selling liquor without a licence. He formerly owned a store in the town, but began selling liquor, then commenced to drink, and was rapidly going to the dogs. After his place had been closed, he went out into the country and took up farming again. It is reported that he is doing well there.

During the year 1905, there were several disturbances in the town which were traced directly to the illicit liquor sellers. Men would come into town on Saturdays to do their marketing, fall to drinking, and end in a fight. Things became so bad at last that a public meeting was held in regard to the matter. As a result of this meeting, the town marshal, the mayor, and the treasurer were appointed to get evidence and secure the conviction of those who were guilty. Six persons were convicted and fined at that time. One of these, a woman, left town. Another is still under suspicion, and the rest, now on their farms, have become respectable citizens.

To my mind, the interesting fact in regard to these prosecutions is that they served not merely to correct a public abuse, but to reform the men who were prosecuted. In most cases, these men went back to the farms and became useful members of the community.

It seems to be pretty well agreed that the moral conditions of the Mound Bayou colony are better than those in other Negro settlements in the Delta. Some years ago, when the question was an "issue" in the community, a committee was appointed from each of the churches to make a house to house canvass of the colony in order to determine to what extent loose family relations existed. The report of this committee showed that there were forty families in the colony where men and women were living together without the formality of a marriage ceremony. As a result of this report, the people of the town gave notice that these forty couples would have to marry within a certain length of time or they would have to be prosecuted. Nearly all of them acted upon this suggestion; the others moved away.

"Since then," said Mr. Montgomery, the founder of the colony, in speaking about the matter, "we have had no trouble of this kind. Upon occasions, the women who are conspicuous in towns and cities, and who travel in the Delta, making the various camps on pay-days, and who more or less infest the larger plantations, have tried to get a footing here, but have never succeeded. They can get no place to stay and have to leave on the next train. This is now generally known and we have no trouble on that score."

When I asked Mr. Montgomery how he explained

the fact that they had been able to obtain such good results in the way of order and morality among the people of the colony, he said: "I attribute it to the force of public opinion. The regulations that we enforce have public sentiment behind them. The people recognise that the laws, when they are enforced, represent the sentiment of the community and are imposed for their own good. It is not so easy for them to realise that where the government is entirely in the hands of white men."

One thing that has helped to maintain order in the colony is the fact that Bolivar County prohibits the sale of liquor. More than once the liquor men have attempted to pass a law that would license the selling of liquor in the county. Some years ago a determined effort was made to repeal the prohibition law. In order to secure the vote of Mound Bayou, which seems to have the balance of power in the county on this question, a "still hunt" was made among the voters in the community. A plan was arranged by which a saloon was to be established in the town and one of the citizens made proprietor.

"This scheme came very near going through," said Mr. Montgomery. "The plan was all arranged before we heard of it. Then we called a meeting and I simply said to the people that experience in our own town had taught us that a saloon was a bad thing to have in the community. I said that if the law was passed, a coloured man might run the saloon here, but in the rest of the county they would be in the hands of white men. We would pay for maintaining them, however, and we would be the ones to suffer. We voted the law down and there has been no serious attempt to open the county to the liquor traffic since."

In a certain sense, it may be said that the Mound Bayou town and colony have been a school in self-government for its colonists. They have had an opportunity there, such as Negro people have rarely had elsewhere, to learn the real meaning of political institutions and to prepare themselves for the duties and responsibilities of citizenship.

It is interesting to note, in this connection, that this is one of the few instances in which Negroes have ever organised and maintained in any Southern state a government which has gained the entire respect of the Southern people. A writer in a recent number of the *Planter's Journal*, published in Memphis, says:

Will the Negro as a race work out his own salvation along Mound Bayou lines? Quien sabe? These have worked out for themselves a better local government than any superior people has ever done for them in freedom. But it is a generally accepted principle in political economy that any homogeneous people will in time do this. These people have their local government, but it is in consonance with the county, state, and national governments and international conventions, all in the hands of another race. Could they conduct as successfully a county government in addition to their local government and still under the state and national governments of another race? Enough Negroes of the Mound Bayou type, and guided as they were in the beginning, will be able to do so.

In view of the oft-repeated statement that Negroes have made a failure of government wherever they have tried it, either in Africa or America, how can we account, we may ask, for the success of the Mound Bayou colony?

In the first place, I should say it was due in part to the fact that the colony is small. I think it will be found that in most cases where a people have learned to govern themselves they have taken their first lessons in small communities. In fact, government in the United States has grown gradually out of the Town Meeting, where the interests of all individuals were so closely knit together that each member was able to feel and understand his responsibility to every other as he could not so readily have done elsewhere.

Another reason why this town has succeeded thus far is, I believe, because it is a pioneer work of Negroes themselves. The men who came and settled in this town have had an opportunity to grow up with it and the growth of the town has been an education to them. Besides, in this town Negroes are not merely inhabitants, but they are owners, and they feel the responsibility of ownership. They possess the land, they own the stores, the cotton-gins, the bank, and the cotton-seed oil mill.

More than any other one thing, however, the
Mound Bayou colony owes its success, I suspect,
to the vision, the enterprise, and the public spirit
of the men who have been its leaders: Isaiah T. Montgomery, the founder, and Charles Banks.   These
have clearly seen that their own permanent success
is identified with the success of the people by whom
they were surrounded, and that their greatest opportunities are in helping to build up the members
of their own race.

I have spoken, in what preceded, of what Negoes
are doing in the way of self-government in towns
like Mound Bayou, and of what Negroes are doing
through the Law and Order Leagues, as in Baltimore,
to secure the enforcement of the law in the communities in which they live.   I should like to say
a word, in conclusion, of another organisation, which
although it has not sought to exercise any direct
influence in securing good government and the
proper enforcement of the law, has done much to
bring about better conditions, in this and other
directions, among the people where it exists.   I
refer to what is known as the Farmers' Improvement Society, of Texas, one of the most interesting
of the many organisations of coloured people which
have sprung up since emancipation, and one that
has exercised an inspiring and helpful influence
upon the people it has reached.

This society, which had a membership, in 1908, of

9,256 among the Negro farmers of Texas, was organised, in 1895, under the leadership of R. L. Smith, of Paris, Texas. It was the outgrowth of a village improvement society which Mr. Smith organised in Freedmantown, which was the name given to the coloured quarter of Oakland, Texas, where he was teaching at the time. It is an interesting fact in this connection that Mr. Smith received the suggestion for the organisation of this society from reading an article in the *Youths' Companion*, describing the work of the Village Improvement Society in Litchfield, Connecticut. This circumstance suggests one of the benefits which the art of reading conferred upon the coloured people of which we do not usually take an account.

While the first purpose of this society was to save money for its members by purchasing provisions in common, and in large quantities, it eventually sought to improve its members in every direction. In order to do this, Mr. Smith decided to adopt the forms of fraternal organisations and confer degrees, first, upon those who succeeded in getting out of the chronic condition of debt in which they lived; and, second, upon those who, in the comprehensive language of Mr. Smith, "made the most progress in civilisation."

The degrees were twelve in number. The first degree was conferred upon the member who succeeded in "running" himself three months, without opening an account; the second, upon the member running himself six months; the third, nine months, and the fourth twelve months; the fifth was conferred upon the members who maintained themselves the entire year, and had a surplus of twenty-five dollars; the sixth, the same, with a surplus of one hundred dollars; the seventh the same, with a surplus of one hundred and fifty dollars; and the eighth, with a surplus of two hundred dollars; and so on, up to the twelfth degree, which was called the Grand Patriarch degree, and entitled its possessor to membership in the annual convocation without election, "thereby creating," as Mr. Smith explains, "a permanent delegateship of successful members, who had worked out their salvation and were actually fitted for leadership by growth in the essentials of civilisation."

In 1907 members of the organisation owned 71,439 acres of land, which were worth considerably over one million dollars. The estimated value of their live-stock was $275,000.

In 1906 the Farmers' Improvement Association, having raised among its members something over twelve hundred dollars, purchased land and started an Agricultural College. The purpose of the society was to provide a school in which their sons and daughters could have the sort of training that would prepare them to stay on the farm, and not leave it for the doubtful advantages of the city.

R. L. Smith is one of the younger generation of coloured men. Born in Charleston, South Carolina, in 1861, he was a student for a while during Reconstruction days at the University of South Carolina, but was eventually starved out when the law passed which cut off the funds for the scholarships of Negro students. He afterward was graduated at Atlanta University, returned to Charleston and ran a Republican paper. That enterprise naturally failed with the downfall of the Reconstruction government in the South, and Mr. Smith decided to go to Texas and begin life anew as a teacher.

Although he had intended to keep out of politics after leaving South Carolina, he found himself, in 1895, running for the Legislature of Texas. Much to his surprise he was elected, a majority of white voters having given him their support. "Since the white people," said Mr. Smith, in relating this experience, "were kind enough to say that a man who felt so much interest in the upbuilding of his own race should be endorsed in some way by the whites, I thought that the race problem was solved sure enough."

Mr. Smith has continued in the work which he began, and, although he had had one or two offices under the Federal Government since that time, he has never permitted that to turn him aside from the important original work which he has undertaken for the improvement of the Negro farmers in Texas.

In spite of Mr. Smith's election to the Legislature, the race problem is not yet solved in Texas. Nevertheless, at our annual Negro Conference at Tuskegee, Mr. Smith has never failed to be present and to report progress.

CHAPTER XV

ONE of the most striking and interesting things about the American Negro, and one which has impressed itself upon my mind more and more in the course of the preparation of this book, is the extent to which the black man has intertwined his life with that of the people of the white race about him. While it is true that hardly any other race of people, that has come to this country, has remained, in certain respects, so separate and distinct a part of the population as the Negro, it is also true that no race, which has come to this country, has so woven its life into the life of the people about it. No race has shared to a greater extent in the work and activities of the original settlers of the country, or has been more closely related to them in interest, in sympathy and in sentiment, than the Negro race.

In fact, there is scarcely any enterprise, of any moment, that has been undertaken by a member of the white race, in which the Negro has not had some part. In all the great pioneer work of clearing forests, and preparing the way for civilisation, the Negro, as I have tried to point out, has had his part. In all the difficult and dangerous work of exploration of the country the Negro has invariably been the faithful companion and helper of the white man.

Negroes seem to have accompanied nearly all the early Spanish explorers. Indeed, it has even been conjectured that Negroes came to America before Columbus, carried hither by trade winds and ocean currents, coming from the west coast of Africa. At any rate, one of the early historians, Peter Martyr, who was an acquaintance of Columbus, mentions "a region in the Darian District of South America where Balboa, the illustrious discoverer of the Pacific Ocean, found a race of black men who were conjectured to have come from Africa and to have been shipwrecked on this coast."

It is said that the first ship built along the Atlantic Coast was constructed by the slaves of Vasquez de Ayllon, who, one hundred years before the English landed there, attempted to found a Spanish settlement on the site of what was later Jamestown, Virginia. There were thirty Negroes with the Spanish discoverer, Balboa, and they assisted him in building the first ship that was constructed on the Pacific Coast of America. Cortez, the Conquerer of Mexico, had three hundred Negro slaves with him in 1522, the year in which he was chosen Captain-general of New Spain, as Mexico was then called, and it is asserted that the town of Santiago del Principe was founded by Negro slaves who had risen in insurrection against their Spanish masters.

In the chronicles of the ill-starred Coronado expedition of 1540, which made its way from Mexico as far north as Kansas and Nebraska, it is mentioned that a Negro slave of Hernando de Alarcon was the only member of the party who would undertake to carry a message from the Rio Grande across the country to the Zunis in New Mexico, where Alarcon hoped to find Coronado and open communication with him.

I have already referred to the story of Estevan, "little Steve," a companion of Pamfilo Narvaez, in his exploration of Florida in 1527, who afterward went in search of the seven fabulous cities which were supposed to be located somewhere in the present state of Arizona, and discovered the Zuni Indians.*

Negroes accompanied De Soto on his march through Alabama, in 1540. One of these Negroes seems to have liked the country, for he remained and settled among the Indians not far from Tuskegee, and became in this way the first settler of Alabama. Coming down to a later date, a Negro servant accompanied William Clark, of the Lewis and Clark Expedition, which, in 1804, explored the sources of the Missouri River, and gained for the United States

---

* R. R. Wright, "American Anthropologist," vol. xiv, 1902.

the Oregon country. Negroes were among the first adventurers who went to look for gold in California; and when John C. Fremont, in 1848, made his desperate and disastrous attempt to find a pathway across the Rockies, he was accompanied by a Negro servant named Saunders.

Recently in looking over the pages of the *National Geographical Magazine*, I ran across an article giving an account of Peary's trip farthest north. Among the pictures illustrating that article I noticed the laughing face of a black man. The picture was the more striking because the figure of this black man was totally encased in the snow-white fur of a polar bear. I learned that this was the picture of Matt Henson, the companion of Peary in his most famous expedition to reach the pole. Just now, as I am writing this, I learn from the newspapers that Peary claims he has reached the North Pole and that Matt Henson was his companion on this last and most famous journey.

One reason why the Negro is found so closely associated with the white man in all his labours and adventures is that, with all his faults, the Negro seldom betrays a specific trust. Even the individual who does not always clearly distinguish between his own property and that of his neighbour, when a definite thing of value is entrusted to him, in nine cases out of ten, will not betray that trust. This is a trait that characterises the Negro wherever he is found.   I have heard Sir Harry H. Johnston, the African explorer, use almost exactly the same words, for example, in describing the characteristics of the native African.

Some years ago I was travelling through Central Alabama, and I chanced to stop at a crossroads country store.   While I was talking with the store-keeper a coloured man, who lived some distance away, chanced to pass by.   It happened that the merchant had a considerable sum of money which he wanted to send to some of his friends some miles distant.   He called the coloured man into the store and put the money into his hands with the request that he deliver it to his friend as he passed by the house on his road home.   My attention was attracted by this trans-action, and I asked the white merchant how it was that he was willing to entrust so large a sum of money to this particular coloured man.   My question brought out the fact that the merchant did not even know the name of the man to whom he had entrusted this money.   He was familiar with his face, knew that he had lived in the neighbourhood for a number of years, and felt quite secure in putting the money in his hands to carry to its destination.

In explanation the merchant told me that, in all his experience in dealing with coloured people in that neighbourhood, he had never been deceived when he asked one of them to perform some specific act which involved direct, personal responsibility.   He went on to say that while the man to whom he had given this money, if the opportunity offered itself, might yield to the temptation of pilfering, he still felt perfectly sure that the money he had entrusted to him would be delivered in exactly the shape in which it had been turned over.

It is a common thing in the South for the heads of the household to leave home and be away for weeks and even months, without a single thing of value in the house being left under lock and key. In such cases Southern white people are willing to entrust, apparently, all their property to the care of Negro servants. In spite of this fact, I have rarely heard of a case of this kind in which the Negro servants have proved dishonest. I very seldom go into any Southern city that some banker, or retail or wholesale merchant does not introduce me to some individual Negro, to whom he has entrusted all that is valuable in connection with his banking or mercantile business.

I have already referred to the part that the Negro took in the wars which were fought to establish, defend and maintain the United States. One of the soldiers of the Revolutionary War who afterward distinguished himself in a remarkable way was Reverend Lemuel Haynes, and as I have not mentioned him elsewhere, I will do so here. Lemuel Haynes was born in West Hartford, Connecticut, in 1753. In 1775 he joined the Colonial Army as a Minute-man, at Roxbury, Massachusetts, having volunteered for the Ticonderoga Expedition. At the close of the War he settled in Granville, New York, where he worked on a farm, meanwhile studying for the ministry. By some means or other he succeeded in securing an exceptionally good education. In 1785 he succeeded in securing a position as a minister to a white congregation in Torrington, Connecticut. As there was objection from some members of the congregation on account of his colour, he removed to Rutland, Vermont, where he served as a minister from 1787 to 1817. In 1818 he went to Manchester, New Hampshire. It was while there that he made himself famous by opposing the execution of the Boone brothers, who had been condemned to death for murdering an insane man. He visited the brothers in the prison, and having listened to their story became convinced of their innocence, whereupon he took up their defence in the face of violent opposition. In spite of his efforts they were convicted, but a few days before their execution the man they were supposed to have killed, Louis Calvin, returned alive to his home. At that time people generally believed it was the coloured minister's prayers that brought him back.

In 1822 Mr. Haynes returned to his former home, at Granville, where he continued to preach until his death. He is most widely known for his "sermon against universalism," which he preached in opposition to Hosea Ballou. This sermon, which was preached impromptu and without notes, created a great impression. It was afterward published and circulated widely all over the United States and in some parts of Europe. Lemuel Haynes died in Granville, in 1832. He was, so far as I know, the first coloured Congregational minister.

During the Civil War there were several Negro officers appointed to take charge of the Negro troops, and immediately after the War several Negroes were admitted to West Point. Three of these have graduated. The only one of these now in the service is First Lieutenant Charles Young, who was Major of the Ninth Ohio Battalion United States Volunteers in the Spanish-American War.

Negro soldiers took a more prominent part in the Spanish-American War than in any previous war of the United States. In the first battle in Cuba the Tenth Cavalry played an important part in coming to the support, at a critical moment, of the Rough Riders under Colonel Theodore Roosevelt, at the Battle of Las Guasimas.

The Twenty-Fifth Infantry took a prominent part in the Battle of El Caney. It is claimed by Lieutenant-colonel A. D. Daggett that the Twenty-fifth Regiment caused the surrender of the stone fort at El Caney, which was the key to all the other positions in that battle for the possession of San

Juan. Eight men of this regiment were given certificates of gallantry for their part in the battle of San Juan Hill. The other Negro regiments which took part in these battles was the Ninth Cavalry and the Twenty-fourth Infantry, both of whom did heroic service in the famous battle for the crest of San Juan hill.

What impresses me still more, however, is the part which these black soldiers played after the battle was over, when they were called to remain and nurse the sick and wounded in the malarial-haunted camp at Siboney, at a time when the yellow fever had broken out in the army.

To engage in this service required another and a higher kind of courage, and I can perhaps give no better idea of the way in which this service was performed by these black soldiers than to repeat here the account given by Stephen Bonsal in his story of the fight for the possession of Santiago. He says:

The Twenty-fourth Infantry was ordered down to Siboney to do guard duty. When the regiment reached the yellow fever hospital it was found to be in a deplorable condition. Men were dying there every hour for lack of proper nursing. Major Markley, who had commanded the regiment since July 1st, drew his regiment up in line and Dr. LaGarde, in charge of the hospital, explained the needs of the suffering, at the same time clearly setting forth the danger for men who were not immune of nursing and attending yellow fever patients. Major Markley then said that any man who wished to volunteer to nurse in the yellow fever hospital could step forward. The whole regiment stepped forward. Sixty men were selected from the volunteers to nurse, and within forty-eight hours forty-two of these brave fellows were down, seriously ill with yellow or pernicious malaria fever.

Again the regiment was drawn up in line, and again Major Markley said that nurses were needed and that any man who wished to do so could volunteer. After the object lesson which the men had received in the last few days of the danger from contagion to which they would be exposed, it was now necessary for Dr. LaGarde to again warn the brave blacks of the terrible contagion. When the request for volunteers to replace those who had already fallen in the performance of their dangerous and perfectly optional duty was made again, the regiment stepped forward as one man.

When sent down from the trenches the regiment consisted of eight companies averaging about forty men each. Of those who remained on duty the forty days spent in Siboney, only twenty-four escaped without serious illness, and of this handful not a few succumbed to fever on the voyage home and after their arrival at Montauk. As a result thirty-six died and about forty were discharged from the regiment, owing to disabilities resulting from sickness which began in the yellow fever hospital.

I have described the manner in which the Negro has adapted his own life to that of the people around him, uniting his interests and his sympathies with those of the dominant white race. Perhaps I should say a word here of the way in which he has managed to keep his life separate and to prevent friction in his dealings with the other portions of the community. Few white people, I dare say, realise what the Negro has to do, to what extent he has been compelled to go out of his way, to avoid causing trouble and prevent friction.

For example, in one large city I know of a business place in which there is a cigar stand, a bootblacking stand, a place for cleaning hats and a barber shop, all in one large room. Any Negro can, without question, have his hat cleaned, his boots blacked, or buy a cigar in this place, but he cannot take a seat in the barber's chair. The minute he should do this he would be asked to go somewhere else.

The Negro must, at all hazard and in all times and places, avoid crossing the colour line. It is a little difficult, however, sometimes to determine upon what principle this line is drawn. For instance, customs differ in different parts of the same town, as well as in different parts of the country at large. In one part of a town a Negro may be able to get a meal at a public lunch counter, but in another part of the same town he cannot do so. Conditions differ widely in the different states. In Virginia a Negro is expected to ride in a separate railway coach, in West Virginia he can ride in the same coach with the white people. In one Southern city Negroes can enter the depot, as they usually do, by the main entrance; in another Southern city there is a separate entrance for coloured people. While in one Southern city the Negro is allowed to take his seat in the main waiting-room he will be compelled at another depot, in the same city, to go into a separate waiting-room. In some cities Negroes are allowed to go without question into the theatre; in other cities he either cannot enter the theatre at all, or he has a separate place assigned to him.

In all these different situations, somehow or other, the Negro manages to comport himself so as to rarely excite comment or cause trouble.

He often hears the opinion expressed that the Negro should keep his place or that he is "all right in his place." People who make use of these expressions seldom understand how difficult it is, considering the different customs in different parts of the country, to find out just what his place is. I might give further illustrations of this fact. In the Southern states the Negro is rarely allowed to enter a public library. In certain parts of the United States the Negro is allowed to enter the public high school, but he is forbidden to enter the grammar school, where white children are taught. In one city the Negro may sit anywhere he pleases in the street car; in another city, perhaps not more than twenty miles away, he is assigned to special and separate seats. In one part of the country the Negro may vote freely, in another part of the country, perhaps across the border of another state, he is not expected to vote at all.

As illustrating the ability of the Negro to avoid the rocks and shoals, which he is likely to meet in travelling about the country, and still manage to get what he wants, I recall an experience of a coloured man with whom I was travelling through South Carolina some time ago. This man was very anxious to reach the railway train and had only a few minutes in which to do so. He hailed, naturally enough, the first hackman he saw, who happened to be a white man. The white man told him that it was not his custom to carry Negroes in his carriage. The coloured man, not in the least disturbed, at once replied: "That's all right, we will fix that; you get in the carriage and I'll take the front seat and drive you." This was done, and in a few minutes they reached the depot in time to catch the train. The coloured man handed the white man twenty-five cents and departed. Both were satisfied and the colour line was preserved.

The facts I have detailed serve to illustrate some of the difficulties that the coloured man has in the North, as well as in the South, with the present unsettled conditions as to his position in the community. The Negro suffers some other disadvantages living in the midst of a people from whom he is so different, with whom he is so intimately associated, and from whom he is, at the same time, so distinctly separate.

In living in the midst of seventy millions of the most highly civilised people of the world, the Negro has the opportunity to learn much that he could not learn in a community where the people were less enlightened and less progressive. On the other hand, it is a disadvantage to him that his progress is constantly compared to the progress of a people who have the advantage of many centuries of civilisation, while the Negro has only a little more than forty years been a free man.   If the American Negro, with his present degree of advancement, were living in the midst of a civilisation such as exists to-day in Asia or in the south of Europe, the gap between him and the people by whom he is surrounded would not then be so wide, and he would receive credit for the progress that he has already made.

In speaking of the progress of the Negro in America, I want to refer to a letter, published in Virginia in 1801, and addressed to a member of the General Assembly of Virginia.   This letter, which in many respects is a remarkable document, is supposed to have been written by the Honourable Judge Tucker, and was occasioned by a slave conspiracy which greatly disturbed the people of Virginia about that time.   This letter is, in part, as follows:

There is often a progress in human affairs which may indeed be retarded, but which nothing can arrest.   Moving with slow and silent steps, it is marked only by comparing distant periods. The causes which produce it are either so minute as to be invisible, or, if perceived, are too numerous and complicated to be subject to human control.   Of such a sort is the advancement of knowl- edge among the Negroes of this country.   It is so striking as to be obvious to a man of most ordinary observation.   Every year adds to the number of those who can read and write; and he who has made any proficiency in letters becomes a little centre of instruction to others.

This increase of knowledge is the principle agency in evolving the spirit we have to fear.

.   .   .   .

In our infant country, where population and wealth increase with unexampled rapidity, the progress of liberal knowledge is proportionately great. In this vast march of the mind, the blacks, who are far behind us, may be supposed to advance at a pace equal to our own; but, sir, the fact is they are likely to advance faster, the growth and multiplication of our towns tend in a thousand ways to enlighten and inform them. The very nature of our government, which leads us to recur perpetually to the discussion of natural rights, favours speculation and inquiry. By way of marking the prodigious change which a few years has made among this class of men, compare the late conspiracy with the revolt under Lord Dunmore. In the one case, a few solitary individuals flocked to that standard, under which they were sure to find protection; in the other, they, in a body, of their own accord, combine a plan for asserting their claims and rest their safety on success alone. The difference is, then, they sought freedom merely as a good; now they also claim it as a right. This comparison speaks better than volumes for the change I insist on.

But, sir, this change is progressive. A little while ago their minds were enveloped in darkest ignorance; now the dawn of knowledge is faintly perceived and warns us of approaching day. Of the multitude of causes which tend to enlighten the blacks I know not one whose operation we can materially check. Here, then, is the true picture of our situation. Nor can we make it less hideous by shutting our eyes to it. These, our hewers of wood and drawers of water, possess the physical power to do us mischief, and are invited to do it by motives which self-love dictates and reason justifies. Our sole security consists, then, in their ignorance of this power and of their means of using it — a security which we have lately found was not to be relied upon, and which, small as it now is, every day diminishes.

I have quoted this letter at some length because it seems to me to describe, in a very remarkable way, the process and the method by which the Negro masses have advanced slowly but steadily before emancipation, more rapidly but not less steadily since.

The story of the American Negro has been one of

progress from the first. While there have been times when it seemed the race was going backward, this backward movement has been temporal, local or merely apparent. On the whole, the Negro has been and is moving forward everywhere and in every direction.

In speaking of his experiences in the South Mr. Ray Stannard Baker, whose articles on Southern conditions are in many respects the best and most informing that have been written since Olmsted's famous "Journey through the Seaboard Slave States," said that before he came into the South he had been told that in many sections of the country the Negro was relapsing into barbarism. He, of course, was very anxious to find these places and see for himself to what extent the Negro had actually gone backward. Before leaving New York he was told that he would find the best example of this condition in the lowlands and rice-fields of South Carolina and Georgia. He visited this section of South Carolina and Georgia, but he did not find any traces of the barbarism that he expected to see. He did find, however, that coloured people in that part of the country were, on the whole, making progress. This progress was slow, but it was in a direction away from and not toward barbarism.

In South Carolina he was told that while the people in that part of the country had not gone back into barbarism, if he would go to the sugar cane regions of Louisiana he would find the conditions among the Negroes as bad as in any other part of the United States. He went to Louisiana, and again he found not barbarism but progress. There he was told that he would find what he was looking for in the Yazoo Delta of the Mississippi. In Mississippi he was told that if he went into Arkansas he would not be disappointed; he went to Arkansas, but there, also, he found the coloured people engaged in buying land, building churches and schools, and trying to improve themselves. After that he came to the conclusion that the Negro was not relapsing into barbarism.

The Negro is making progress at the present time as he made progress in slavery times. There is, however, this difference: In slavery the progress of the Negro was a menace to the white man. The security of the white master depended upon the ignorance of the black slave. In freedom the security and happiness of each race depends, to a very large extent, on the education and the progress of the other. The problem of slavery was to keep the Negro down; the problem of freedom is to raise him up.

The story of the Negro, in the last analysis, is simply the story of the man who is farthest down; as he raises himself he raises every other man who is above him.

In concluding this narrative I ought to say, perhaps,

that if, in what I have written, I seem to have emphasised the successes of the Negro rather than his failures, and to have said more about his achievements than about his hardships, it is because I am convinced that these things are more interesting and more important. To me the history of the Negro people in America seems like the story of a great adventure, in which, for my own part, I am glad to have had a share. So far from being a misfortune it seems to me that it is a rare privilege to have part in the struggles, the plans, and the ambitions of ten millions of people who are making their way from slavery to freedom.

At the present time the Negro race is, so to speak, engaged in hewing its path through the wilderness. In spite of its difficulties there is a novelty and a zest as well as an inspiration in this task that few who have not shared it can appreciate. In America the Negro race, for the first time, is face to face with the problem of learning to till the land intelligently; of planning and building permanent and beautiful homes; of erecting schoolhouses and extending school terms; of experimenting with methods of instruction and adapting them to the needs of the Negro people; of organising churches, building houses of worship, and preparing ministers. In short, the Negro in America to-day is face to face with all the fundamental problems of modern civilisation, and for each of these problems he has, to some extent, to find a solution of his own. The fact that in his case this is peculiarly difficult only serves to make the problem peculiarly interesting.

We have hard problems, it is true, but instead of despairing in the face of the difficulties we should, as a race, thank God that we have a problem. As an individual I would rather belong to a race that has a great and difficult task to perform, than be a part of a race whose pathway is strewn with flowers. It is only by meeting and manfully facing hard, stubborn and difficult problems that races, like individuals, are, in the highest degree, made strong.

THE END

INDEX

Abbott, Dr. A. R., coloured graduate Canadian University, II, 244.

Abolition, of slavery, in Canada, II, 239; in New York, 313; effect of, on free coloured people, I, 200.

Acadians, in Louisiana, I, 122.

Adams, first slave on Calhoun plantation, I, 150.

Adams, Lewis, responsible for location of Tuskegee Institute, II, 28, 29; on extent to which slaves were educated in the trades, 63, 64.

Addison, Nancy, endows St. Francis Academy, Baltimore, II, 346.

Africa, Coloured Baptist Mission in, II, 333; Ethiopian movement in, 334, 335; mission of A. M. E. Church in, 334; native method of smelting ores in, I, 32; slave trade in, 95; intermingling of races in, 22.

African Colony, Mobile, Ala., I, 103; visited by members of Alabama Coloured Medical Society, II, 138.

African, folk-tale of the origin of music, II, 259.

African Free Schools, New York, II, 132.

African Law, I, 70-72.

African Literature, I, 72, 73.

African Kings, artistic sceptres, I, 47.

African Medicine, I, 67, 68.

African Methodist Episcopal Church, founded 1790, I, 255; first general conference of, Philadelphia, 1816, 255.

African Methodist Episcopal Zion Church, started New York, 1800, I, 255, 256; founded 1820, 256; missionary of, to freedmen, II, 16, 17.

African Natives, at Tuskegee, I, 39.

African Native Markets, I, 49, 50.

African Natives, skill in hand-crafts of, I, 46-49.

African Religion, I, 65.

African Story Tellers, I, 72.

African Students, at Oxford, Eng., II, 285.

African Union Methodist Protestant Church, II, 345.

African Women, distrust white man's civilisation, I, 61.

Afro-American Presbyterian Church, see Presbyterian Church.

Agriculture, need of better in South emphasised by former slave, I, 308.

Agriculture, number of Negroes engaged in, II, 67, 68.

Aimes, II. II. S., slavery in Cuba, I, 120.

Alabama, Negro first settler in, II, 385; number of Negro banks in, 211; State Association of Coloured Physicians of, 175.

Albany, O., Station of Underground Railway in, II, 197.

Alarcon, Hernando de, Negro slave of, in 1540 carries message from Rio Grande to New Mexico, II, 385.

Aldridge, Ira, famous coloured actor, I, 294; II, 282.

Allen, Bishop Richard, founder of Free African Society, I, 253-255; founder and first bishop of the A. M. E. Church, 252-255; Abolitionist, 288; Associated with Lundy in Haitian colonisation movement, II, 237, 332.

Allen, Macon B., first coloured attorney in the United States, II, 185.

Allen, William G., editor National Watchman, coloured anti-slavery newspaper, I, 294.

Chavis, John, first Negro educated at Princeton, I, 274; school for whites of, in North Carolina, 274, 275.

Cheatham, II. P., coloured congressman, II, 25.

Cherokees, Indian slave-owners of Georgia, I, 133.

Chesnutt, Charles W., coloured novelist, I, 203; descended from free Negroes of North Carolina, II, 289, 290.

Chew, Benjamin, master of Richard Allen, I, 253.

Cheyney, Pa., industrial school for Negroes in, II, 132.

Chicago, Negro crime in, II, 86; Provident Hospital, coloured, in, II, 174.

Chickasaws, conspiracy of with slaves of New Orleans, I, 133.

Chretien, Paul, wealthy Creole Negro, I, 208.

Christianity, relation of to slavery, I, 115, 116, 238.

Christian League, organisation of by ex-Gov. Northen, II, 107, 108.

Christmas in Virginia, II, 57.

Church, Negro, the richest, in United States, 307.

Church Institute, for Negroes, of Protestant Episcopal Church, II, 345.

Churches, Negro, amounts collected annually by, for education, 342, 343.

Churchill, Winston, the Kingdom of Uganda, described by, I, 76, 77.

Cincinnati, Negro refugees in, I, 227; Negro crime in, II, 86; High School for Negroes in, 133.

Civic League, organisation of in Altanta II, 107, 108.

Claflin University, Orangeburg, S. C., II, 140.

Clark, Col. Elijah, referred to, I, 316.

Clark, William, accompanied by Negro servant in exploration of Oregon Country, II, 385.

Clay, Cassius M., publishes anti-slavery paper in Kentucky, I, 193.

Cleopatra, death of, represented by coloured sculptress, II, 293.

Cleveland, President Grover, effect of appointment on a Negro politician, II, 208.

Clinton, Bishop George W., reminiscences of Reconstruction, II, 38, 39.

Clinton, Bishop I. C., spiritual adviser of former masses, II, 39.

Clinton, Sir Henry, invites Negro to enlist in King's Army, I, 319.

Coffin, Levi, Quaker, abolitionist, President Underground Railway, I, 240.

Coke, Bishop Thomas, Negro companion of, I, 257.

Cole, Bob, Negro comedian, II, 281.

Coleman, organiser of coloured cotton-mill company, II, 76, 77.

Coleridge-Taylor, S., Negro composer, I, 13.

Colleges, for Negroes, II, 140.

Collins, Captain Jack, free Negro, I, 209.

Collins, Winfield N., on domestic slave trade, I, 96, 98; on kidnapping free Negroes, I, 196, 197.

Colonisation, African, interest of Virginia Negroes in, II, 235.

Colonisation, see Liberia.

Colour line, difficulty of defining, I, 21; II, 393, 394.

Coloured American, Ante-bellum coloured newspaper, I, 293.

Coloured Citizen, Ante-bellum newspaper, I, 204.

Coloured Conservators, meets at Nashville, Tenn., adopts resolutions, II, 15, 16.

Coloured High School, record of the Baltimore, II, 363.

Coloured Library, of Louisville, Ky., promoted by coloured Y. M. C. A., II, 354.

Coloured Methodist Church organised, 1866, I, 256; schools supported by, II, 344.

Coloured Methodists, of Mississippi, money raised by, for support of schools, II, 345.

Coloured Patriots of the Revolution, the, I, 310.

Mohammedan Fanatics, among Negroes of Uganda, I, 28; Negro, 54.

Mon Louis Island, Creole settlement on, I, 209.

Montamal, John, incident of Reconstruction in New Orleans, II, 7, 8.

Montgomery, Benjamin, manager of Davis plantation, I, 154-156.

Montgomery, Thornton, former slave of Joseph Davis, I, 155, 156; letter to Mrs. Jefferson Davis, 157.

Montgomery, Isaiah T., referred to, I, 24; former slave of Joseph Davis, 155; founder of Mound Bayou, II, 246, 247, 371; opinions of, in regard to moral and political conditions in Mound Bayou, 374-376.

Moore, Rev. George W., coloured field superintendent, A. M. Association, II, 269.

Moore, George Henry, on law of slavery in Massachusetts, I, 130.

Moorland, Dr. J. E., secretary coloured Y. M. C. A., II, 352.

Moravians, Negro, II, 119; established missions for Negroes, 119; of Salem, N. C., II, 253.

Moral Education Association of Boston, coloured woman a member of, II, 328.

Morris, Albert, Free Negro in North Carolina, I, 202.

Morris, Freeman, Free Negro in North Carolina, I, 202.

Morris, Robert, coloured attorney admitted to bar on motion Charles Sumner, II, 185.

Mosaic Templars of America, founded 1882, business of, II, 162.

Moten, Major Robert R., commandant Hampton Institute, I, 25; great-grandfather of, kidnapped from Africa, 102, 103.

Mott, James and Lucretia, aid in escape of Henry Box Brown, I, 218.

Moultry, Francis, J, coloured caterer, II, 196.

Mound Bayou, Miss., Negro colony in Yazoo Delta, I, 156, II, 246-248; self government in, 371; moral conditions in, 374.

Mount Meigs, Reformatory for coloured children at, II, 113.

Murray, George W., coloured congressman, II, 25, 26.

Music, of native Africans, II, 260.

Myers, George A, successful barber, II, 199, 200.

Mystery, Ante-bellum coloured newspaper, I, 287.

Napier, James C., founder One Cent Savings Bank, Nashville, Tenn., II 212.

Narvaez, Panfilo de, Spanish explorer, Negroes accompany, I, 88; accompanied by Negro Estevan, II, 385.

Nash, Charles E., Negro soldier and congressman, I, 324.

Nassau, Rev. R. II., on African religion, I, 65.

Natchez Indians, sold as slave to Santo Domingo, I, 130.

National Bank, Chelsea, N. Y., stock owned in, by Negro, II, 202.

National Baptist Publishing Company, II, 340, 341.

National Medical Association, coloured, sketch of, II, 179-181.

Nazarites, coloured secret order, II, 148.

Neau, Elias, establishes, 1704, school for Indian and Negro slaves in New York, II, 119.

Negro, The, in Africa, as represented in school books, I, 8; American, natives of Africa, 10, 18; colour, basis of solidarity of, 33, 34; the true, better than the Asiatic, 43; in the country districts of the South, 62, 63; power of adaptation of, 77; compared with the Indians, 125-143 part of, in slavery, 144; as an individual and as a race, in the South, 179; the educated, II, 91, 92; literacy of, compared with European nations, 117, 118; colonies, value of, 252; gift of poetic expression of, 284; mission for, in Maryland, 121; natural eloquence of, 318; relation to white man in slavery and freedom, 399.

www.ingramcontent.com/pod-product-compliance
Lightning Source LLC
Chambersburg PA
CBHW051440270326
41932CB00024B/3368